Dealing with Dictators

The BCSIA Studies in International Security book series is edited at the Belfer Center for Science and International Affairs (BCSIA) at Harvard University's John F. Kennedy School of Government and is published by The MIT Press. The series publishes books on contemporary issues in international security policy, as well as their conceptual and historical foundations. Topics of particular interest to the series include the spread of weapons of mass destruction, internal conflict, the international effects of democracy and democratization, and U.S. defense policy.

A complete list of BCSIA Studies appears at the back of this volume.

Dealing with Dictators

Dilemmas of U.S. Diplomacy and Intelligence Analysis, 1945–1990

Ernest R. May and Philip D. Zelikow, editors
with Kirsten Lundberg and Robert D. Johnson

BCSIA Studies in International Security

The MIT Press
Cambridge, Massachusetts
London, England

This book was typeset in Palatino by Sarah B. Buckley at the Belfer
Center for Science and International Affairs and bound in the United
States of America. Cover image: Photos clockwise from left: "Chiang
Kai-Shek Seated at Microphone," © Bettmann/CORBIS; "Iraqi President
Saddam Hussein," © Hulton-Deutsch Collection/CORBIS; "Philippine
President Ferdinand Marcos and His Wife Imelda, © Reuters/CORBIS;
"President Mobutu," © Reuters/CORBIS. All photos used with
permission. Cover image by Donna Whipple.

MIT Press books may be purchased at special quantity discounts for
business or sales promotional use. For information, please email
special_sales@mitpress.mit.edu or write to Special Sales Department,
The MIT Press, 55 Hayward Street, Cambridge, MA 02142.

Library of Congress Cataloging-in-Publication Data

Dealing with dictators : dilemmas of U.S. diplomacy and intelligence
    analysis, 1945–1990 / edited by Ernest R. May and Philip D. Zelikow ;
    with Kirsten Lundberg and Robert D. Johnson.
        p. cm. — (BCSIA studies in international security)
    Includes bibliographical references and index.
    ISBN-13: 978-0-262-13459-0 (hc.: alk. paper)—978-0-262-63324-6 (pbk.: alk.
        paper)
    ISBN-10: 0-262-13459-4 (hc.: alk. paper)—0-262-63324-8 (pbk.: alk. paper)
        1. United States—Foreign relations—1945–1989—Case studies.
    2. Dictators—Case studies.   3. Intelligence service—United States—
    History—20th century—Case studies.   4. Totalitarianism—Case studies.
    I. May, Ernest R.   II. Zelikow, Philip, 1954–   III. Lundberg, Kirsten.   IV.
    Johnson, Robert David, 1967–   V. Series.

E840.D392 2006
327.73009'045—dc22

                                                                    2005058420

Contents

Preface

From 1986 to 2002, Harvard University's John F. Kennedy School of Government had an executive program for senior managers in the U.S. intelligence community, known as the Intelligence and Policy Program. It ran once or twice a year for one to three weeks. Participants typically had twelve to twenty years of experience. Most came from the Directorate of Intelligence (DI) in the Central Intelligence Agency (CIA). Some came from CIA's Directorate of Operations (DO), the home of the U.S. clandestine service; end-of-course certificates for the latter had blanked-out names because the names under which they enrolled were not their own. Some other participants came from the National Security Agency, the center for U.S. signal interception and code-breaking; the National Reconnaissance Organization, which oversees collection of intelligence by satellites; the Defense Intelligence Agency, the military establishment's not-so-mini-CIA; and intelligence branches of the armed services, the Department of State, and the Department of Energy. A handful came from federal law enforcement agencies.

This executive program was the brainchild of Robert M. Gates, who in 1986 had just become Deputy Director of Central Intelligence. He would later be Deputy National Security Adviser for President George H.W. Bush as well as Bush's Director of Central Intelligence. In 2002, he became president of Texas A&M University. As he outlines in his unique, revealing, and quite wonderful memoir, Gates was a career analyst in the CIA who chanced early on to have tours of duty in the White House, first under Henry Kissinger, then under Zbigniew Brzezinski.[1] It struck him that his work in the White House on policy issues did not connect often with the work of his former colleagues in the intelligence community. When back in that community, he puzzled over the fact that work there connected so

---

1. Robert M. Gates, *From the Shadows: The Ultimate Insider's Story of Five Presidents and How They Won the Cold War* (New York: Simon and Schuster, 1996).

little with what was being done by his whilom colleagues in the National Security Council staff and other parts of the government where policy decisions were framed, taken, and executed.

Gates devised the Kennedy School's new executive program after consulting with, among others in the School, Richard E. Neustadt and Ernest R. May, Dean Graham T. Allison and Academic Dean Albert Carnesale, and Peter B. Zimmerman and Nancy Huntington, who managed other executive programs. The Intelligence and Policy Program aimed to teach managers in the intelligence community how to think about needs in the policy community and about ways in which they and their associates might better serve those needs. This would be done in part by exposing them to elements of decision, bargaining, and organization theory, but primarily through Socratic discourse centered on case studies.

Neustadt and May had, for several years, taught a case-based course, on the basis of which they had then just published *Thinking in Time: The Uses of History for Decisionmakers*.[2] The first cases used in the new program were cases that they had developed, with assistance from the National Endowment for the Humanities, all focused on presidential choice-making but tangentially involving use of intelligence. Of these cases, those that seemed best-suited for the new program concerned the Pearl Harbor attack, the onset of the Korean War, the Bay of Pigs affair, the 1962 missile crisis, and the Americanization of the Vietnam War.

A contract between the Kennedy School and CIA's Center for the Study of Intelligence provided not only for the new executive program but also for development of one to three new case studies annually, designed specifically to foster learning about the intelligence-policy nexus. The cases were to be wholly unclassified and subject to no constraints other than those normal in any academic research project. The CIA undertook, however, to facilitate the effort, particularly by declassifying documents and identifying potential interviewees.

A steering committee helped guide the selection of topics for case studies. Chaired jointly by the Dean of the Kennedy School and the Director of Central Intelligence, the committee consisted of senior faculty from Harvard University, current and former high-level officials from Washington's intelligence and policy communities, and majority and minority members of the two Congressional intelligence oversight committees.

Between 1986 and 2002, the Program developed more than forty cases, some of which had multiple parts and two of which became books: one on

---

2. Richard E. Neustadt and Ernest R. May, *Thinking in Time: The Uses of History for Decisionmakers* (New York: The Free Press, 1986).

the 1962 missile crisis, the other on Germany's defeat of France in 1940.[3] This volume contains six of those cases that have enough similarities to yield cumulative insight into the intelligence-policy relationship.

The CIA-Harvard contract was itself necessarily unclassified, for Harvard has since World War II been unbending in its refusal to do classified research. The CIA had as little experience of writing unclassified contracts as Harvard had of concluding contracts with an intelligence agency. On the Harvard side, with memories of Vietnam-era riots still all too fresh, deans and professors worried lest news of the contract lead to protest demonstrations. Although the Harvard sponsors had agreed that the objective was important enough to justify running such a risk, they tried to minimize it by issuing a low-key press release late on a Friday afternoon, when it was least likely to catch the attention of newspaper editors. The ploy failed; the story was featured both in Harvard student newspapers and in the Boston press. However, to the wonderment of the Harvard contingent, the headlines lauded Harvard for "opening up" the CIA.

The CIA had already placed a certain number of senior officials in universities as "officers-in-residence" to teach, do research, or just provide information about the intelligence community. The program at the Kennedy School benefited from having a succession of such officials, whom the School designated as research associates, who stayed for at least a semester, and who helped develop teaching cases for the program. Occupants of this post included William Kline and James Worthen from the Directorate of Intelligence and two others who, after their retirement from the CIA, spent some additional years at Harvard: Charles Cogan, who had headed the Near East Division of the Directorate of Operations and been station chief in Paris, and Douglas MacEachin, an analyst of strategic forces, who had been head of the Directorate of Intelligence.

Neustadt and May managed the program from the Harvard side— May from beginning to end, and Neustadt keeping a hand in long after his formal retirement in 1989. They were joined from time to time by, among others, Gregory F. Treverton, who went on to become Vice Chairman of the National Intelligence Council and then a Senior Policy Analyst for the RAND Corporation; Richard Haass, later Director of Foreign Policy Studies at the Brookings Institution, head of policy planning for Secretary of State Colin Powell, and president of the Council on Foreign Relations; Robert Blackwill, later Ambassador to India and then a deputy to National Security Adviser Condoleezza Rice; Kurt Campbell, later senior vice president of the Center for Strategic and International Studies; and

---

3. Ernest R. May and Philip D. Zelikow, eds., *The Kennedy Tapes: Inside the White House during the Cuban Missile Crisis* (Cambridge, Mass.: Harvard University Press, 1997); and Ernest R. May, *Strange Victory: Hitler's Conquest of France* (New York: Hill and Wang, 2000).

Jessica Stern, a member of the Kennedy School faculty and an expert on terrorism.

From his arrival at the Kennedy School in 1991, Philip D. Zelikow became, along with May and Neustadt, a central figure in the program. After Neustadt retired, May and Zelikow became the principal teachers in the executive program and the principal architects, editors, and sometimes authors of its case studies. The executive program in its early years depended, like most such programs in Harvard's professional schools, on cameo appearances by a variety of faculty and visitors. Later, the program was taught almost exclusively by May and Zelikow, who were sometimes in the classroom six to eight hours a day.

May and Zelikow—coached, of course, by fellow faculty members and by friends outside—gradually developed a set of precepts which participants in the executive program reported in feedback to have proved of real use in their work. These precepts are sketched in the introductory chapter. The reader is warned that they are less than fully meaningful absent the opportunity to discuss them along with the case studies, which serve to explain them and amplify them.

We hope that this volume and the individual cases will be widely used in the study and teaching of intelligence analysis. We also hope that they will be used by students of government and history and that they will be read by citizens interested in how intelligence analysis interacts with policy-making. We hope further that anyone who looks at this book will reflect on its arguments and communicate to us any thoughts about how those arguments might be amplified, amended, or corrected.

—Ernest R. May
Cambridge, Massachusetts

—Philip D. Zelikow
Washington, D.C.
September 2005

Acknowledgments

Many programs and individuals deserve thanks for their contributions to this book. Three of the case studies were written for the Harvard Intelligence and Policy executive program described in the Preface. Though May and Zelikow oversaw the preparation of these cases, the original drafts were prepared by others: the Congo case by Charles Cogan, a retired senior office of the clandestine service, who has been a research fellow at Harvard (and a productive scholar) for more than a decade; the Philippine case by William Kline and James Worthen, both of them senior officers from CIA's Directorate of Intelligence serving at Harvard as research fellows for the executive program; and the Iraq case by Zachary Karabell, a much-published historian and also an investment analyst. May or Zelikow or both did enough early rewriting on these cases to have a sense of partial authorship. Robert D. Johnson of the History Department at Brooklyn College, drafted the Nicaragua case. Kirsten Lundberg and Johnson revised and polished all the cases and brought them up to date. May did more rewriting as the cases became part of this book. (Zelikow, meanwhile having become Counselor of the Department of State, lacked the time to do more than look over May's shoulder.)

The two outliers are the China and Iran cases. The former was originally a small book by May, *The Truman Administration and China, 1945–1949* (Philadelphia: J.B. Lippincott, 1975) appearing in "The America's Alternatives Series," edited by Harold M. Hyman. The Iran case was prepared by Gregory F. Treverton, with the assistance of James Klocke, when Treverton was a member of the Kennedy School faculty teaching in the Intelligence and Policy executive program. The auspices of and funding for the Iran case were, however, those of the Diplomatic Training Initiative of the Pew Charitable Trusts. Lundberg and Johnson also brought these cases up to date, and May did a good deal of additional revision on the China case.

For the cases produced within the Intelligence and Policy program, the authors are grateful to the Central Intelligence Agency for funding and other support. We are all also grateful to the case program of Harvard's Kennedy School of Government, which has kept all of these cases in circulation.

We want also to express appreciation to the successive deans of the Kennedy School—Graham T. Allison, Robert Putnam, Albert Carnesale, Joseph Nye, and David Ellwood—for their support and encouragement; to Peter Zimmermann and Nancy Huntington, who managed the executive program; and to Howard Husock, who oversees the Kennedy School Case Program. We have already said in the Preface how grateful we are to Robert Gates. We are also grateful to his successors in the office of Director of Central Intelligence (DCI), James Woolsey, John Deutch, and George Tenet, and to the overseers of the DCI's Center for the Study of Intelligence, David Gries, Brian Latell, Lloyd Salvetti, and Paul Johnson.

Finally, we want to record heartfelt thanks for the sensitive, tactful, and efficient work of our editor, Teresa Lawson and to register our gratitude to Sean Lynn-Jones and Sarah Buckley of the Belfer Center for managing the process of converting a project into a book.

Introduction

Seven Tenets

Ernest R. May and Philip D. Zelikow

Almost from the beginning, a central theme of U.S. foreign policy has been support for democracy against dictatorship. For practical reasons, nevertheless, the U.S. government has tolerated, aided, and even allied itself with dictators. In the World War II contest with Nazi Germany and the other Axis powers, the United States allied with the Soviet Union. In the Cold War, when the Soviet dictatorship was the chief adversary, the United States had as allies a dictator in Spain, previously on the side of the Axis, and a dictator in Yugoslavia who had been an ally of the Soviet Union, had broken with Moscow, but remained a dedicated Communist.

Though such examples testify to opportunism and moral relativism, links with dictators caused Americans qualms even when conflict with the Axis or the Soviet bloc was most intense, and the management of those links posed chronic dilemmas for American decisionmakers. On one hand, officials have felt some obligation to nudge dictators toward democracy, or at least to appear to do so. On the other hand, they have felt a strong obligation to be cautious, not only for fear of losing the benefits of an alliance but also because of a countervailing commitment to the principle of national self-determination and the corollary of non-intervention.

These dilemmas were apparent in U.S. relations with Latin America from the time that the United States became dominant in its region. They became much more prominent and bothersome during the Cold War, for several reasons: because the United States had a much wider array of allies; because many opponents of dictators, posing as champions of democracy, were actually Communists working in the interest of the Soviet Union; and because the U.S. government had significantly greater capacity for attempting to influence internal affairs in other nations. The United States provided economic and military assistance to these nations, sometimes on a large scale, and it had a new and large intelligence establishment collecting and analyzing data about other governments, recruiting secret agents within those governments, and developing and maintaining capacities for covert action—officially defined as "action undertaken at the direction of the President to further U.S. foreign policy aims without leaving visible traces of American involvement."

The case studies in this book illustrate how these moral and political dilemmas presented themselves to the U.S. government at a variety of points during the Cold War when almost nothing else of relevance was constant. External circumstances, domestic climates of opinion, institutions of government, and the resources available to presidents were not what they had been earlier or would be later. The first case, that of Chiang Kai-shek and China, concerns the Truman administration not long after World War II, when the Cold War was in its early stages and a "national security state" had only begun to emerge.[1] The second case, that of the Congo from Patrice Lumumba to Joseph Mobutu (later Mobutu Sese Seko), concerns the Eisenhower and Kennedy administrations at the high point of the Cold War—in the interval between the Berlin and Taiwan Straits crises of 1958 and the détente that began to develop after the great Cuban missile crisis of 1962—when the U.S. defense and intelligence establishments were at the peak of their power and autonomy. The third and fourth cases (Nicaragua and Iran in the late 1970s) arose after the Vietnam War and the Watergate affair, when consensus about foreign policy seemed to have dissolved, and Congress and the news media were holding the executive branch to much more demanding standards of accountability. The fifth case, that of Ferdinand Marcos in the Philippines, comes from the 1980s, when tension with the Soviet Union had revived, and some of the post-Vietnam, post-Watergate restraints on the executive had loosened. The sixth and last case, that of Iraq's Saddam Hussein, comes from the late 1980s, when the long Cold War was giving way to what President George H.W. Bush characterized hopefully as "a new world order."

The cases illustrate the chronic dilemmas inhering in U.S. dealings with dictators not only in different periods but in different parts of the world. They are intended to provide students of the Cold War with in-depth examples of the types of problems that confronted every U.S. administration in almost every part of the world. They are intended also to provide students of decisionmaking with examples of the types of challenges that are apt in the future to face anyone attempting to manage U.S. relations with the developing world, even though the Cold War is now in the distant past.

These examples are of a particular type. Written for students not only of history or political science but also of management and organization,

---

1. See Michael J. Hogan, *A Cross of Iron: Harry S. Truman and the Origins of the National Security State, 1945–1954* (Cambridge, U.K.: Cambridge University Press, 1998).

they are designed for use in case-method teaching and have been so used, in progressively improved drafts, by students at many levels, from college freshmen on up through senior officials and flag and general officers participating in professional-school executive programs at Harvard and elsewhere. Each is self-contained and designed to be read or studied without necessary reference to other cases or to this introduction or the concluding chapter in this volume.

A reader or student not familiar with case-method teaching and study may need a few pointers to understand the character and potential uses of these case studies. Each case is written as if by a newspaper reporter trying simply to set forth facts. Although some interpretation inheres in any narrative, the effort here is to minimize retrospective comment or analysis. The objective is to enable the reader to participate in the case and to ask at various points: "What would I do if I had been a character in this story and had had to take or recommend action on the basis of no more evidence than is here?"

The potential educational value of such exercises of imagination is hard to overstate. We usually see the past through eyes of second-guessers, focusing on whether a past choice was right or wrong. Historical controversies pit one set of second-guessers against others. Regarding the episodes that are bookends here, concerning China in 1945–1948 and Iraq in 1988–1990, most writings to which one might turn are organized around post-hoc judgments. Some authors argue that President Harry S. Truman made a huge mistake in not trying to keep Chiang Kai-shek in power, others that he should have sought an accommodation with the Communists before Mao Zedong locked himself into an alliance with the Soviet Union. Similarly, some authors upbraid President George H.W. Bush for not having taken a hard line against Iraq from the beginning of his administration, while others argue that if he had been more conciliatory, he could have prevented the 1991 Gulf War.

Such disputes about the past, valuable as they can be, make it hard for readers or students to understand how difficult and uncertain are the forces that produce policy choices. More often than not, decisionmakers have little sure knowledge. They have to act mostly on the basis of shaky presumptions about actual conditions and even shakier guesswork about the consequences of alternative courses of action.

Attentive readers of these cases, or teachers and students who discuss them in class, can experience vicariously the processes of formulating policy under conditions of high uncertainty. In doing so, they can arrive, not at a more certain verdict on the rightness or wrongness of past choices, but at a deeper understanding of how uncertainty and cross purposes, both practical and moral, penetrate the processes. This vicarious experience can be at least as instructive as trying to second-guess the wisdom of the actual choices. It is a kind of study of history that has potential for yielding real lessons. The question to ask is not: did Truman or Bush make the right choices? Instead: did Truman, Bush, and their aides—given the inevitable fog of uncertainty and the inevitable pressure to make some kind of decision, even if there is a fifty-fifty chance that it may be wrong—ask all of the questions that could have been asked and answered?

By studying historical episodes in this way, one can build a checklist of generic questions worth asking about other episodes in the past or about problems of the present or future that in any way resemble the cases in hand. We do not maintain that these cases necessarily offer lessons directly applicable to dealing with dictators today. We do argue that efforts to relive cases can equip one for better understanding of such relationships now and in the present. We are influenced by Mark Twain, who reportedly said that history never repeats itself, but sometimes it rhymes.

Precepts

The following are general precepts that Neustadt, May, Zelikow, and their collaborators developed from studying and teaching about the cases in this volume and a large number of others.

PRECEPT ONE

Information, whether raw or analyzed, enters the policy stream as part of policymakers' "appreciations." In his classic work, *The Art of Judgment*, Sir Geoffrey Vickers defines "appreciation" as the product of interaction among reality judgments ("What is going on?"), value judgments ("What difference does it make?"), and action judgments ("What do we do about it?").[2] An appreciation comprises both an action decision and the rationale that underpins it. The quality of the decision depends on the thought devoted to each component and the thought applied to relating one component to another. Perfect knowledge of reality is not of much use without criteria for separating the important from the unimportant. Knowing clearly what is important is not much use in practical affairs without capacity for matching knowledge to action.

Vickers, who was a lawyer and public official in Britain, gives a simple private-sector example. He describes the dilemma of an employer who concludes that a long-serving and loyal manager is not up to a job for which he seems to be in line. The employer goes back and forth in reality judgments about the manager's qualities and abilities; value judgments

---

2. Geoffrey Vickers, *The Art of Judgment: A Study of Policy Making (Rethinking Public Administration)* (Thousand Oaks, Calif.: Sage, 1995; orig. Chapman and Hall, 1965).

Figure 1. The Appreciative System.

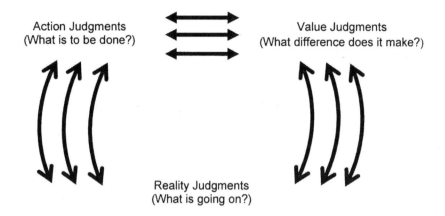

Action Judgments
(What is to be done?)

Value Judgments
(What difference does it make?)

Reality Judgments
(What is going on?)

about possible effects on the individual, the morale of others, and the prospective performance of the firm. Reviewing again and again alternative action judgments, he hits eventually on moving the individual to a different part of the company, promoting him, but keeping him doing work that he can do well. Vickers uses the term "innovative appreciation" to describe this kind of analytical discovery of how to match up understanding of facts, assessment of their relative importance, and creative thought about what to do.

PRECEPT TWO
None of the elements of appreciation is fixed; they change rapidly and sometimes unpredictably. When one element changes, the others are likely also to change. Figure 1 illustrates the process, but someone looking at it needs to bear in mind that it captures Vickers' concept only if one imagines that the arrows are constantly in motion until the process is sufficiently complete so that action can actually be taken.

That this is a dynamic, not a static, image is critically important, because both intelligence analysts and decisionmakers often make the mistake of assuming that one set of judgments or another is fixed. This mistake is most often made regarding value judgments, for it is all too easy to suppose that the actions or policies of another person or organization or government derive from ascertainable and more or less permanent interests. Such a supposition is often alluring because it is seldom wholly wrong. Interests are ascertainable and are more or less permanent. But the mix that answers the question "So what?" can change almost from moment to moment.

The final case study in this volume provides a memorable example. It deals with U.S. policy toward Iraq in 1988–1990. Participants in class discussion never have any trouble naming U.S. interests affected by Iraq at that time or, for that matter, at almost any other time: oil, regional stability, security of Israel, hope for an accord between the Israelis and the Palestinian Arabs, U.S. agricultural exports, proliferation of weapons of mass destruction, human rights, and so on. The only item for 1988–1990 that would be missing later is concern about Soviet influence.

The interests that mattered at particular moments in 1988–1990 depended, however, on changing judgments as to what was going on and what the United States could possibly do. In the autumn of 1989, President George H.W. Bush signed a National Security Directive defining U.S. policy toward Iraq as one of "constructive engagement." The directive had originated in the Department of State, where the dominant concern of Secretary of State James Baker and his aides was to get some progress in Israeli-Palestinian negotiations. Iraq, originally the hardest-line opponent of any such negotiations, had recently softened its position and moved toward an apparent entente with some of the more moderate Arab states. Iraq had also recently accepted an inconclusive end to a long and exhausting war with Iran. Baker and his aides believed that Iraq might help their negotiating effort, especially if they could capitalize on Iraq's need for funds for postwar reconstruction. Hence, "constructive engagement": the United States would put up a billion dollars in Commodity Credit Corporation (CCC) funds, guaranteeing that U.S. firms would be paid if they sold wheat or other commodities to Iraq. This was not direct aid to Iraq: the money would never leave the United States, but it would enable Iraq to get better terms from American suppliers than it could get based just on its unsupported promise to pay.

In the spring of 1990, the U.S. government backed away from "constructive engagement" and cut off the CCC credits. The dominant interest then was one hardly in play the previous autumn: evidence had come to light suggesting mismanagement of CCC funds passing through the Atlanta branch of the Italian-based Banco Nacional de Lavoro (BNL). Iraqi dictator Saddam Hussein had meanwhile shown few signs of really relenting in his antagonism toward Israel. Instead of concentrating on domestic reconstruction, he had resumed the build-up of his armed forces, taking some steps toward acquisition of advanced weaponry, including possibly nuclear weaponry. Ignoring protests from Washington and London, he had publicly executed a British journalist whom he alleged to be a spy. Footage of the execution figured in prime-time news throughout the United States. The decision to reverse "constructive engagement" originated in the Department of Agriculture, which managed CCC credits. Agriculture Department officials had said little earlier. Now, their voices dominated. State Department representatives argued for continuing the existing policy but lost.

In the summer of 1990, after sending many signals that were missed or misunderstood in Washington and among Iraq's Arab neighbors, Iraqi dictator Saddam Hussein invaded Kuwait. This new reality brought to the foreground interests previously subordinated: oil, regional stability, and, more broadly, the maintenance of international order. The chief framer of the "appreciation" from which U.S. leadership in the first Gulf War emerged was President Bush himself.

The moral of this case study is that value judgments change along with changes in reality judgments and action judgments. While the interests may be constant, priorities among those interests are not.

PRECEPT THREE

As argued in some detail by Neustadt and May in *Thinking in Time*, initial reality judgments can be sharpened by taking care to distinguish clearly what is known from what is merely presumed to be true. Presumptions often have great influence in appreciations. Participants in the policy process frequently push particular presumptions because they suit either their value preferences or their action preferences. *Thinking in Time* goes into reasons why separating the known from the presumed can help protect against this risk. Here, the point expands, for intelligence analysts need to note presumptions of their own (and of other analysts) that might have distorting effects; they need to gauge the mixture of known and presumed in the reality judgments of the other governments or organizations; and—at least as important—they must try to sort out what is known and presumed by the policymakers they hope to inform.

The injunction to think about what is in the minds of U.S. policy-makers sits uncomfortably with many intelligence analysts. They have been schooled not to let their own policy preferences intrude into assessments. This salutary teaching has often, however, encouraged deliberate inattention to, or attempts to avoid any appearance of attention to, ongoing debates about alternative courses of action. The consequence has sometimes been Sergeant Friday–style "just the facts, ma'am" reportage, which contributes to the lack of connection between the intelligence and policy communities that Robert Gates observed and experienced during his tours in the White House.

The precept here is not counsel to intelligence analysts to become advocates of particular courses of action. It is counsel to become as sensitive as possible to the differing presumptions in the minds of users of intelligence analysis. That is how they can best help decisionmakers convert judgments about what is going on into judgments about what matters and what to do about it.

The point is illustrated by the next to last case in this volume. It concerns the Philippines in the mid-1980s. Intelligence analysts as well as decisionmakers recognized that the regime of Philippine dictator Ferdinand Marcos was increasingly shaky. The intelligence analysts recognized also that the decisionmakers came to this reality with varied sets of values. Those in the State and Defense departments and in the U.S. mission in Manila were much of one mind. They were concerned about U.S. base rights, the stakes of U.S. investors, and the ability of Marcos or a successor to keep peace in the islands.

But the circle of decisionmakers was wider, and so was the range of their concerns. Some individuals in Congress wanted Marcos to fall, in part because he had ordered the murder of an opponent whom they admired. In the executive branch, the ultimate decisionmaker, President Ronald Reagan, regarded Marcos as a personal friend and thought in addition that the United States owed him loyalty as a longtime ally in the Cold War.

Analysts in the State Department's Bureau of Intelligence and Research (INR) and in the Central Intelligence Agency (CIA) collaborated to an unusual degree both with one another and with the individuals working out action choices on the seventh floor of the Department of State, the E-ring of the Pentagon, the embassy in Manila, and National Security Council (NSC) staff in the Old Executive Office Building. As a reader of Chapter 5 will see, intelligence estimates and other analytic products were specifically tailored to take into account President Reagan's particular outlook. Though they agreed that the Marcos regime was probably doomed, they kept saying only that Marcos was part of the problem but possibly also part of the solution. This language made it more likely that the president would not simply reject the estimates as prejudiced against Marcos and that he would, as a result, be influenced by the evidence, which showed that Marcos was the problem.

Purists may think that these analysts were wrong to skew what they said for the sake of getting the attention of the president. They might, however, note that this is the one case in this volume where the United States can be said to have been most successful in managing a relationship with a dictator.

A case not included in this collection illustrates the price paid when analysts do not engage decisionmakers' presumptions. It concerns U.S. involvement in Lebanon in the early 1980s. At the time, Secretary of State George Shultz and Secretary of Defense Caspar Weinberger were open antagonists, quarreling about almost every visible issue. Lebanon was then suffering civil warfare, compounded by the occupation of parts of the country by elements of the Palestine Liberation Organization and by the armed forces of Syria and of Israel. Shultz supported special envoy Philip Habib, who was attempting to broker a truce that would lead to Syrian and Israeli withdrawal. A key presumption for Habib and therefore for

Shultz was that the Syrians and Israelis had forces in Lebanon only to off-set one another; hence, if one party seemed credibly willing to withdraw, the other would agree to do likewise. Weinberger did not directly dispute Habib's presumption; he simply took the position that the chance of a truce and mutual withdrawal was too slim to justify keeping a substantial contingent of U.S. Marines in Lebanon, especially since the Marines were increasingly viewed by the Lebanese as supporters of one particular faction in their civil war.

Analysts in the intelligence community, seldom in perfect agreement about any subject, were in this instance harmonious to a degree that would have delighted a choir director. They believed unanimously that Habib's key presumption was wrong, and that the Syrians intended to stay in Lebanon regardless of what the Israelis did. Although they were aware of differences of opinion within the Israeli government, they believed that the person in charge, Defense Minister Ariel Sharon, had no more intention of voluntarily withdrawing from Lebanon than of abandoning Arab lands conquered in the Six-Day War.

For practical reasons, however, the intelligence analysts kept their opinions to themselves. Even Robert Ames, the highly respected and personally forthright National Intelligence Officer for the Middle East who was on good personal terms with Shultz, kept his mouth shut. No analyst was willing to appear to intervene in a dispute between Shultz and Weinberger unless the White House specifically asked for an estimate. Even when that happened — at much too late a date to matter — the resulting estimate was guarded and ambiguous. For the most part, all that the analysts did to influence the policy debate was to insert into the National Intelligence Daily, and other such publications, bits of information that hinted at their doubts concerning Habib's presumption. For example, they highlighted a report that the Israelis, throughout their zone of occupation, were putting up road signs in Hebrew. But the fact that the whole intelligence community thought the U.S. government to be guided by a false presumption remained virtually unknown until after Lebanese terrorists drove an explosives-laden truck into the Marine barracks in Beirut, killing 241 Marines and prompting President Reagan to, as he put it, "redeploy to sea" and back off from any role as mediator.

In this instance, the intelligence community would have served the United States better if analysts had volunteered their assessments of Syrian and Israeli policies. They would not have been weighing in on the side of Weinberger against Shultz, but simply identifying reigning presumptions and laying out the evidence that caused them to question those presumptions. As was said to May once by Robert Bowie, former overseer of CIA's analysts and before that an assistant secretary of state for policy planning, "if analysts see that there's a cliff on one side of the road, it's their duty to warn the people who are driving the bus."

PRECEPT FOUR

In framing reality judgments, it can be useful to test alternative paradigms of explanation. The classic book *Essence of Decision*, written by Graham Allison and recently revised by Allison and Zelikow, describes three essentially different paradigms that can account for the observed behavior of another government or organization.[3]

One paradigm—the unitary rational actor—seeks explanations in the interests and motives (that is, in the collective value judgments) of the entity in question. Reliance on this paradigm would lead one to say that road signs in Hebrew went up in Lebanon because "Israel" planned permanent occupation of the area.

The second paradigm, organizational behavior, seeks explanations in the standard operating procedures or routines of the government or organization in question or in processes that organizational theorists label "satisficing," that is, processes that settle on the first minimally acceptable course of action rather than "maximizing" or searching for the best course. This paradigm could yield a conclusion that the road signs might have gone up because Israeli Defense Force manuals prescribed putting up such signs, or because the Israeli command in Lebanon was concerned to minimize road mishaps.

The third paradigm, governmental politics (originally mislabeled "bureaucratic politics") seeks explanations in political bargaining within a government or organization. The observed outcome reflects not so much the purposes of the government or organization as the conflicting purposes of leaders within the government or organization, one-upping or compromising with one another. From this paradigm, the road signs could be interpreted as a maneuver by Sharon, or possibly the result of an internal bargain in Jerusalem.

Figure 2 offers a matrix suggesting questions to be asked in the framing of any and all reality judgments.

PRECEPT FIVE

Regarding value judgments, understanding can be sharpened by use of a different matrix. Broadly considered, value judgments derive from axiomatic beliefs or from calculations of interest, advantage, opportunity, and the like.[4] At the end of World War II, the United States occupied

---

3.   Graham T. Allison, *Essence of Decision: Explaining the Cuban Missile Crisis* (Boston: Little, Brown, 1972); Graham T. Allison and Philip Zelikow, *Essence of Decision: Explaining the Cuban Missile Crisis*, 2nd ed. (New York: Longman, 1999).

4.   This matrix is sketched in Ernest R. May, "The Nature of Foreign Policy," in Akira Iriye, ed., *Rethinking International Relations: Ernest R. May and the Study of World Affairs* (Chicago: Imprint Publications, 1998), pp. 3–14.

Figure 2. Tests for Reality Judgments.

Product of:	Known	Presumed
Unitary Rational Actor?		
Organizational Processes?		
Internal Organizational or Governmental Politics?		
Something Else?		

southern Korea while the Soviet Union occupied northern Korea. Negotiations about creating a unified nation broke down. After 1948 there was an independent Republic of Korea in the south and a nominally independent People's Republic of Korea in the north. President Harry S. Truman and his top advisers formally reviewed the question of what, given the burgeoning Cold War with the Soviet Union, should be U.S. policy regarding the Korean Peninsula. Not just once but twice, the president accepted a recommendation from his National Security Council to act on the premise that the United States had no strategic interest in Korea. In June 1950, however, when North Korea invaded South Korea, President Truman decided almost at once to defend South Korea. A costly two-and-a-half year war ensued. The president and his advisers had seen the North Korean action as sponsored by Moscow (which, indeed, it was) and as an act of aggression that called into play the axiom derived from experiences of the 1930s, namely that aggression, if not resisted immediately, would feed upon itself and lead eventually to large-scale war. In this instance, the axiom overwhelmed calculation. Something similar occurred in 1990, when President Bush reacted to Saddam Hussein's aggression against Kuwait.

But value judgments, whether derived from axioms or calculations, vary in their substantive emphasis. A reality judgment may seem to "make a difference" because of inherent characteristics or because of anticipated consequences. (This is similar to the distinction made by students of ethics between the deontological and the consequentialist.) Many of the cases in this volume show decisionmakers and analysts concerned about a dictatorship, but with the center of concern on the one hand the fact of being a dictatorship or, on the other hand, the potential consequences of supporting it or not supporting it. The case studies here concerning Nicaragua and Iran illustrate sharply how the axiom that dictatorship is bad can conflict with calculations either that the dictator has his uses or that an alternative government might be unfriendly.

Figure 3 offers a simple matrix for disaggregating value judgments.

PRECEPT SIX

Action judgments also fall into two broad categories. They answer one of two questions: *what* to do? And what to *do*? In other words, what strategy

Figure 3. Tests for Value Judgments.

		Principal basis	
		Axiom	Calculation
Center of concern	Inherent characteristics		
	Possible consequences		

or broad course of action is appropriate, given the mix of reality and value judgments, and what tactics, or specific actions, could implement a strategy? There are at least five levels of disaggregation for these choices, applicable to both categories of action judgments, though in differing degrees.[5]

First comes definition of the operational objective. Though an individual or organization or government may have general objectives such as security or prosperity, an action judgment should include a definition of a measurably attainable objective. In the Philippine case in this volume, the United States had general hopes, but its operational objective narrowed down to peaceful removal of President Marcos from office.

Second, an action judgment depends on some type of theory as to how the operational objective can be attained. In the Lebanon case described above, Shultz and Habib acted on a theory that the United States would be accepted as an honest broker by Syria, Israel, and the various factions in Lebanon. This theory turned out to be wrong.

Thirdly, an action judgment involves some type of plan that applies the theory to the particular case. The fourth and fifth considerations are resources and implementation. Are the necessary resources available? Can the plan actually be carried out? In several cases here—the Congo, Iran, and Nicaragua—the reader will find that these considerations did not receive adequate attention within the U.S. government.

Figure 4 gives a matrix for calling attention to the most important elements of action judgments.

PRECEPT SEVEN
Effective intelligence analysts have to estimate not only the appreciations of other analysts and of the decisionmakers to whom they are responsible,

---

5. The argument here is amplified in Philip D. Zelikow, "Foreign Policy Engineering: From Theory to Practice and Back Again," *International Security*, Vol. 18, No. 4 (Spring 1994), pp. 143–171.

Figure 4. Tests for Action Judgments.

	What to do	**What to do**
Operational objective		
Theory		
Plan		
Resources		
Implementation		

but also those of prospective decisionmakers in other governments. They have to take into account the ways in which presumptions, axiomatic beliefs, calculations, and action plans can vary with histories, cultures, and circumstances. After defeating Saddam Hussein's armed forces and occupying Iraq in 2003, Americans expected to find stocks of weapons of mass destruction. They found none. They found it hard to understand why Saddam had not tried to prove that he had no such weapons. Had he done that, he might have dissuaded the United States from attacking him. Only in retrospect did analysts recognize that he had probably not been thinking of Washington as much as of Teheran. The possibility that this might be the case should have, but apparently did not, figure in intelligence estimates given to U.S. decisionmakers before the war. Good intelligence analysis ought to involve a disciplined imaginative effort to understand and describe processes of thought and decision in foreign areas. Metaphorically, intelligence analysts should think of themselves as always using bifocals or even trifocals.

These precepts emerged from discussion of the many cases developed for the Intelligence and Policy Program. Each of the cases that follows can be thought of as a laboratory for trying out and testing some or all of them.

Chapter 1

China, 1945–1948: Making Hard Choices

Ernest R. May, with assistance from Kirsten Lundberg and Robert D. Johnson

Two years after World War II, the United States faced the possibility of becoming involved in a civil war in China. Nationalist China's dictator, Generalissimo Chiang Kai-shek, who had been America's ally against Japan, was challenged by a Communist Party led by Mao Zedong.[1] As of mid-1947, U.S. experts agreed that Chiang was in danger of losing to Mao. President Harry S. Truman, his advisers, and the U.S. Congress had to decide whether or not to give Chiang the support needed to prevent Communist success.

Truman's Secretary of State, General George C. Marshall, concluded, as he said to the Senate Foreign Relations Committee and House Foreign Affairs Committee in executive session in February 1948, that such support for Chiang would require "sizeable forces and resources over an indefinite period." It would involve "obligations and responsibilities on the part of this Government which I am convinced the American people would never knowingly accept."[2] His judgment prevailed. The United States gave some economic aid to Chiang but left him militarily on his own.

By mid-1949, Communist military success had been sufficient so that Chiang's supporters prepared for retreat to the island of Taiwan. By the end of the year they had surrendered all of mainland China. President

---

1. In Pinyin spelling, which is current today, Chiang Kai-shek is Jiang Jie-shi. His Nationalist Party, which we render as Kuomintang, is Guomintang. Because U.S. documents of the 1940s use the older Wade-Giles spellings, we use them in the text wherever not doing so might cause confusion. When that is not the case, we use Pinyin, as, for example with Mao, who was Mao Tse-tung in Wade-Giles and Mao Zedong in Pinyin but was referred to in the 1940s simply as "Mao."

2. Executive session testimony before the Senate Foreign Relations Committee and the House Foreign Affairs Committee, February 21, 1948, in *U.S. Department of State, United States Relations with China with Special Reference to the Period 1944–1946* (Washington, D.C.: U.S. Government Printing Office [U.S. GPO], 1949), pp. 380–384 (hereafter referred to as *The White Paper*).

Harry S. Truman had meanwhile been elected to a full second term, and in August 1949 Marshall's successor, Secretary of State Dean G. Acheson, issued a "White Paper," documenting in detail the assessments behind decisions regarding Chiang. Over succeeding years, critics of Truman, Marshall, and Acheson would gain increasing support for a thesis that the administration had unnecessarily "lost" China, possibly because of the machinations of Communist subversives inside the government.

Background

Some background is needed to understand the U.S. dilemma. After the fall of its last emperor in 1911, China had declared itself a republic. In the 1920s it had become a one-party state, deliberately modeled after the Soviet Union. The ruling party was the Kuomintang or Nationalist Party. The Chinese Communist Party was originally a faction within the Kuomintang.

In 1927 Chiang had emerged as leader of the Kuomintang. A soldier who had had some training in Japan and had also had vague links with gangsters in Shanghai, he had successfully forced China's provincial warlords to subordinate themselves to his Nationalist government. Almost at the moment of victory, he turned on the Communists within the Kuomintang and tried to suppress them. They rescued themselves by banding together in a "long march" from southern China to an area in the north around Yenan, which they proved able to defend against Chiang's armies.

Though both the Nationalists and the Communists used the Soviet Union as a model, neither imitated the Soviets in creating a government separate from the party. Both ruled through party cadres, which exacted taxes, drafted soldiers, and otherwise gave orders through local and provincial governments. Many of the Kuomintang cadres made common cause with landlords, merchants, and other local elites, leaving conditions for the local population little better, if not worse, than under the emperor. The Communists, by contrast, maintained tight discipline but were perceived as honest, fair, and genuinely offering peasants and townspeople hope of better material conditions in the future.[3]

In 1937, when Imperial Japan commenced an effort to conquer China, the Kuomintang and the Communists temporarily joined forces. After the

---

3. See the contemporaneous reportage in Theodore H. White and Annalee Jacoby, *Thunder Out of China* (New York: William Sloane Associates, 1946); and the retrospective assessments in *Cambridge History of China*, vol. 13: John K. Fairbank and Albert Feuerwerker, *Republican China, 1912–1949*, part 2 (Cambridge, UK: Cambridge University Press, 1986).

Japanese occupied most of coastal China but slowed their drive toward the interior, Kuomintang and Communist forces continued to defend against the invader but began to fight one another. In November 1938, Mao described the Communists' aim as "the seizure of political power by force of arms" and added, memorably, that "political power grows out of the barrel of a gun."[4]

Though the American public had generally sympathized with China against Japan, the U.S. government became an ally of China only after the Japanese attack on Pearl Harbor in December 1941. The first U.S. priority was the war against Germany and Italy in Europe. The second was an amphibious campaign against Japanese-held islands in the Pacific. China was one of several theaters with lower priority.

The United States established a military mission in Chiang's temporary capital at Chungking. Its head was Lieutenant General Joseph W. Stilwell, who spoke Chinese and had had extended periods of service in China. By agreement between Chiang and America's wartime president, Franklin D. Roosevelt, Stilwell was to be the channel for military aid to China, to command all U.S. military forces in mainland Asia, and to be Chiang's chief of staff for whatever Chinese forces Chiang assigned to him. The purpose of Stilwell's mission was to maximize Chinese military pressure on Japan.

Stilwell was not by nature either diplomatic or patient. His nickname was "Vinegar Joe." He quickly became frustrated, and he grew more frustrated and angry by the day, for Chiang was plainly reluctant even to let Stilwell arrange for equipping and training Chinese forces, let alone commanding them in battle. Stilwell and most Americans who visited China during the war concluded that Chiang was not interested in improving the efficiency of troops that might prove loyal to one of his rivals within the Kuomintang. Nor did he seem interested in committing his own best soldiers to any operations against the Japanese other than those that protected his base areas. He wanted to save them for his contest with Mao and the Communists. "The Japanese," he said in 1941, "are a disease of the skin; the Communists are a disease of the heart."[5]

By 1944 the U.S. relationship with Chiang seemed to be moving toward crisis. Victory in Europe was near, and the amphibious campaign in the Pacific had brought U.S. forces within striking distance of Japan's home islands. Roosevelt and his military advisers urgently wanted operations in China that would erode or tie down Japanese forces that might

---

4. "Problems of War and Strategy," November 6, 1938, *Selected Writings of Mao Zedong*, vol. 2 (Oxford, UK: Pergamon Press, 1965), p. 224.

5. White and Jacoby, *Thunder Out of China*, p. 129.

otherwise be sent to defend the last Japanese island redoubts or to resist a U.S. invasion of Japan. Guided by Stilwell, the U.S. government became increasingly insistent that Chiang follow U.S. advice, improve the quality of his armies, and commit them against the Japanese.

In the early summer of 1944, Roosevelt sent Vice President Henry A. Wallace to China. As Barbara Tuchman comments in her history of Stilwell's work in China, Roosevelt had more than one motive. "Wallace had made many enemies. The President...was considering dumping Wallace in favor of some more generally acceptable running mate, and it was a natural instinct in the circumstances to want him out of sight."[6] But, as the most highly placed American ever to have visited China, Wallace symbolized the importance that Roosevelt now attached to Chinese military cooperation.

Wallace pressed Chiang to follow Stilwell's recommendations. He also pressed him to compose his differences with the Communists so that all Chinese armies could engage the Japanese. Wallace left Chungking moderately optimistic that Chiang would do as asked. One token was Chiang's consent that the U.S. military mission could post an observer group in Yenan. But Stilwell and other Americans in Chungking warned Washington insistently that the Japanese had resumed offensive operations in China and that Kuomintang forces were in danger of being put to rout.

In December 1944, with victory in Europe virtually certain but with the duration and cost of the war against Japan very uncertain, Roosevelt sent a new special emissary to Chungking, instructing him to press for unification of the Nationalist and Communist armies and, in the longer run, for absorption of the Communists into a unified Chinese government. The emissary was Major General Patrick J. Hurley, a flamboyant Oklahoma oil prospector who had been secretary of war under Herbert Hoover.

Though Hurley initially lent strong support to Stilwell, Chiang and his family and friends demanded that Stilwell be replaced, and Hurley eventually gave way. Lieutenant General Albert C. Wedemeyer arrived as Stilwell's replacement.

One issue for Hurley was how hard to press Chiang on cooperation with the Communists. To Wallace, Chiang had denounced the notion that the Communists were "agrarian democrats." He said that they followed orders from Moscow, which would "not feel safe if the Communists were not in power in China." They were, he said, "more communistic than the

---

6. Barbara W. Tuchman, *Stilwell and the American Experience in China, 1911–1945* (New York: Macmillan, 1971), p. 464.

Russian Communists."[7] But Hurley had seen contradictory evidence that Wallace had cited to Chiang, as well as a dispatch from the U.S. ambassador in Moscow, W. Averell Harriman, which quoted Soviet dictator Joseph Stalin as saying that the Chinese Communists "are not real Communists, they are 'margarine' Communists."[8] Hurley himself had chosen to go to Chungking via Moscow, where Soviet Foreign Minister Vyacheslav Molotov assured him that the Chinese Communists "had no relation whatever to Communism" and that the Soviet Union would be happy to see them brought under Chiang's control.[9]

Hurley thus arrived in China believing that the Chinese Communists would not have Soviet support and that he could successfully persuade them to come to terms with Chiang. Knowing that Chiang's government was fast running out of money, Hurley also believed that he would have little trouble getting Chiang to offer the Communists reasonable terms.

In November 1944, Hurley flew to Yenan. He surprised the Communist welcoming committee by descending from his plane, whipping his Stetson around his head, and emitting an Oklahoma Indian war whoop. Mao and his foreign minister, Chou En-Lai, gave Hurley a cordial reception and sent him back to Chungking even more persuaded that his mission would prove successful.

In fact, as it turned out, neither the Nationalists nor the Communists proved interested in the kind of accord that Hurley sought to forge. Receiving from the United States both money and equipment and recognizing that Japan would eventually have to surrender, Chiang did begin to devote more effort to fighting the Japanese. Since a Japanese offensive in the winter of 1944–1945 ate into Nationalist territory and even threatened Chungking, Chiang perhaps had little choice. In any case, Hurley came to think that Chiang was pliable while the Communists were not. Homesick and not in good health, he also came to think that his efforts as mediator were being sabotaged by pro-Communist China hands in the observer mission in Yenan and in the State Department at home.

While Hurley's suspicion of sabotage was wholly unfounded, he was not wrong in believing that most of the Americans in Yenan (and many in Chungking) had a higher opinion of the Communists than of the Nationalists. For at least one Foreign Service officer — John Stewart

---

7. Summary notes of conversations between Vice President Henry A. Wallace and President Chiang Kai-shek, June 1944: June 22, *The White Paper*, p. 553.

8. U.S. Department of State, *Foreign Relations of the United States* (Washington, D.C.: U.S. GPO, 1861–) (hereafter FRUS), vol. 6, 1944, p. 799.

9. Russell Buhite, *Patrick J. Hurley and American Foreign Policy* (Ithaca, N.Y.: Cornell University Press, 1973), pp. 151–152, citing an unsent dispatch in Hurley's manuscripts in the library of the University of Oklahoma in Norman, Oklahoma.

Service—this was sufficiently true so that he could properly be labeled pro-Communist. And Service had company in this respect among civilians in the observer mission who represented the Office of Strategic Services, the forerunner of the Central Intelligence Agency (CIA), and also among American journalists who traveled to Yenan. The majority of members of the observer mission, however, regarded the Communists as simply more honest and efficient than the Nationalists; they assumed both that a Communist regime in China would resemble Stalin's dictatorship in the Soviet Union and that Mao and his associates would follow orders from Moscow.

The State Department's China hands were even less pro-Communist than those on the spot in Yenan or Chungking. They were concentrated in the Division of Chinese Affairs, which was part of the State Department's Office of Far Eastern Affairs. During the early part of Hurley's mission in China, the chief of the Division of Chinese Affairs was John Carter Vincent, a Georgian who had spent most of his diplomatic career in China, including a stint as deputy chief of mission in Chungking under Clarence Gauss, who was ambassador until October 1944, when Hurley took that post himself. Like most of the American China hands in China, Vincent had a low opinion of the Nationalist leadership but presumed that the Communists were Stalinists and, at the very least, were subject to Soviet influence. Like Hurley, Vincent hoped that the Soviets would encourage the Chinese Communists to come to terms with the Nationalists in order to avoid a Soviet-American conflict in Asia. But more than Hurley—or, indeed, virtually any other China hand—Vincent looked for a third force of liberal, pro-Western Chinese, opposed to both Chiang and the Chinese Communist Party (CCP), who could emerge as the dominant force in post-war China.[10]

Harry S. Truman, who became president after Roosevelt's death in April 1945, preferred more orderly procedures than those of his predecessor. Instead of relying heavily on personal aides, special emissaries, and new organizations like the OSS, he sought to have the State Department become once again, as before Roosevelt, the chief channel for information and advice about issues of foreign policy. This did not, of course, stop other agencies from gathering data so that their chiefs could challenge the State Department's views, but Truman's decree did give State Department officials more authority than they had had for some time. Foreign Service officers' estimates of situations abroad thus had a higher likelihood of being accepted as bases for policy decisions.

---

10. Gary May, *The China Scapegoat: The Diplomatic Ordeal of John Carter Vincent* (Washington, D.C.: New Republic Books, 1979), pp. 130–150.

Truman reinforced the State Department—or so he thought—by naming as Secretary of State James F. Byrnes, a former senator from South Carolina, onetime Supreme Court justice, and wartime "assistant president" under Roosevelt. Byrnes then chose Dean Acheson to be undersecretary. During a previous tenure as assistant secretary in the department, Acheson had had a falling out with the Japan hands who then dominated the Far Eastern Office. Not of a forgiving nature, Acheson removed these men as soon as he had power to do so. He then made Vincent director of the Far Eastern Office. Moreover, Byrnes and Acheson told Vincent to report directly to them, bypassing the assistant secretary to whom he was nominally subordinate.

Vincent's former job as chief of the China Division went to Everett Drumwright, a China hand with close ties to missionaries who were fiercely anti-Communist and pro-Chiang. Memoranda from the China Division became more reflective of such attitudes. For example, a communication of mid-November to Acheson via Vincent declared that Communist success in any part of China would "bring about a situation...little different from that obtaining before the defeat of Japan. Instead of a Japanese-dominated puppet regime we should probably find in its place one dominated by the USSR."[11]

Others in the State Department contributed reports and memoranda that buttressed Drumwright's arguments. The embassy in Moscow cautioned against any optimism about Soviet cooperation in the Far East. Officers in the Division of Eastern European Affairs were intent on teaching President Truman and his advisers to be less trusting than their predecessors about Communist ambitions and tactics. They predicted Soviet use of the Chinese Communists as "an effective machine to build upon and expand their influence in a somewhat similar manner to the methods they have used in central and eastern Europe."[12] There seemed thus to be consensus within the State Department that the Chinese Communists were acting on behalf of Moscow.

Hurley had meanwhile managed to rid his mission, including both the military mission and the observer group in Yenan, of most of the men whom he suspected of sabotage. Their replacements were mostly not experienced China hands. They were, however, Foreign Service officers who prided themselves on accurate reporting. Setting forth the facts as they observed them, they reported unequivocally that there was still no evidence of Soviet advisers, arms, or supplies among China's Communists. They pointed out that Russian occupying forces seemed to

---

11. Drumwright memo, November 16, 1945, FRUS, vol. 7, 1945, pp. 629–634.

12. Harriman, September 1, 1945, FRUS, vol. 7, 1945, pp. 982–984; memo by Durbrow, Chief of Division of East European Affairs, May 10, 1945, ibid., p. 864.

be seizing all movable goods in Manchuria and sending them home, not turning them over to Chinese allies.

Other Americans in China, particularly military and naval officers, concentrated on seeking and sending back to Washington evidence, mostly in the form of rumor, that the Chinese Communists were acting on behalf of the Soviet Union. A constant theme of reports from the U.S. embassy in Moscow was that the Russians planned to use the Chinese Communists as instruments for controlling some or all of China.

By November 1945, President Truman and nearly all members of his cabinet accepted this assessment of what was going on in China. The chief exception was Wallace, now secretary of commerce, but his expressions of doubt had little apparent impact.[13]

Late that month, Hurley came back to the United States on what was supposed to be simply a period of leave. To the total surprise of Truman, all his advisers, and the entire State Department, Hurley called in some news reporters and announced that he was resigning because State Department careerists had continued to sabotage his work and he wanted to be free to fight his "enemies."[14]

When Truman learned of Hurley's resignation, his immediate concern was to defend the administration against attacks from Republicans and admirers of Chiang. The news had come while the president was lunching with his cabinet. According to Secretary Wallace's diary, Truman said in response that "we were the one big nation that wanted a united democratic China. The President said that unless we took a strong stand in China, Russia would take the place of Japan in the Far East." Secretary of Agriculture Clinton Anderson then suggested that the president ask General George C. Marshall, the wartime army chief of staff and a national hero, to step in. Truman accepted the suggestion and acted upon it that afternoon, asking Marshall to serve as his special representative to China.[15]

When the Senate Foreign Relations Committee held hearings on Hurley's resignation and Marshall's nomination as the president's special representative for China, Secretary of State James Byrnes testified that America's aim was "a strong, united, and democratic China." This language was quoted in Truman's formal instructions to Marshall.[16] Marshall

---

13. John Morton Blum, ed., *The Price of Vision: The Diary of Henry A. Wallace 1942–1946* (Boston: Houghton Mifflin, 1973), pp. 519–522.

14. Buhite, *Patrick Hurley*, pp. 165–170; May, *China Scapegoat*, pp. 140–143.

15. Blum, *The Price of Vision*, pp. 519–522.

16. U.S. Congress, Senate Committee on Foreign Relations, *Investigation of Far Eastern Policy*, 79th Cong., 2nd sess., 1945, published in U.S. Congress, Senate Committee on Foreign Relations, *United States–China Relations*, 92nd Cong., 1st sess., 1973, Appendix, p. 96; *The White Paper*, pp. 764–814.

was to go to China to carry on what had been begun during the war: he should try to get the Nationalists and Communists to compose their differences, allow the merger of their armies into a single nonpolitical national army, and agree to compete peacefully within some mutually acceptable constitutional system.

In order to obtain Nationalist concessions, Marshall was empowered to use almost any form of enticement or threat. For example, he could offer to keep the U.S. forces in place or threaten to withdraw them. There were more than 100,000 U.S. troops in China, mostly Marines. They had helped Chiang's forces move from south China to north China and Manchuria; indeed, without this assistance, Manchuria and much of northeastern China almost certainly would have fallen to the CCP.[17] By controlling key ports and railroads, the American military had kept open Nationalist supply lines and freed Nationalist troops for other purposes. Marshall could offer to continue this assistance or threaten to curtail it. He could also offer to release or threaten to withhold relief funds and military supplies that were still being shipped in fulfillment of wartime commitments. He had authority to tell Chiang that the United States would support him if the Nationalists were reasonable and the Communists were not, but that it would desert him if the Communists were reasonable and the Nationalists were not.[18]

Although Marshall accepted the president's commission, he insisted that Truman and Byrnes look at the possibility that the stated objective of the United States might prove unattainable. He asked whether they agreed with him that if the United States were to abandon Chiang, "there would follow the tragic consequences of a divided China and of a probable Russian reassumption of power in Manchuria, the combined effect of this resulting in the defeat or loss of the major purpose of our war in the Pacific." According to Marshall's notes, "the President and Mr. Byrnes concurred in this view."[19]

Like virtually every U.S. policymaker of the period, Marshall believed that the United States could not tolerate a CCP victory because it would give the Soviets a foothold in East Asia. Marshall obtained from Truman and Undersecretary Acheson a secret codicil to his instructions that, "in the event that I was unable to secure the necessary action by the Generalissimo, which I thought reasonable and desirable, it would still be

17. Steven Levine, "A New Look at American Mediation in the Chinese Civil War: The Marshall Mission and Manchuria," *Diplomatic History*, Vol. 3 (1979), pp. 349–377.

18. Gordon Chang, *Friends and Enemies: The United States, China, and the Soviet Union, 1948–1972* (Stanford, Calif.: Stanford University Press, 1990), pp. 3–8.

19. Memorandum of conversation, Truman, Leahy, Byrnes, and Marshall, December 11, 1945, FRUS, vol. 7, 1945, pp. 767–769.

necessary for the US Government, through me, to continue to back the National Government of the Republic of China." Thus, even though the United States adhered to the wartime definition of its policy objective of a united China, there was already a high-level consensus that the U.S. government should back a non-Communist regime rather than its Communist opponents.[20]

Marshall was no stranger to China. In the 1920s, when foreign residents still enjoyed extraterritoriality and protection by military forces of their own, Marshall had spent three years as deputy commander, then commander, of a U.S. infantry regiment garrisoned at Tientsin. He had even learned enough Chinese to sit in judgment in legal proceedings involving Chinese witnesses. It was in this period that he had come to know and admire Stilwell. During the war he had done his utmost to keep Stilwell in Chungking. Though Wedemeyer was a younger favorite of Marshall's, it is almost certain that Marshall came to China at least a little prejudiced against Chiang by reason of having heard some of Stilwell's complaints.

Marshall arrived in China on December 20, 1945. By January 10, 1946, he had succeeded in inducing both the Nationalists and Communists to agree to a cease-fire. He had placated the Nationalists by allowing them to continue to move forces into Manchuria. He had placated the Communists by persuading Chiang to call off advances into Communist-held parts of Jehol and Chahar provinces. The cease-fire was supposed to be policed by tripartite teams of Nationalists, Communists, and Americans, all overseen by a tripartite executive on which Marshall was the representative of the United States.

Despite sporadic fighting, the cease-fire seemed to hold for about three months. Then, in mid-April, Chiang's troops in Manchuria's Jili province assaulted and captured Changchun, forcing Communist troops to flee. The Communists counterattacked at several points, eventually regaining Changchun. Another cease-fire arranged in June had little or no effect on either Nationalist or Communist military movements. Civil war raged in many parts of Manchuria, north China, and even central China.

Marshall had originally urged parallel negotiations for new constitutional arrangements. Though he avoided formal use of the term "coalition," he clearly hoped for compromises that would allow Nationalists and Communists to be members of a single government under conditions that neither would see as requiring capitulation to the other. But political undertakings proved even more elusive than military undertakings. Chiang had no interest in any constitution except one guaranteeing a strong national executive and a weak legislature, both under Kuomintang

---

20. Truman to Marshall, December 15, 1945, FRUS, vol. 7, 1945, p. 770.

control, and vesting minimal power in local governments. Aware of Chiang's priorities, the Communists could safely call for a weak executive, a strong and broadly representative legislature, and maximum local autonomy.

By August 1946 Marshall had concluded provisionally that his mission was hopeless. He told Chiang that he intended to ask Truman to recall him. He also cautioned Chiang that, though the Nationalists seemed to be gaining ground militarily, much of the gain was illusory. He gave Chiang his professional opinion "that the long lines of communication and the terrain favored the employment of the Communist guerrilla tactics" and that continued warfare "would probably lead to Communist control in China."[21]

Chiang made enough verbal concessions to persuade Marshall not to ask immediately for recall. Seeing little besides continued military movements by both sides, Marshall in October 1946 advised Chiang that he was in fact asking to be recalled. Once again he offered a pessimistic assessment of Nationalist military prospects. Chiang, however, seemed confident of Nationalist victory. "Given time," he said to Marshall, "the ripe apple will fall into our laps."[22] He again promised enough concessions to induce Marshall not to leave just yet. In fact, Marshall remained in China until early January 1947.

In May 1946 Marshall had been told privately that Truman wanted him to succeed Byrnes as secretary of state. Approaching his sixty-sixth birthday and in uncertain health, Marshall did not crave the post. Duty, however, obliged him to say yes.[23] On January 8, 1947, he departed China. On the same day his nomination to be secretary of state was announced from the White House. On a stopover in Hawaii, he reported publicly on his mission. He blamed its failure on the irreconcilable ambitions of both parties. While he seemed to condemn the Communists more than the Nationalists, he spoke of "irreconcilable groups within the Kuomintang, interested in the preservation of their feudal control of China."[24]

Debates within the U.S. Government

Toward the end of his time in China, Marshall had turned to economic coercion as potential means of influencing Chiang. He had arranged for an

---

21. *The White Paper*, p. 176.

22. *The White Paper*, p. 214.

23. Forrest C. Pogue, *George C. Marshall*, 4 vols. (New York: Viking, 1973–87), vol. 4, p. 113.

24. *The White Paper*, p. 688.

embargo on deliveries of small-arms ammunition and other items still in the wartime supply pipeline. The embargo had had no apparent effect on Chiang.[25] Now that Marshall was to have overall responsibility for U.S. foreign relations, he would have to decide whether to continue or to rescind the embargo. More broadly, he would have to decide whether, in spite of the faults of the Nationalist regime, the United States should give it backing in order, if possible, to prevent victory by the Communists.

From the American diplomatic mission in China, Marshall received advice that, in differing degrees, argued for backing the Nationalists. Though Marshall had had plenary powers in China, he had not held the title of ambassador. He had chosen a genuine old China hand for that post. John Leighton Stuart, who became ambassador in July 1946, was a New Testament scholar, formerly a Presbyterian missionary in China, and more recently president of Yenching University in the traditional Chinese capital of Beijing. He had all the attitudes of a bearer of the "white man's burden," viewing the Chinese with a mixture of impatience, affection, and zealous optimism. He would point out to Washington that the Chinese had a "lack of self-reliance...partially accounted for by the family system and other age-long patterns," and that there was a "Chinese trait of denouncing some other person for one's mishaps." At the same time, he would profess confidence "in the capacity of the Chinese people to master modern techniques and to acquire truly democratic standards of public morality." He recalled telling Chiang that "the greatest help that America could give was not money nor military advice but the dynamic force of our ideals."[26]

Although Stuart acknowledged and deplored defects in the Nationalist regime, he had affection for Chiang, who was a Christian convert, and he had little doubt that the United States ought to guarantee Chiang's survival and success. He viewed the Chinese Communists as wholly tied to Moscow and, in any case, "cruelly authoritarian." There was in progress a "struggle between Communists and democratic ways of life," he believed, with the Chinese Communists on one side while the Nationalists and the United States were on the other. To aid Chiang's regime, he declared in a cable to Washington, "is the delicate but splendidly creative opportunity for American statesmanship."[27]

---

25. Tang Tsou, *America's Failure in China, 1941–50* (Chicago: University of Chicago Press, 1963), pp. 427–429.

26. Stuart, January 23, 1947, January 30, 1947, April 19, 1947, April 22, 1947, May 8, 1947, November 19, 1947, FRUS, vol. 7, 1947, pp. 24–26, 29–30, 101–104, 105–107, 115–117, 367–368. See also John Leighton Stuart, *Fifty Years in China* (New York: Random House, 1954).

27. Stuart, January 23, 1947, FRUS, vol. 7, 1947, p. 26.

In Stuart's opinion, the Nationalists needed more than material aid and more than exhortation to adopt American ideals. As a practical matter, he felt, they need tutelage, guidance, and direction. He envisioned an "American-directed army reorganization," U.S. training for the armed forces, placement of "qualified American advisers and auditors" in the railway system, and participation by U.S. agencies in the development of industry. Chiang, he reported, "has recognized with cold realism the inherent weaknesses of his country both human and material and has disciplined himself to pay the price for American monetary aid in having it accompanied by a large measure of American control."[28]

Working mostly in his residence, Stuart seldom visited the embassy, and relied more on the Chinese secretary he had brought from Yenching University than on any of his official aides. Foreign Service officers in the mission viewed Stuart with misgivings: because he was a non-careerist, because they suspected his secretary of being an agent for Chiang, and because, as one of them wrote, Stuart "had learned how to be just as oblique and, when necessary, just as devious as any Chinese."[29]

The embassy, left quasi-autonomous by Stuart, was supervised by Minister Counselor W. Walton Butterworth. Though a newcomer in the Far East, Butterworth was a career diplomat close to both Vincent and to Acheson, who remained undersecretary until mid-1947. Along with some of his junior colleagues, Butterworth regarded Stuart as excessively pro-Chiang. When Marshall was about to ask for recall, Butterworth pleaded with him to hang on, for "he felt General Marshall's departure would be catastrophic, and in view of Dr. Stuart's inclinations, would cause the United States, as far as its policy is concerned, to drift toward full support of the Nationalist Government."[30]

Butterworth and most of his colleagues agreed with Stuart that it was critical that the Communists not prevail. Continuing to choke off aid to the Nationalists, they advised the State Department, "would ultimately result in a chaotic condition in which the Chinese would find themselves at the mercy of Soviet machinations." However, they argued much more strongly than Stuart that political and economic reforms should be demanded as the price of U.S. aid and, unlike Stuart, they regarded Chiang as a liability rather than an asset. By 1948, officers of the diplomatic mission were engaged in clandestine efforts to encourage Kuomintang leaders to

---

28. Stuart, May 8, 1947, FRUS, vol. 7, 1947, p. 116.

29. John F. Melby, *The Mandate of Heaven: Record of a Civil War, China 1945–49* (Toronto: University of Toronto Press, 1968), p. 137.

30. Minutes of a meeting between Marshall and Butterworth, December 1, 1946, FRUS, vol. 10, 1946, p. 575.

replace Chiang with either General Li Tsung-jen, the Nationalist vice-president who was thought to be more liberal, or Marshal Li Chi-shen, who headed a Kuomintang Revolutionary Committee based in Hong Kong.[31] In the end, however, nearly all of the American diplomats in China advocated U.S. aid for the Nationalists and predicted that, given favorable circumstances, such aid could prevent Communist success.

For the most part, U.S. military and naval officers in China argued even more ardently than the diplomats for aid to the Nationalists. However, they were careful not to get too far in front of the policymakers. General Wedemeyer, when still commanding what remained of the wartime military mission, had been generous in providing supplies to the Nationalists. When he reported to Washington, however, he had always asked for clarifying instructions to assure him that he was acting properly. This was a common practice in the military establishment, usually based on a well-founded presumption that Washington would not repudiate initiatives taken in the field.[32]

With the rapid postwar drawdown of forces, Wedemeyer in mid-1946 had to close down his command. He and other officers had, however, drawn up plans for postwar Army and Navy advisory groups. Vincent had protested that what they envisioned would amount to "a de facto protectorate with a semi-colonial Chinese army under our direction," and, at his urging, Secretary of State Byrnes signed a memorandum objecting to the proposed advisory groups.[33] The War and Navy Departments then scaled back these plans and limited the functions of the advisory groups. Nevertheless, following the closure of Wedemeyer's command, about 750 Army officers and 165 Navy officers remained in China with orders to advise Chiang and his commanders on how to run the Nationalist armed forces. U.S. Marines remained ashore to assist in the protection of fuel transport. And both in the field and in Washington, the military establishment kept recommending expansion in the number of advisers and in the breadth of their missions.[34]

Heading the new Army Advisory Group was Major General John P. Lucas, a West Point graduate who had been a corps commander in the

---

31. Freeman (Consul, Beijing) to Stuart, July 1, 1947, FRUS, vol. 7, 1947, pp. 218–222; Memorandum prepared for Butterworth, July 5, 1947, ibid., pp. 222–228; Sprouse to Wedemeyer, July 31, 1947, ibid., pp. 690–691; Melby, *Mandate of Heaven*, p. 268.

32. Melvyn P. Leffler, *A Preponderance of Power: National Security, the Truman Administration, and the Cold War* (Stanford, Calif.: Stanford University Press, 1992), p. 85.

33. Leffler, *A Preponderance of Power*, p. 128; May, *China Scapegoat*, pp. 148–149; Byrnes memorandum, January 5, 1946, FRUS, vol. 10, 1946, pp. 810–811.

34. See the various memoranda exchanged among departments between January and December 1947, FRUS, vol. 10, 1946, pp. 811–848.

Italian theater during World War II. Like his wartime predecessors in China, he judged the Chinese to be potentially excellent soldiers who needed only proper equipment and military training. If Washington would give him the authority and wherewithal, Lucas felt sure that he and his advisory group could build a first-rate army and defeat the Communists. He estimated that he could do the job in about two years, if the United States would provide arms and supplies equivalent to those needed for ten U.S. divisions, and if he could exert some control over Chinese strategic and operational planning.[35] Brigadier General John P. McConnell headed an almost autonomous section of Lucas's group, advising on military aviation. Having served in Southeast Asia and China during the war, he had more pertinent background than Lucas. His reports to Washington described the Nationalist air force as being in pitiable condition. Nevertheless, he advised that it could rapidly be made efficient and effective, if it were suitably equipped and trained.[36]

The Naval Advisory Group had as its chief Rear Admiral Stuart S. Murray, who had commanded submarines in the southwest Pacific during the war. His reports to Washington warned in strong terms of the strategic advantage the Russians would gain if the Chinese Communists won control of any part of China and if the United States were therefore prevented from keeping the base at Tsingtao it maintained under an informal understanding with Chiang. Like Lucas and McConnell, he advocated aid to the Nationalists accompanied by supervision of their military training, plans, and operations, and his recommendations were strenuously seconded by Admiral Charles M. Cooke; commanding the Seventh Fleet, he was the senior U.S. officer in the region.[37]

Cooke had been the U.S. Navy's chief planner in World War II, and his nickname "Savvy" reflected his reputation. When Marshall was in China, Cooke had fought unsuccessfully against reductions in the marine forces there. He argued persistently that the loss of Tsingtao base would be catastrophic, and he urged on Washington a variety of schemes for training Chinese marines and for using U.S. naval forces to aid the Nationalists.[38]

---

35. Lucas to Stuart, June 28, 1947, FRUS, vol. 7, 1947, pp. 860–863.

36. Stuart, March 21, 1947, FRUS, vol. 7, 1947, pp. 73–80.

37. Murray to Stuart, June 19, 1947, FRUS, vol. 7, 1947, pp. 864–871; Stuart (on Cooke), February 3, 1947, ibid., pp. 944–945.

38. See testimony by Cooke, U.S. Congress, Senate Committee on the Judiciary, International Security Subcommittee, Hearings, *The Institute of Pacific Relations*, 81st Cong., 1st and 2nd sess., 1949–50, pp. 1492–1515. Cooke boasted to British acquaintances about how many Nationalist sailors and marines he was training at the naval base at Tsingtao; Lanxin Xiang, *Recasting the Imperial Far East: Britain and America in China, 1945–1950* (London: M.E. Sharpe, 1995), p. 84.

In Washington, the fate of recommendations from the diplomatic and military missions in China depended as much on the military establishment as on the State Department. In part, this was because military aid was at issue, and in part, it was because civilian policymakers had respect for and confidence in their military advisers. Roosevelt, for example, had deferred to Marshall and the other chiefs of staff more than to anyone else around him. Although Truman tried initially to make himself less dependent on the professional military, he was disappointed in State Department staff work, and he, too, turned to the Pentagon. His selection of Marshall as secretary of state in 1947 evidenced his esteem for the professional military. Despite his persisting uneasiness about reliance on military agencies, Truman respected the judgment of his service secretaries and of military chiefs such as Dwight Eisenhower, Army chief of staff from 1945 to 1948, and Omar Bradley, the next Army chief of staff who then became JCS Chairman in 1949.

In 1947, the involvement of the military establishment in foreign policymaking was formalized through the National Security Act. In reorganizing the military establishment, this legislation created the post of secretary of defense and separated the Air Force from the Army. The act did not create an overall chief of staff for the three services, although there had been agitation to do so. Instead, it gave formal status to the Joint Chiefs of Staff (JCS), previously an ad hoc committee comprising the heads of the three uniformed services (the chiefs of staff of the Army and the Air Force, and the chief of naval operations), as well as the chief of staff to the commander in chief—at this time, Fleet Admiral William D. Leahy—who served as the JCS liaison to the president. The 1947 measure also established the National Security Council, with the secretary of state, secretary of defense, and the three civilian service secretaries among its members. The existence of this council was supposed to ensure that foreign policy decisions would not be made without consideration of their military implications.

The military establishment arrived at its positions on issues of foreign policy through a variety of processes. In the Army, the critical body was the Plans and Operations Division of the General Staff. After the spring of 1947, its chief was Wedemeyer, who advised both the army chief of staff and the secretary of the army on all policy issues. In the Navy, various sections of the office of the chief of naval operations divided up work on policy questions. Since major commands in the Navy were not yet subject to centralized control like that exercised by the general staff over the army, staff officers in Washington deferred to the views of the various fleet headquarters. Thus, the basic evaluation of the proposals by Admiral Murray's advisory group for training and assisting the Nationalists was made in the Seventh Fleet, led by Admiral Cooke. Officers in Washington introduced amendments only after consultation with Seventh Fleet headquarters. Cooke's views thus influenced the chief of naval operations and his deputies and, through them, the secretary of the navy.

The key committee supporting the Joint Chiefs consisted of Wedemeyer, as Chief of Plans and Operations for the Army General Staff, and his opposite numbers from the other services. The collective position of the Joint Chiefs resulted from negotiations among Army and Navy staff officers and their counterparts in the Air Force. Agreements among these officers produced papers that would be approved, usually with relatively little change, by the chiefs of staff. Since the civilian service secretaries and the secretary of defense had almost no other sources of expert advice on such issues as aid to China, they, too, tended to accept the views communicated to them through individual chiefs of staff or collectively by the Joint Chiefs. Few in the military establishment contested the belief of General Wedemeyer and Admiral Cooke that Communist victory in China would have grave consequences for the United States and that the Nationalists should therefore be given military aid as proposed by General Lucas, General McConnell, and Admiral Murray of the U.S. military advisory groups in China.

However, the service staffs also had officers who were concerned about other theaters, particularly the Middle East and Western Europe, where Communist takeover seemed even more imminent. Moreover, successive army and air force chiefs all tended to regard Europe as more important to the United States than Asia. As a result, staff processes produced, in the spring of 1947, a memorandum by the Joint Chiefs. Although it acknowledged that Communist victory in China could produce "very grave long-range jeopardy to our national security interests," it assigned China relatively low priority as a claimant for American military aid.[39]

A few weeks later, on June 9, 1947, the Joint Chiefs signed another memorandum that seemed, in some respects, to contradict the low priority they had just given China. Concerned only with China, it had passed through fewer hands and showed more of Wedemeyer's influence. In this memo, the chiefs said categorically that the Chinese Communists "are tools of Soviet policy" and that "the military security of the United States will be threatened if there is any further spread of Soviet influence and power in the Far East." The chiefs therefore recommended "carefully planned, selective and well-supervised assistance to the National Government, under conditions which will assure that this assistance will not be misused." Spelling out the implications of this recommendation, they said that the United States should abandon the policy

---

39. JCS 1769/1, May 12, 1947, FRUS, vol. 1, 1947, pp. 734–750.

of not interfering in the civil war. In a nod toward their earlier statements giving China a low priority, they offered the hope that "even small amounts of United States assistance to the National Government will materially strengthen its morale and at the same time weaken the morale of the Chinese communists."[40]

The civilian secretaries at the head of the military service departments concurred with the Joint Chiefs.[41] Earlier in 1947, Secretary of War Robert B. Patterson had questioned whether the United States should adhere to the policy of staying out of the Chinese civil war. Naval officers who championed a larger American role in China got a sympathetic hearing from Secretary of the Navy James V. Forrestal, who would become, in July 1947, the first secretary of defense. On more than one occasion, he argued to Marshall that the United States should make a major effort to set Nationalist China on its feet.[42]

The China experts in the State Department continued to be doubtful of Nationalist prospects. In July 1946, when Drumwright had moved on to become first secretary of the Embassy in London, Arthur Ringwalt took his place as head of the Division of Chinese Affairs; Philip Sprouse became Ringwalt's deputy. Both Ringwalt and Sprouse had served under Vincent in Chungking during the early part of the war, and tended to share his skepticism about aid to Chiang more than Drumwright's pro-Chiang views.

Memoranda from the China Division and from Vincent himself, as director of the Office of Far Eastern Affairs, consistently warned against over-optimism about the Nationalists. Vincent wrote to Marshall that, "it is the opinion of the Far Eastern Office that a USSR-dominated China is not a danger of sufficient immediacy or probability to warrant committing ourselves to the far-reaching consequences which would ensue from our involvement in the Chinese civil war on the side of the National Government," namely, an all-but-certain Soviet intervention on the side of the Chinese Communists and a massive U.S. strategic commitment outside Europe.[43]

While the China Division and the Office of Far Eastern Affairs were the primary advisers to the State Department policymakers, they were not the only ones. A bureaucratic battle was then in progress which would

---

40. JCS to State-War-Navy Coordinating Committee, June 9, 1947, FRUS, vol. 7, 1947, pp. 838–848.

41. Minutes of meeting of secretaries of state, war, and navy, June 26, 1947, FRUS, vol. 7, 1947, pp. 850–851; Leffler, *A Preponderance of Power*, p. 169.

42. Patterson to Marshall, February 26, 1947, FRUS, vol. 7, 1947, pp. 799–803; Forrestal to Marshall, June 20, 1947, ibid., pp. 968–970.

43. Vincent to Marshall, June 20, 1947, FRUS, vol. 7, 1947, p. 849.

result in creation of the Central Intelligence Agency (CIA) as a new version of the OSS. Some veterans of the OSS had gone to the State Department, where they were segregated in special units, particularly the Office of Intelligence Research. Eyed with suspicion by Foreign Service officers, they were kept subordinate to the regular geographic sections as much as possible. Nevertheless, there were China specialists in the Office of Intelligence Research, and they succeeded on at least one occasion in reaching Secretary Marshall with their estimate that rescuing Chiang would entail $2 billion in economic aid over a two-year period, plus equipment for thirty to sixty Chinese divisions.[44] These intelligence analysts were thus more pessimistic than the military establishment in predicting costs. Unlike Vincent and the Foreign Service China hands, they took the view that military aid to Chiang deserved consideration, but unlike the military, they were less concerned about the dangers of a Communist China. They reasoned that, to fully exploit China, the Soviet Union would need to "allocate from its scarce domestic resources capital equipment and possibly consumers' goods," thus becoming weaker rather than stronger.[45]

Other views came from analysts in the State Department's other geographic bureaus and divisions. Although departmental protocol inhibited one bureau from challenging another about affairs in the latter's sphere, the preeminent Office of European Affairs took care to pass on to the secretary all cables from Moscow that reported Soviet support for the Chinese Communists. They and their colleagues in the Office of Near Eastern Affairs emphasized the ruthlessness of the Soviet Union and the magnitude of its ambitions. Army liaison officers commented in 1946 that the State Department's European and Middle East experts believed that, "we should preserve a position which will enable us effectively to continue to oppose Soviet influence in China...[and] that failure to maintain this position would have the gravest effect on our long-range security."[46] Thus, apart from Vincent's Office of Far Eastern Affairs, State Department attitudes tended to resemble those within the military establishment.

A crucial factor in America's relationship to China in 1947 was the attitude of Secretary of State Marshall. Experience in China had convinced him that the Chinese Communists were "playing the Russian game," but also that Chiang's regime was incompetent. When the military establishment first began to press for aid to China, he responded that he was not yet sure

---

44. Office of Intelligence Research Report 4517, September 18, 1947, FRUS, vol. 7, 1947, pp. 286–287.

45. Ibid.

46. Marshall S. Carter to General Marshall, August 14, 1946, Marshall Mission Files, Lot 54-D270, National Archives and Records Administration.

whether it was necessary or desirable, but he indicated that, if there were a program, it would require close U.S. supervision. Even the granting of credits, he said, should probably be accompanied by an economic advisory mission with "more authority than is implied in the word 'advisory'."[47]

Reports from China in the first half of 1947 were discouraging. The Nationalists' advantage in manpower seemed to be diminishing, while Communist forces were growing in size and becoming more confident, and there were gloomy predictions that Nationalist units might defect. Chiang's hold on cities in Manchuria seemed to become more and more precarious, and Ambassador Stuart warned that the Nationalists might not be able to hold even northern China.[48] As Marshall read bulletins from the embassy, the military mission, and American reporters, he grew more and more worried that the Nationalists might collapse. There were no obvious remedies for the weaknesses of Chiang's regime. Briefing a group of businessmen in early June, Marshall said candidly, "I have tortured my brain and I can't now see the answer."[49]

The Joint Chiefs' June 1947 memorandum recommending aid to Chiang reached Marshall while he was adjusting to a new undersecretary. On June 30, Acheson had resigned after a six-month transition period. His successor was Robert A. Lovett, a Wall Street banker who had served as assistant secretary of war for air during World War II and whom Marshall had come to know well and to respect. Forrest Pogue, Marshall biographer, writes of Lovett: "His tongue, like Acheson's, could cut with suavity, but he had no condescension in dealing with politicians, and he handled those on the Hill more easily than did Acheson."[50]

Almost as soon as Lovett was formally installed, Marshall confided his thinking about China. He agreed with Vincent, he said, that although the Joint Chiefs' advice was "not quite realistic," nevertheless, "the situation is critical and it is urgently necessary I feel that we reconsider our policy to see what changes may be necessary." Marshall had not decided what to do, but he had decided on a procedure: unless Lovett saw reasons not to do so, he proposed to ask Wedemeyer, who was then Chief of Plans and Operations for the Army General Staff, to revisit China and to recommend a course of action for the U.S. government.[51]

---

47. Melby, *The Mandate of Heaven*, p. 98; Marshall to Patterson, March 4, 1947, FRUS, vol. 7, 1947, p. 808.

48. Stuart, March 26, 1947, FRUS, vol. 7, 1947, pp. 84–86.

49. David E. Lilienthal, *Journals: The Atomic Energy Years 1945–1950* (New York: Harper and Row, 1964), p. 201.

50. Pogue, *Marshall*, vol. 4, p. 150.

51. Marshall to Lovett, July 2, 1947, FRUS, vol. 7, 1947, pp. 635–636.

Historians have examined the motives behind Marshall's decision. It is possible that Marshall settled on Wedemeyer as simply the best man for the job; Wedemeyer had been one of his principal staff aides during the early part of the war and helpful to him in China. Moreover, Wedemeyer knew Chiang and other Chinese leaders, and had their confidence.[52] Sending Wedemeyer, rather than the State Department's nominees, Dean Acheson or Robert Lovett, promised to score points at home, especially with the Republican Congress. On the other hand, Marshall was not a guileless man. He believed, he once told Acheson, "not [in] antagonizing people but managing them."[53] Marshall may have regarded Wedemeyer as a man who could be managed. If Wedemeyer returned with a report that counseled against military involvement, it would give Marshall a stout club against the missions in China, the chiefs of staff, the service secretaries, and other "hawks."[54]

After Lovett concurred in the plan, Marshall arranged for Wedemeyer's appointment as special representative of the president. He allowed the general to draft his own instructions, but amended them so that they did not categorically promise "a program of rehabilitation and stabilization provided the Chinese Government stipulates, guarantees and accepts definitive supervisory measures to be maintained by representatives of the United States." Instead, Wedemeyer was instructed that the United States could "consider assistance in a program of rehabilitation only if the Chinese Government presents satisfactory evidence of effective measures looking towards Chinese recovery and provided further that any aid…be subject to the supervision of representatives of the United States Government."[55]

Accompanied by a small staff, Wedemeyer made a month-long tour during late July and early August 1947, visiting the Nationalist capital of Chungking as well as Formosa, Canton, Shanghai, areas in the north and northeast, and Korea. Soon after arriving, he reported to Marshall that conditions had grown worse since Marshall's departure a little over six months earlier. The Nationalists seemed to him "spiritually insolvent" and paralyzed by corruption and incompetence. After touring regions where the civil war was hotly in progress, he commented cynically that the Nationalists would do all they could to get the United States to fight their war. He was not disposed, however, to wash his hands of them. Rather, he

---

52. William Stueck, *The Wedemeyer Mission* (Athens: University of Georgia Press, 1984), p. 11.

53. Dean G. Acheson, *Present at the Creation* (New York: W.W. Norton, 1969), p. 216.

54. Stueck, *Wedemeyer Mission*, p. 8.

55. May, *China Scapegoat*, pp. 150–162.

wrote, "we must...compel them to make realistic contributions in the global effort first to retard, then stop Soviet aggression, and later to penetrate peacefully through political, economic and psychological means those areas within the Soviet orb."[56]

In Hawaii, Wedemeyer prepared his report. The instructions that he gave to the drafting officers indicated that his basic views remained unchanged. He said that he wished to recommend "moral encouragement and material aid," and that he wanted direct U.S. supervision. His comment that he looked for a program comparable to that in Greece implied that he foresaw active military assistance involving U.S. supervision of plans and operations. In addition, he introduced a notion that he had developed in 1946 while still in China. He proposed that Chiang be relieved of responsibility for Manchuria.[57] Wedemeyer had concluded that Chiang had little chance of retaining a foothold there, but he did not want to concede the strategically vital region to the Communists, so he proposed establishing a UN trusteeship similar to that in Korea. That would allow some Soviet forces to return, but U.S., British, and French forces would also come in. Manchuria could then be turned into a buffer zone and Nationalist troops that might otherwise be committed there or on the Manchurian borders could be released to fight the Communists elsewhere.[58]

The final report that Wedemeyer delivered to Marshall and the president on September 19, 1947, included a strong recommendation for UN action in Manchuria. It was, he argued, "necessary to prevent that area from becoming a Soviet satellite." In addition, he urged large-scale economic aid to the Nationalists, accompanied by close supervision; military aid in the form of vehicles, weapons, ammunition, aircraft, and transport vessels; and an expanded role for U.S. military and naval advisers. Wedemeyer stopped short of proposing that these advisers accompany Nationalist units in the field, but he said that they should "provide advice indirectly to tactical forces" by carrying out reconnaissance missions, determining which units should remain in combat and which should be withdrawn for retraining, and directly supervising training, outfitting, and the maintenance of services of supply.[59]

Wedemeyer's recommendation for a UN trusteeship for Manchuria came as an unwelcome surprise to Marshall. The State Department had all

---

56. Wedemeyer to Marshall, July 29, 1947, FRUS, vol. 7, 1947, pp. 682–684; Wedemeyer to Marshall, August 8, 1947, ibid., pp. 712–715; Wedemeyer to Marshall, August 17, 1947, ibid., pp., 725–726.

57. Leffler, *A Preponderance of Power*, p. 86.

58. Memo by Wedemeyer, September 7, 1947, FRUS, vol. 7, 1947, pp. 769–770.

59. *The White Paper*, pp. 764–814.

but written off Manchuria by this time, and Wedemeyer's revival of the issue was evidence of a continuing split between State and Defense per-spectives on China. Moreover, involving the United Nations in such a sticky issue as Manchuria would surely test the new organization's ability to survive. The proposal also had potentially harmful global implications. At the time, U.S. missions in Greece were reporting hopefully about progress in defeating the Communists there; Marshall feared that publici-ty for Wedemeyer's proposal might lead to agitation by Communist states for a UN takeover of Greece as well.[60] It could revive debate in Congress, where some key members had already criticized the U.S. program of aid to Greece and Turkey for being unilateral rather than UN-sponsored, and others had attacked it for focusing on the Communist threat to Europe rather than Asia.[61] Failing to persuade Wedemeyer to delete the recom-mendation on Manchuria, Marshall decided to treat the document as a top-secret advisory report, to be shared with as few people as possible and not to be communicated even in summary to Congress or the press.

Public Debate

The months following Wedemeyer's mission were an anxious period for Marshall, but China was only one of his concerns. Shortly before receiving Wedemeyer's report, Marshall had been told by one of his Soviet experts that "all indications point towards a major political showdown crisis between the Soviet Union and the non-Soviet world.... It is not a matter of several years in the future. It is more likely a question of months."[62] His staff identified Western Europe as the probable theater for a Soviet offen-sive. Not until November 1947 did Marshall's planners begin to assure him that war was not imminent. They predicted, however, that the Soviets would probably take over Czechoslovakia (as they did six months later) and would attempt to foment civil wars in Italy and France.[63] The secre-tary had little leisure for torturing his brain further about China.

---

60. These concerns mattered less to Wedemeyer, who had written that he did "not understand how our government can send four hundred million dollars to Turkey and Greece...and then fail to send similar assistance to China where the spread of commu-nism is just as dangerous and even more advanced." Stueck, *Wedemeyer Mission*, p. 17.

61. Thomas Paterson, "If Europe, Why Not China? The Containment Doctrine, 1947–1949," *Prologue* (National Archives and Records Administration), Vol. 13 (1981), pp. 19–38.

62. Memo by Charles Bohlen, August 30, 1947, FRUS, vol. 1, 1947, pp. 763–765.

63. Report by the Policy Planning Staff, November 6, 1947, FRUS, vol. 1, 1947, pp. 770–771.

However, Marshall faced increasing pressure to do something for Chiang. Demands by the diplomatic and military missions in China and the military establishment in Washington were unrelenting. With Wedemeyer's backing, Lucas and the Army Advisory Group for China came up with detailed plans for training ten Chinese divisions.[64] The new Department of the Air Force urged enlarging the air advisory mission and providing more planes. Admiral Cooke, Commander of the Seventh Fleet, presented schemes for turning additional supplies over to the Nationalists to develop and train a Nationalist marine corps.

Meanwhile, press and public support for aiding Chiang was growing. Henry R. Luce had taken up the cause in 1946. The son of missionary parents who had brought him up in China, Luce felt passionately that Chiang, a Christian convert, merited U.S. support. His widely circulated news and picture magazines, *Time* and *Life*, passed up no opportunity to editorialize or slant reportage so as to laud the Nationalists and blacken the Communists. In the autumn of 1947, Luce commissioned and gave widespread publicity to "China: A Report to the American People" by William C. Bullitt, who had been Roosevelt's first ambassador to the Soviet Union and ambassador in Paris at the time of the fall of France in 1940. Bullitt warned that Russia was on the verge of taking over China, and warned that "the independence of the United States will not live a generation longer than the independence of China."[65] He urged turning over command of a revived China theater to General Douglas MacArthur, then commanding the occupation of Japan and a hero of the American right who boasted of his superior knowledge of the "Oriental mind."

Roy Howard of United Press and of the Scripps-Howard newspaper chain joined Luce's campaign. So did newspaper tycoon William Randolph Hearst, Robert R. McCormick of the *Chicago Tribune*, Eleanor Patterson of the *New York Daily News*, and other anti-Communist publishers who had been critical of the Roosevelt and Truman administrations for emphasizing interests in Europe over those in Asia. Some voices opposed them, most prominently the left-wing weekly, *The New Republic*.[66] But the loudest clamor came from Luce and his fellow publishers, assisted by critics from inside the administration, including Wedemeyer.[67]

A bloc in Congress also agitated for aid to Chiang. Foremost in its ranks was Republican Representative Walter Judd of Minnesota, who had spent his youth as a Congregationalist medical missionary in China. With

---

64. Lucs to Stuart, June 28, 1947, FRUS, vol. 7, 1947, pp. 861–862.
65. William Bullitt, "China: A Report to the American People," *Life*, October 13, 1947.
66. *The New Republic*, July 21, 1947.
67. Stueck, *Wedemeyer Mission*, pp. 94–110.

assistance from the Chinese embassy, which the Nationalists had inherited along with the rest of the Chinese government infrastructure, and from lobbyists for the Nationalists, Judd delivered extensively documented and powerfully argued speeches on Chiang's behalf. As an expert on China, he made his influence felt on the House Foreign Affairs Committee. Military officers such as General Wedemeyer and Admiral Cooke, meanwhile, made converts of many members of the newly created House Armed Services Committee. A junket to China and long interviews with Chiang and other Nationalist leaders confirmed their faith. The Senate had no exact counterpart to Representative Judd, but the persuasive powers of Nationalist lobbyists, coupled perhaps with campaign contributions, resulted in aggressive support from Senator Styles Bridges of New Hampshire, senior Republican on the Appropriations Committee.[68]

Through 1946, some voices on Capitol Hill had challenged Representative Judd and Senator Bridges. Indeed, Byrnes and Acheson had feared lest public and congressional opposition might prevent the United States from helping Chiang even to move troops into parts of China disputed with the Communists.

However, the progress of the Cold War had tended to silence questions about active opposition to international communism. An overwhelming Republican victory in the 1946 Senate and House elections removed from Congress most of those who had been outspokenly critical of Chiang. Hence, in the fall of 1947 Marshall and his associates were mostly reading and hearing public and congressional commentary that paralleled the advice they were getting from Ambassador Stuart, General Lucas, General Wedemeyer, and the military services. Meeting with the Chinese ambassador in November, Marshall acknowledged a "wave of sentiment in favor of aid to China."[69]

In confronting these pressures, Marshall no longer had Vincent nearby to articulate the counterarguments. Since 1945, when Vincent had been attacked by Hurley, he had also been subjected to repeated criticism by partisans of Chiang, Chinese Nationalist officials, and—more important—U.S. military officers and hard-line Foreign Service officers. Once Acheson left in June 1947, Vincent had no State Department protector. By Foreign Service rules, he was due for rotation to an overseas assignment, and Marshall chose not to bend the rules in order to retain Vincent as director of the Office of Far Eastern Affairs. Instead, Vincent was sent off to head

---

68. Ross Y. Koen, *The China Lobby in American Politics* (New York: Macmillan, 1960), p. 62.

69. Memorandum of conversation by Butterworth, November 13, 1947, FRUS, vol. 7, 1947, p. 1215.

the U.S. diplomatic mission in Switzerland. To take his place, Marshall brought Butterworth back from China.[70]

Butterworth had fewer misgivings than Vincent about a U.S. commitment to prevent Communist victory. He remained skeptical, however, as to the wisdom of betting on Chiang. His memoranda therefore did not argue categorically against U.S. involvement in the civil war, but they were clearly intended to prompt the secretary and undersecretary to ask searching questions about the probable effectiveness of specific measures proposed.

With Marshall and Lovett preoccupied by Europe, Chiang's partisans pushing his cause, Vincent no longer in Washington, and his successor offering only cautionary advice, piecemeal decisions threatened to draw the United States willy-nilly into the Chinese civil war. Although the embargo on arms shipment had been lifted in May 1946, Chiang and his supporters complained continuously of shortages of ammunition. They kept saying that the United States had given them weapons but now denied them cartridges and shells. The U.S. military attaché reported that no one actually knew whether ammunition was in short supply or not, because the Nationalists had no system of inventories.[71]

Nevertheless, Marshall approved arrangements for the Chinese to buy U.S. ammunition. During the autumn of 1947, he agreed to subsidize some Chinese arms purchases. He also agreed to keep sending military equipment originally allocated to the Chinese Nationalists for the war against the Japanese. He accepted the rationale that the United States remained bound by a wartime commitment to outfit China with thirty-nine divisions and eight and one-third air groups.

At the beginning of November 1947, Marshall went further, authorizing the Army Advisory Group to commence a limited training program for Chinese combat forces on the island of Formosa. He also approved enlargement of the advisory group's mission, giving a go-ahead for it to reorganize and supervise the Nationalist army's supply services. Meeting with the secretary of defense and the service secretaries, Marshall described his position; everyone now agreed, he said, "that we wish to prevent Soviet domination of China." Although still deploring the character of Chiang's regime, Marshall said the United States had no choice but to keep it in power. Marshall added "that the immediate problem is to determine what we can do effectively," short of what Wedemeyer termed "direct U.S. involvement in fratricidal warfare."[72]

---

70. May, *China Scapegoat*, pp. 110–161.

71. *The White Paper*, pp. 989–990.

72. Stuart, October 14, 1947, FRUS, vol. 7, 1947, pp. 893–895; Minutes of meeting of committee of two, November 3, 1947, ibid., pp. 908–912; Marshall to Stuart, November 23, 1947, ibid., p. 923.

At the end of 1947, the Nationalists still had more troops than the Communists. They had not lost Manchuria, as had seemed likely when Wedemeyer visited China in late summer. By mounting a counteroffensive, the Nationalists had pushed the Communists back in some areas. Although ceding more and more of the countryside in Shantung, Hopei, and Shansi provinces, they retained control of most of the cities and rail lines in north China. In a much publicized but militarily insignificant campaign, they captured the deserted Communist headquarters at Yenan. Most of the Yangtze valley and all of China to the south remained free of Communist forces. Crude statistics seemed to show Nationalists not only holding their own but possibly headed toward victory.

U.S. diplomats in China, however, described the Nationalists' military position as at "a critical state." Lewis Clark, a Foreign Service officer who had served in China from 1926 to 1935 and subsequently in Paris and Ottawa, had replaced Butterworth as Minister Counselor when Butterworth went to Washington to replace Vincent. In December 1947 Clark filed a dispatch warning that "measures taken to guard against a Government military collapse must be adopted promptly." Military supplies alone would be of no use, whatever their quantity; instead, he insisted, it was essential for U.S. officers effectively to take over central military planning, and to ensure the implementation of their plans by placing liaison units with the Nationalist field commands. Ambassador Stuart and the embassy united in reiterating and reemphasizing this recommendation, and it was vigorously seconded by General Lucas, Admiral Murray, and Admiral Cooke in the Far East, and by General Wedemeyer and other military and naval planners in Washington.[73]

At the top of President Truman's international agenda at the time was the Marshall Plan for Europe. The administration estimated the project would cost $17 billion over the next four years, with more than a third of that coming due within eighteen months. The president summoned Congress into special session to consider the necessary legislation, but the act had to pass through Senator Bridges' Senate Appropriations Committee, and it was clear that Bridges would take the occasion to press for aid to China.

During hearings on the measure early in 1948, Senator Bridges called Wedemeyer as a witness and elicited from him public testimony to the effect that China was as important to the United States as Europe; that economic and military aid was urgently needed by Chiang; and that any such aid should be closely supervised. Bridges also provided a forum for Representative Judd and for Alfred Kohlberg, the principal Nationalist

---

73. Stuart, October 4, 1947, FRUS, vol. 7, 1947, pp. 893–895.

lobbyist. William Bullitt got headlines for his testimony disclosing the U.S. embassy recommendations for military assistance to the Nationalists, and urging, as in his "Report to the American People," that General Douglas MacArthur be sent from Japan, where he oversaw the postwar occupation, to take command of Chiang's armies.[74]

State Department witnesses before Bridges' committee did not directly challenge Wedemeyer and the others. Pleading for prompt aid to Europe, they simply promised a specific proposal for aid to China in the near future. This did not satisfy Senator Bridges or his counterparts in the House Appropriations and Foreign Affairs committees. It became evident that the administration would not get aid to Europe without aid to China.

In the State Department, economic affairs specialists had been studying a possible aid program for China since the autumn of 1947. For China, as for Europe, the economic planners thought primarily of enabling the recipient country to rebuild productive capacity and to finance imports without balance-of-payments deficits; they gave little consideration to military needs.

The department's Far East specialists, when consulted by these economic planners, pointed out that Congress would be particularly interested in China's munitions supplies. They suggested that China's prospective earnings from exports be underestimated by about $50 million so that Chiang would have that amount to spend for military purchases. The alternative would be a special appropriation for military assistance, wrote Butterworth to the assistant secretary of state for economic affairs, and "the consequences of the adoption of such a program by the U.S. Government are too serious and too obvious to require elaboration."[75] The State Department sent Capitol Hill a proposal for a one-year appropriation of $570 million for economic aid to China.

Marshall and Lovett recognized that this proposal would not satisfy Senator Bridges and the others who sought military aid for China, but they were uncertain about what to expect. Arrangements were already in progress to reassign Lucas and to put in his place, as head of the Army Advisory Group, Major General David G. Barr, who had been on Eisenhower's staff in Europe during World War II. Ambassador Stuart and others argued that this change should not be made without an accompanying change in instructions to assure that Barr could render "effective aid." However, Marshall's own preference by this time was plain: any ear-

74. U.S. Congress, Senate Committee on Appropriations, Hearings, Third Supplemental Appropriations Bill for 1948, 80th Cong., 1st sess., 1947, pp. 122–173.

75. "Formulation of Program for Aid to China," December 20, 1947–February 17, 1948, FRUS, vol. 8, 1948, pp. 442–478.

lier inclination to consider U.S. intervention in China had disappeared. Marshall cabled Stuart that he feared "acceptance of responsibility for a military campaign with its inevitable international perils and probable tremendous demands of one kind or another." But he could not gauge accurately the will of Congress, and thus took the position that the precise scope of Barr's mission would have to be determined later.[76]

Marshall Opts for Caution

Proposed legislation for aid to China went first to the House Foreign Affairs Committee and the Senate Foreign Relations Committee. After the two houses had acted on a bill authorizing appropriations, the Appropriations committees of the two chambers would consider funding.

Marshall stated his position candidly and vigorously before a joint executive session of the House Foreign Affairs Committee and the Senate Foreign Relations Committee in February 1948. Although, he explained, he could not say so publicly because it would hurt Nationalist morale, it was his considered judgment that the Communists could not be wholly defeated by the Nationalists and that, in fact, they might win. For the United States to underwrite the Nationalists would involve "obligations and responsibilities...which I am convinced the American people would never knowingly accept." The United States, said Marshall, "would have to be prepared virtually to take over the Chinese government" and to commit "sizeable forces and resources over an indefinite period." He could not, he said, estimate the probable requirements, but he felt sure that "the magnitude of the task and the probable costs thereof would clearly be out of all proportion to the results to be obtained."[77]

Marshall's testimony did not convince the members of the House Foreign Affairs Committee. They seemed more persuaded by Wedemeyer, Bullitt, and others who argued that limited military aid could be effective. With Representative Judd taking the lead, the committee resolved that funds should be earmarked for such a purpose, and that U.S. military advisers should be assigned to China, as they were in Greece. Its report was adopted by the House.

The Senate Foreign Relations Committee, however, was much more inclined to agree with Marshall. Republican and Democratic members were equally firm in regarding military aid as unwise. Henry Cabot Lodge (R-Mass.) told his colleagues, "I will be willing to vote to send them some

---

76. *The White Paper*, pp. 989–990.
77. *The White Paper*, pp. 380–384.

money, but I'll be damned if I want to send them manpower." Alexander Wiley (R-Wisc.) expressed a similar view, as did Bourke B. Hickenlooper of Iowa, the most conservative Republican in the group. Hickenlooper told his colleagues that, just after graduating from law school in the 1920s, he had considered going to China because he had been assured that it stood on the verge of great progress. So far as he could tell, he said, no progress had in fact occurred during the subsequent twenty years.

Senator Arthur Vandenberg (R-Mich.), the chairman of the Foreign Relations Committee, summed up the opinion of his colleagues in the observation that the House and Senator Bridges might be appeased by allocating some funds for military supplies, but that the United States should assume no responsibility for how the funds were spent. The bill, he said, would be "essentially three cheers for the Nationalist Government."[78]

Vandenberg was acknowledged as one of the two most powerful Republicans in the Senate, and he faced no opposition on this issue from the other, Robert A. Taft (R-Ohio). Vandenberg had little difficulty persuading the upper house to follow his lead. A conference committee of the Senate and House crafted compromise legislation following Vandenberg's formula. The China Aid Act of April 3, 1948, authorized $338 million for economic support and $125 million for military supplies for China, but declared that there was no "express or implied assumption by the United States of any responsibility for policies, acts, or undertakings by the Republic of China or for conditions which may prevail at any time." Both the House and the Senate approved this language.[79]

When appropriations were to be made, Senator Bridges and his counterpart on the House Appropriations Committee, Representative John Taber (R-N.Y.), revived the proposal that the United States assume responsibility for how military aid would be used in China. The appropriations bills that cleared Taber's committee and were passed by the House reduced economic aid to $275 million, but retained $125 million for military aid. The bill also stipulated that the military aid should be administered under supervision similar to that for military aid to Greece. Despite Bridges' enthusiasm for this provision, however, Vandenberg and his allies were successful in keeping such language out of the Senate bill and the conference committee report. Like the authorizing act, the final appropriations act raised "three cheers" for Chiang without committing the United States to do more than give him money.

---

78.   U.S. Congress, Senate, Executive Sessions of the Committee on Foreign Relations, Historical Series, 80th Cong., 2nd sess., March 14, 1948, pp. 422–444.

79.   Public Law 472, Title IV.

By early 1948, if not before, Marshall and Lovett had reached a decision on which policy alternative they preferred. Marshall may still have been influenced by his frustrating experience in China. The cautious views of Butterworth and the China Division, under Ringwalt and Sprouse, probably also carried some weight with both the secretary and undersecretary. So did counsel from George F. Kennan, the Soviet expert heading the State Department Policy Planning staff, who recommended concentrating on building up Japan, while conceding that "there is not much we can do in China." As evidenced by Marshall in his congressional testimony, and by Lovett in talks with his good friend Senator Vandenberg, the secretary and undersecretary had become convinced that the United States should not in any way engage militarily in China.[80]

Marshall and Lovett at first simply advocated such a policy, disputing the contrary views of the diplomatic and military missions, the military establishment, and public figures such as Representative Judd and William Bullitt. Although Marshall had unique standing with the president and had White House backing in pressing his views on Congress, he apparently did not expect Truman to back him if Congress failed to agree with him. At any rate, until they were reasonably sure how Congress would act, Marshall and Lovett temporized in their responses to questions from the military establishment. They kept open the option of enlarging the mandate of the military mission until the outcome of the debate in Congress gave them room to insist upon their position.

Those who regarded as unwise the policy of giving the Nationalists military assistance without U.S. supervision did not take the "three cheers" decision as final, even though it had Congress's imprimatur. As reports flowed in during 1948 of Nationalist reverses, Chiang supporters raised their voices ever louder. Exercising influence in a joint congressional committee set up to keep track of all foreign aid expenditures, Bridges and Taber employed Bullitt as a consultant, sent him to China, and publicized his pro-Nationalist reports. Henry Luce's publications became more and more shrill in denouncing the administration's China policy.

The diplomatic and military missions and the military establishment passed up few opportunities to press for reconsideration. The embassy filed frequent recommendations that U.S. officers should assume a larger role in planning and guiding Nationalist operations. Soon after his arrival in China as head of the Army Advisory Group, General Barr proposed a scheme to this effect that was more ambitious than any put forward by Lucas, his predecessor. It was enthusiastically seconded by Admiral Oscar

---

80. U.S. Congress, Senate, Executive Sessions of the Committee on Foreign Relations, Historical Series, 80th Cong., 2nd sess., November 4, 1947, pp. 517–518.

Badger, who had succeeded Cooke as the senior U.S. naval officer in the western Pacific. Barr and Badger urged that U.S. officers should take responsibility for operational planning in key Nationalist field commands. In Washington, the Joint Chiefs formally endorsed the issuance of such orders. The new National Security Council, however, balked, noting that the scheme would require the United States "virtually to take over the Chinese government and administer its economic, political, and governmental affairs."[81]

In response to the Barr and Badger proposal, Marshall met with the secretary and undersecretary of the Army, the Army chief of staff, and General Wedemeyer. He said that he had no objections to the Army Advisory Group's providing limited training well away from combat areas, but he categorically opposed placing any U.S. advisers with Nationalist operational commands. He also insisted that the advisory groups exercise no supervision over Chinese decisions as to what to purchase with the $125 million, nor over what to do with the matériel thus purchased. He said that "the important thing was...do this without 'getting sucked in'." He insisted that the proposal by Barr and Badger be dropped.[82]

Time and again thereafter, Marshall or Lovett suppressed similar initiatives. The most extreme came from Admiral Badger, who proposed that, if the Communists attacked Tsingtao, which the United States still used as a naval base, Badger's forces should join with the Nationalists in repelling them. In private, Badger confessed that he did not see any valid rationale for retaining the base, but officers on his staff and in Washington were resolute that, since the United States had the base, it should not give it up. Over the objections of the State Department, the Joint Chiefs gave Badger the orders he requested, and Secretary of Defense Forrestal backed them up. Only by going to the president were Marshall and Lovett able to overrule them and get a ruling that Badger should be ordered to evacuate Tsingtao in the event of a Communist attack and not to be drawn into a shooting war alongside the Nationalists.[83]

As late as October 1948, Ambassador Stuart and other Americans in China were still pleading for a U.S. takeover of Nationalist military planning. In a long cable to the ambassador, Marshall reemphasized all the points made eight months earlier in his February 1948 presentation to the

---

81. Memo by Executive Secretary of the National Security Council, with enclosures, March 26, 1948, FRUS, vol. 8, 1948, pp. 44–50.

82. Memo of conversation, Forrestal, Royall, Marshall, and others, June 7, 1948, FRUS, vol. 8, 1948, pp. 84–85.

83. Badger to CNO, May 3, 1948, FRUS, vol. 8, 1948, pp. 310–325.

House Foreign Affairs and Senate Foreign Relations committees, and he emphasized that Congress had accepted his reasoning. So far as he was concerned, he indicated, the issue was closed.[84] Public opinion polls, meanwhile, documented growing support for this stance: a Gallup Poll taken in late 1948 showed more people opposed to than supporting military aid to the Nationalists.[85]

Most of the embassy staff had already concluded that Chiang's cause was hopeless. In the Army Advisory Group, General Barr, too, conceded that the Nationalists were finished. The Pentagon reluctantly accepted his estimate. Although the bureaucracy went through the motions of developing a follow-up aid program for China, State and Defense Department policymakers turned to such issues as whether or not to recognize a Communist government if it took control of all China. The possibility of military backing for Chiang received no further serious consideration. In December 1949, the Nationalists lost their hold on the mainland.

---

84. Marshall to Stuart, May 7, 1948, FRUS, vol. 8, 1948, pp. 512–517.

85. *Public Opinion Quarterly*, Spring 1949.

Chapter 2

The Congo, 1960–1963: Weighing Worst Choices

Charles G. Cogan and Ernest R. May,
with assistance from Kirsten Lundberg and
Robert D. Johnson

On June 30, 1960, the former Belgian Congo became independent. Within weeks, mutinous soldiers were terrorizing civilians, especially Belgians and other Europeans; the richest of the country's six provinces had declared independence; and the Congo government's new republic had appealed for outside military aid. U.S. President Dwight D. Eisenhower refused unilateral aid but supported policing of the Congo by the United Nations (UN), deploying forces from nations not aligned with either side in the Cold War. Seeing a possibility that the Congo would make itself dependent on the Soviet Union, the Eisenhower administration complemented its open support for the UN with secret plans for covert action, including a plan to assassinate Congolese prime minister Patrice Lumumba.

The Congo remained a scene of crisis in 1961, when John F. Kennedy succeeded Eisenhower as president. Though Kennedy entered office hoping for "dramatic new directions" in Congo policy, he, too, combined open support of the UN with covert action. Eventually, he took an initial step toward overt military action. At that point the crisis eased. Though Kennedy's successor, Lyndon B. Johnson, would also have to cope with trouble in the Congo, the basic decision had already been made to depend on a military strong man as an alternative to communism or chaos. For more than thirty years thereafter, the United States would be identified with what became one of the most despotic and corrupt regimes on earth, that of Mobutu Sese Seko. He would be, as one book title put it, "America's tyrant."[1]

Background

Among more than a score of colonies that became independent between 1946 and 1960, the Belgian Congo was probably least ready to govern

---

1. Sean Kelly, *America's Tyrant: The CIA and Mobutu of Zaïre* (Washington, D.C.: The American University Press, 1993).

itself. Almost as big as India, with a population of around 14 million, it was rich in rubber, ivory, diamonds, copper, cobalt, and uranium. Belgians and large Belgian and British companies had exploited these resources chiefly for their own benefit. Very few natives received any education beyond the primary level. There were no native engineers and no native civil servants above the level of clerk. In the colony's army, the *Force Publique*, all officers and most non-commissioned officers were white Europeans.[2]

Like the Congolese and most of the rest of the world, the Eisenhower administration had been surprised by Belgium's decision to make the Congo independent. Only very recently had pro-independence demonstrations broken out in the colony. Conscious of how much it had cost France to resist nationalism in Indo-China and Algeria, members of the Belgian government decided to surrender control voluntarily. In January–February 1960 they held a round table meeting in Brussels with advocates of Congolese independence. At the end of the meetings, they declared that the Congo would become independent in a matter of months. The Congolese at the round table rushed home to prepare for nationwide elections.

Most of what would become the Congo Republic still consisted of sprawling savanna or, as Joseph Conrad had described it in *The Heart of Darkness*, "trees, trees, millions of trees, massive, immense, running up high." The Congo River remained the country's chief transportation system. A few roads and railroads existed so that goods and travelers could bypass the river's wilder stretches.

On a map, the contours of the new country resembled a battered Wehrmacht helmet. In the west, the brim touched the Atlantic at the country's one port, Matadi, just west of Léopoldville, the capital both of the nation and of the province of Léopoldville. In the east, the lower part of the back of the helmet was the province of Katanga, bordering on Portuguese Angola and British Northern Rhodesia and Tanganyika, with Elisabethville its capital. South Katanga had most of the country's copper and cobalt. Between Léopoldville and Katanga lay Kasai province, the center for production of industrial diamonds. The province north of Léopoldville was Equateur. The province in the mountainous northeast was Orientale, with its capital Stanleyville. Between Orientale and Katanga stood the province of Kivu. All these provinces were artificial

---

2. Catherine Hoskyns, *The Congo Since Independence: January 1960–December 1961* (London: Oxford University Press, 1965), gives a detailed and comparatively objective account of conditions and developments in the Congo during its first year and a half of independence.

creations of Belgians. The actual divisions among the population were familial, tribal, linguistic, and religious. Ethnologists counted more than 250 distinctive tribes. A political map of the Congo that ignored the inventions of the Belgians would have resembled a canvas by Jackson Pollock.[3]

Native political organizations in the Congo were local and rarely even province-wide. The Belgians nevertheless wrote for the republic a makeshift constitution, a *Loi Fondamentale*, modeled on Belgium's own constitution, which prescribed a national parliament under a national chief of state. In the short period between the Brussels round table and independence, Congolese politicians began to form coalitions within provinces and across provincial lines.

The most successful organizer was Patrice Lumumba.[4] Thirty-five years old in 1960, born in Kasai, he had become a postal clerk in Stanleyville. He had natural gifts for making friends and for enthralling crowds through passionate oratory. He also had a gift for languages and could orate in French, Swahili, or a number of Congolese tongues. His *Mouvement National Congolais* (MNC), which was the only nationwide political party, won forty of the 137 seats in the new parliament, and Lumumba himself won election by the parliament as prime minister.

The parliament chose as chief of state Joseph Kasavubu.[5] Forty-three or thereabouts, Kasavubu had studied to become a Catholic priest but never finished seminary. His political base was the *Alliance des Bakongo* (ABAKO), an organization designed to protect the privileges of the Kongo people against the supposedly less cultured peoples of the interior, including the Mongo, from which Lumumba sprang. On many levels, Kasavubu and Lumumba would find it difficult to cooperate.

At the handover ceremony, Baudouin, the young Belgian king, gave a paternalistic speech. Kasavubu responded politely but tersely. Lumumba used the occasion for a denunciation of colonialism. He described the condition of Congolese under Belgian rule as "humiliating slavery which was

---

3. There have been, confusingly, two Congo republics over the years, one which had previously been the Belgian Congo, the other formerly an adjacent French colony, with its capital at Brazzaville. Even more confusingly, the republic formed from the former Belgian Congo came to be known from 1971 to 1997 as Zaïre and since 1997 as the Democratic Republic of Congo. Mobutu Sese Seko, who dubbed the country Zaïre, also Africanized the names of most cities. Léopoldville became Kinshasa, Stanleyville Kisangani, and Elisabethville Lubumbashi. Here, we use the place names current in 1960–1963.

4. See Robin McKown, *Lumumba, A Biography* (Garden City, N.Y.: Doubleday, 1969).

5. See Charles-André Gilis, *Kasa-Vubu, au coeur du drame congolais* (Brussels: Editions Europe-Afrique, 1964); and Zuzu Justine M'Poyo Kasa Vubu, *Kasa-Vubu et le Congo indépendant* (Brussels: Le Cri, 1997).

imposed on us by force." He brought his African audience to its feet by declaring: "We are going to show the world what the black man can do when he works in freedom."[6] Lumumba's words caused obvious discomfort to Baudouin and all the Belgians present.

Five days later, Congolese soldiers began to mutiny against their Belgian commanders. Incidents of indiscriminate firing, looting, and rape caused Belgians and other Europeans to begin fleeing the country. President Kasavubu and Prime Minister Lumumba joined in trying to mollify the soldiers. They promised to "Africanize" the Force Publique, renaming it the Armée Nationale Congolaise (ANC). Although they kept many Belgians as advisers, they replaced white officers with Congolese, and they gave every soldier a one-rank promotion with a consequent rise in pay.

Belgian officials meanwhile became alarmed for the safety and property of the 100,000 Europeans, mostly Belgians, living in the Congo.[7] Most of the Europeans and European-owned properties were in Kasai or south Katanga. The companies with the largest holdings were the Société Générale de Belgique, the British-owned Tanganyika Concessions, Ltd., and their joint subsidiary, the Union Minière du Haut Katanga. Although the *Loi Fondamentale* and a pact between Belgium and the new republic forbade foreign troops to enter the country except at the invitation of the Congolese government, the president of Katanga province, Moïse Tshombe, asked for Belgian military protection, and the Belgian government obliged by sending paratroopers to both Katanga and Kasai. On July 11, as soon as the Belgian paratroopers were in place, Tshombe declared Katanga independent.

When Kasavubu and Lumumba tried to fly to Katanga, they were denied permission to land at Elisabethville airport. The ministers whom they left behind in Léopoldville had meanwhile met and agreed to ask help from both the United States and the UN. Through U.S. ambassador Clare Timberlake, they asked for 3,000 U.S. troops to quell the soldiers' revolt.

By the time Kasavubu and Lumumba returned to Léopoldville, the situation had worsened: Belgian marines, acting with no legal pretext at all, had seized the port facilities at Matadi and in the process killed a number

---

6. An English version of the full text of Lumumba's speech is in McKown, *Lumumba*, pp. 101–104.

7. Hoskyns, *The Congo Since Independence*, pp. 1–2, estimates that there were 100,000 Europeans in the Congo at the time of independence. Ernest W. Lefever, *Uncertain Mandate: Politics of the U.N. Congo Operation* (Baltimore, Md.: The Johns Hopkins University Press, 1967), p. 131, estimates that 87,000 of these were Belgians.

of Congolese. Kasavubu and Lumumba both believed, nonetheless, that the ministers had gone too far. While they had no objection to asking for help from the UN, they had no desire to be seen as calling in American imperialists to offset Belgian imperialists. Effectively annulling the earlier message, they appealed to UN Secretary-General Dag Hammarskjöld for "urgent...military assistance" to "protect the national territory against acts of aggression committed by Belgian metropolitan troops." They stipulated that UN troops should come only from countries not aligned with either side in the East-West Cold War.[8]

The first message from Léopoldville posed for the U.S. government the question of whether or not it should intervene militarily in the Congo. While the second message cut across the first, it suggested a different question, for U.S. diplomats and journalists in the Congo speculated that Kasavubu and Lumumba, if disappointed by the answers from the UN and the United States, might turn to the Soviet Union for help. The crisis in the Congo was thus from the outset a Cold War crisis.

Partly because of nuclear weapons but partly also because of the burst of nationalism among peoples in European colonies, the United States and the Soviet Union had increasingly shifted their competition to the Third World. In Southeast Asia, as in Korea, each side had protégés. In most of the countries of Asia and the Middle East and among newly independent states in Africa, the most common preference was nonalignment, which permitted efforts to play one side off against the other. But Washington and Moscow each remained constantly vigilant lest the other convert a nonaligned state into an ally or satellite.

The Soviet Union had gained an important edge in this competition just at the end of the 1950s. In Cuba, guerrillas led by Fidel Castro overthrew a corrupt dictatorship. As Castro consolidated power, he became increasingly anti-American and increasingly linked with members of the small Cuban Communist Party. In February 1960, Castro openly aligned Cuba with the Soviet Union. Khrushchev jubilantly promised aid and support, including defense of Cuba were it to be attacked by the United States.

Cold War events affected U.S. domestic politics. Eisenhower and Kennedy could both recall how demagogues such as Wisconsin Senator Joe McCarthy had successfully attacked Democrats with a charge that they had "lost" China to Communists. These recollections influenced

---

8. Summary of a telephone report from Timberlake, July 12, 1960, Department of State, *Foreign Relations of the United States* (FRUS), 1958–1960, Vol. XIV, *Africa* (Washington, D.C.: U.S. Government Printing Office, 1992), pp. 293–295 (hereafter FRUS, 1958–1960, Vol. XIV); Andrew W. Cordier and Wilder Foote, eds., *Public Papers of the Secretaries-General of the United Nations*, Vol. 5: 1960–1961, *Dag Hammarskjöld* (New York: Columbia University Press, 1975), p. 19 (hereafter cited as Hammarskjöld Papers).

discussion of the possibility of the Congo's joining Cuba as a new ally of the Soviet Union.

Another domestic development deep in the background of the Congo crises was the rising protest of African-Americans against racial discrimination within the United States. In 1954 the U.S. Supreme Court outlawed racial segregation in public schools. In 1957 Eisenhower found himself having to use federal troops to enforce this ruling against segregationist state and local officials in Arkansas. Kennedy would come to office just as young African-Americans began militant protests against other manifestations of segregation. When thinking about the Congo, members of the Eisenhower, Kennedy, and Johnson administrations recognized that the attitudes of Congolese and other Africans could be influenced by perceptions of what was happening to African-Americans and that, by the same token, African-Americans were a bloc at home particularly attentive to U.S. actions in Africa.

When inaugurated in 1953, Eisenhower was already, at sixty-two, the oldest person thus far to become president. In the autumn of 1960 he turned seventy. He had had a severe heart attack in 1955 and had needed gastric surgery in 1956. On July 27, 1960, when the Congo crisis was just beginning, Eisenhower's vice-president, Richard M. Nixon, became the Republican nominee for president, running against Kennedy, the Democratic nominee. U.S. policy in the Congo crisis thus took shape under a physically weakened lame-duck president in the midst of an election year.

Eisenhower nevertheless remained in firm control of policymaking down to his last day in office.[9] He had inherited the organizational structure created under his predecessor, Harry S. Truman. A National Security Council (NSC) provided some coordination, particularly among the State and Defense departments and the intelligence community. As in Truman's time, the State Department dominated both the formulation and execution of presidential decisions on foreign affairs. The secretary of defense and the Joint Chiefs of Staff (JCS) weighed in only when actual use of military force seemed in prospect. The intelligence community, although mostly under the Department of Defense, was coordinated by a Director of Central Intelligence (DCI), who acted as chief intelligence officer for the

---

9. At the time, it was common, especially among Democrats, to assume that Eisenhower left most business to subordinates, spending much of his own time playing golf and bridge. On the basis of archives and manuscripts later opened, together with interviews, Fred I. Greenstein, *The Hidden-hand Presidency: Eisenhower as Leader* (New York: Basic Books, 1982), makes it clear that this was a carefully cultivated illusion, which permitted Eisenhower to use subordinates as lightning rods.

president and as head of the Central Intelligence Agency (CIA), which recruited spies and conducted clandestine operations abroad.

Eisenhower had named as DCI Allen W. Dulles, the brother of his first secretary of state, John Foster Dulles. Within the World War II Office of Strategic Services, the forerunner of the CIA, Allen Dulles had managed from Switzerland a number of secret operations against Nazi Germany. He was a strong advocate of mounting like operations against the Soviet Union and its allies. A committee headed by former Air Force general James Doolittle had recommended to Eisenhower and his NSC in 1954 that they put no curbs on CIA operations. "It is now clear," said the Doolittle committee, "that we are facing an implacable enemy whose avowed objective is world domination by whatever means and at whatever cost. There are no rules in such a game. Hitherto acceptable norms of human conduct do not apply." Though Eisenhower accepted the Doolittle committee's advice, he set up yet another committee under the NSC—usually called the Special Group—to monitor CIA secret operations.[10]

The waning months of the Eisenhower administration would see judgments about the Congo develop according to processes Eisenhower had ordained, with an especially important role for DCI Dulles and the Special Group.

The UN Steps In

Hammarskjöld moved with speed to respond to the appeals from Kasavubu and Lumumba. As UN secretary general since 1953, he had taken many initiatives to give the UN a larger role in international affairs, especially in what he called "preventive diplomacy" and in peacekeeping.[11]

On July 14, just three days after receiving the Congolese appeal, Hammarskjöld obtained from the UN Security Council a resolution calling

---

10. See John Ranelagh, *The Agency: The Rise and Decline of the CIA* (New York: Simon and Schuster, 1986), especially pp. 276–285. The Special Group was known initially as the Special Group 5412 after the NSC document which set it up. The Kennedy administration would create a separate and larger Special Group (CI) (for Counter-Insurgency), and the Special Group 5412 would become the "40 Committee," after the room in which it met. An offshoot, the Special Group (Augmented), which included Attorney General Robert Kennedy, devoted itself specifically to plans to assassinate or otherwise attack Fidel Castro. As either 5412 or 40, the Special Group that oversaw covert action plans for the Congo consisted of the president's national security assistant, the number-two officials from State and Defense, and the DCI and his deputy for operations. Charles Cogan interview with Thomas Parrott, former secretary of the Special Group.

11. See Brian Urquhart, *Hammarskjöld* (New York: Knopf, 1972).

on Belgium to withdraw its troops from the Congo. The resolution authorized the secretary general to provide the Congo "with such military assistance as may be necessary until, through the efforts of the Congolese government with the technical assistance of the United Nations, the national security forces may be able, in the opinion of the government, to meet fully their tasks."[12] Though neither France nor Britain chose to exercise its veto, both abstained from voting for the resolution. Like the Belgians, they feared that Kasavubu and Lumumba would be unable to protect Europeans, and they welcomed Katanga's quasi-independence as safer for European property in case Lumumba followed in the footsteps of Castro. U.S. Ambassador Timberlake shared this view, commenting that Katanga's secession "should keep bears out of the Congo caviar."[13]

Eisenhower saw Katanga's secession differently. He judged that, without Katanga, the new Congo republic would find it much harder to avoid chaos or communism, and he believed—accurately—that Africans would see the Belgians in Katanga as agents of Western imperialism. Eisenhower thought that a UN presence in all of the Congo would reassure Africans and others in the nonaligned world. He thought it would also help to deter Soviet intervention. After seeing the Congolese appeal for 3,000 U.S. troops, but perhaps before seeing the message from Kasavubu and Lumumba that asked only for UN troops, Eisenhower had his press secretary issue a statement saying "any assistance to the Government of the Congo should be through the United Nations and not by any unilateral action by any one country." The statement added, "it is the opinion of the President...and the Secretary of State that...military assistance would be better for the Congo if it did not come from the United States or any of the large Western nations."[14]

During the following week, the possibility loomed larger that the Congolese leaders might turn to the Soviets for aid. Soviet Premier Nikita Khrushchev said that, if Belgian aggression continued, the Soviet Union might take "more active measures."[15]

No one in the U.S. government was well prepared for dealing with the Congo. Neither in the State Department nor among intelligence agencies had sub-Saharan Africa been an interest of high-fliers. When, on July 31, DCI Dulles briefed the NSC on the developing crisis in the former Belgian

---

12. *Hammarskjöld Papers*, Vol. 5, p. 25.

13. FRUS, 1958–1960, Vol. XIV, p. 287.

14. *New York Times*, July 13, 1960, quoted in Stephen R. Weissman, *American Foreign Policy in the Congo, 1960–1964* (Ithaca: Cornell University Press, 1974), p. 59.

15. Madeleine G. Kalb, *The Congo Cables: The Cold War in Africa—from Eisenhower to Kennedy* (New York: Macmillan, 1982, pp. 15–17.

colony, he was almost certainly summarizing what he had learned from Belgian sources. According to the minutes:

> Mr. Dulles said that in Lumumba we were faced with a person who was a Castro or worse.... There were strong Leftist and Communist trends in his background.... It is safe to go on the assumption that Lumumba has been bought by the Communists.[16]

Timberlake cabled Washington that he was unable to confirm communist influence on Lumumba. The only relevant evidence, he said, was "Communist-line type speeches" by associates of Lumumba. But Dulles's words were echoed by the U.S. ambassador in Brussels, who recommended presuming that a "Lumumba government threatens our vital interests in Congo and Africa generally" and that the U.S. objective "must therefore be to destroy Lumumba government."[17]

The minutes of the NSC meeting do not indicate that Eisenhower saw any immediate need to reconsider his earlier decision to rely on the UN. The Security Council was scheduled to discuss the Congo again on July 22. Lumumba himself was due to attend the UN General Assembly soon afterward and then to visit Washington. Eisenhower's advisers would be able to appraise the Congolese prime minister for themselves.

With the U.S. government still firmly supporting Hammarskjöld and pressing European governments to do likewise, the Security Council on July 22 had little difficulty unanimously (11-0) passing a resolution that called on Belgium to withdraw "speedily" and that authorized the secretary general to "take all necessary action to this effect." The resolution also called on individual states not to intervene unilaterally in the Congo, a provision obviously aimed as much at the Soviet Union as at Belgium. Although the Soviet Union voted for both of the UN resolutions, First Deputy Foreign Minister Vasily V. Kuznetsov warned that the July 22 vote "should not...be considered a precedent for the future."[18]

Lumumba a Threat?

Lumumba's speech at the handover ceremony had sketched a political program. While the speech had socialist overtones, it had hardly been a

---

16. FRUS, 1958–1960, Vol. XIV, pp. 338–339.

17. Timberlake cable, July 17, 1960, in Kalb, *The Congo Cables*, pp. 26–27; William Burden cable (from Brussels), ibid., p. 27.

18. Kalb, *The Congo Cables*, pp. 44–45.

call for Sovietization. Lumumba said, "Together, we are going to establish social justice and make sure everyone has just remuneration for his labor." He also said, however: "I ask you unconditionally to respect the life and property of your fellow citizens and of foreigners living in our country." Begging Congolese to put aside tribal animosities and "to limit themselves strictly to legal and democratic channels," he called "on all Congolese citizens, men, women, and children, to set themselves resolutely to the task of creating a prosperous national economy which will assure our economic independence."[19] Little in this speech or indeed in any of his speeches or writings was more radical than what had been said time and again by Kwame Nkrumah of Ghana, the foremost champion of a united and nonaligned Africa.

The threads of argument in Lumumba's speeches and writings were sufficiently coherent and complex that, when a collection of them was published after Lumumba's death, the French writer and philosopher Jean-Paul Sartre contributed a generally complimentary introduction. Although himself often allied with Communists in France, Sartre did not see Lumumba as even a crypto-Marxist-Leninist. Lumumba's ideology, wrote Sartre, was not proletarian; it was petit-bourgeois, built on the dreams of clerks who wanted to become proprietors.[20]

U.S. officials who met Lumumba at the UN or during his one-day visit to Washington on July 24 did not appear to see much evidence supporting Dulles's characterization of Lumumba as "a Castro or worse." Some said later that they had found Lumumba assertive, jumpy, and unpredictable, but told U.S. newspaper and magazine reporters at the time that he had made a good impression. Answering one reporter's query about Lumumba's reputation for being "crazy," Secretary of State Christian Herter said he was "crazy like a fox."[21]

Pressed by Washington to be especially on watch for signs of Soviet influence, the U.S. embassy and the new, rapidly growing CIA station in Léopoldville reported that, after his return from North America, Lumumba began having suspiciously frequent meetings with Soviet and

---

19. McKown, *Lumumba*, pp. 101–104.

20. Jean-Paul Sartre, "Preface," in Jean Van Lierde, *La pensée politique de Patrice Lumumba* (Paris: Présence africaine, 1963).

21. *Christian Science Monitor*, July 28, 1960, and *Time*, August 8, 1960, both cited in Weissman, *American Foreign Policy in the Congo*, p. 66. Assertions that Lumumba seemed irrational or, in Bissell's words, "a mad dog," were made years later by men defending the decision to try to assassinate Lumumba. This testimony is scattered through U.S. Senate, *Alleged Assassination Plots Against Foreign Leaders: An Interim Report of the Select Committee to Study Governmental Operations with Respect to Intelligence Activities* (New York: W.W. Norton, 1976), referred to hereafter as the Church Committee Interim Report.

East European technicians and that one of his intimates was a mulatto woman from Guinea, a state usually classified as a Soviet ally. Eisenhower's top advisers nevertheless remained uncertain. Herter told the U.S. ambassador in Brussels that he found Lumumba's "reliability open to serious question" but his "intentions and sympathies unclear."[22]

By the end of July 1960, just over 11,000 troops had arrived in the Congo under the UN banner. The majority came from African countries, mainly Morocco, Ghana, and Tunisia. Instructed to fire only in self-defense, they took up positions in all provinces except Katanga. On August 4, Hammarskjöld's personal representative, Ralph Bunche, an African-American, managed to get to Elisabethville, but he had no success persuading Tshombe to allow UN troops into Katanga.

On August 9, Hammarskjöld obtained yet another Security Council resolution. This one specifically authorized action in Katanga. By stating that the UN force was not to be used to influence the outcome of any internal conflict, the resolution sought to reassure Tshombe and the Europeans in Katanga that UN troops would not be used to impose rule by Léopoldville.[23]

In view of this new resolution, Tshombe agreed to let a token UN force enter Katanga. On August 13, Hammarskjöld arrived in person in Elisabethville, with two companies of Swedish troops. He and Tshombe then signed a joint communiqué promising that Belgian troops would be replaced by UN troops, but emphasizing that the UN force would "not be a party to or in any way intervene in or be used to influence the outcome of any internal conflict, constitutional or otherwise."[24]

Although the Belgian government felt compelled to yield to the UN, ministers in Brussels remained doubtful that UN troops could either maintain order or protect Katanga against the Léopoldville government's army. They decided to assign several hundred officers to a new Katanga gendarmerie, which would be built upon Katangan elements of the Force Publique. They also transferred to the Katanga government all of the Belgian military aircraft remaining in the Congo.[25] On the surface, nevertheless, Hammarskjöld, the UN, and the United States seemed to have secured their ends.

Now, however, conflict developed between the UN and Lumumba. The arrangement made between Hammarskjöld and Tshombe outraged

---

22. Herter cable, August 1, 1960, Kalb, *The Congo Cables*, p. 38.

23. *Hammarskjöld Papers*, Vol. 5, p. 76.

24. *Hammarskjöld Papers*, Vol. 5, p. 106.

25. Alan James, *Britain and the Congo Crisis, 1960–63* (New York: St. Martin's, 1996), pp. 49–52.

Lumumba, precisely because it did not call for or even imply that Katanga should cease to be independent. Hammarskjöld had said not a word protesting the fact that Katanga flew its own flag, had its own currency, and communicated through foreign consuls in Elisabethville as if they were ambassadors. He had raised no objections to Belgium's measures for reinforcing the Katanga regime. Hammarskjöld had been meticulous, moreover, in insisting that no outside aid of any kind should go to the Congo except through the UN, thus denying the central Congolese government the means to build up military forces capable of forcing submission by Katanga.

When Hammarskjöld passed through Léopoldville on August 14 on his way back to New York, Lumumba upbraided him for not taking the side of the Congo's central government against Tshombe. On the following day, Lumumba declared publicly that he had lost confidence in Hammarskjöld.

Very soon thereafter, Lumumba secretly turned to the Soviet Union, seeking the aid that the UN seemed to have denied him. He had a plan for gathering ANC troops in Stanleyville and moving them across Kasai for an invasion of Katanga. In response to his appeal, the Soviet Union sent fifteen Ilyushin transport planes to Stanleyville. The Soviets also turned over to Lumumba a hundred trucks that had been shipped to the Congo for use by the UN. On August 26, the Ilyushin planes ferried ANC troops to Bakwanga in south Kasai.[26]

The arrival of the Soviet planes and trucks, together with large contingents of technicians and advisers from the Soviet bloc, seemed to confirm the fears voiced earlier by Belgians and by DCI Dulles. Lawrence Devlin, the forceful French-speaking operative sent by Dulles and Bissell to head the CIA station in the Congo, cabled on August 18:

Embassy and station believe Congo experiencing classic Communist effort takeover government. Many forces at work here: Soviets...Communist party, etc. Although difficult determine major influencing factors to predict outcome struggle for power, decisive period not far off. Whether or not Lumumba actually Commie or just playing Commie game to assist his solidifying power, anti-West forces rapidly increasing power Congo and there may be little time left in which take action to avoid another Cuba.[27]

When the NSC met at Newport later on the same day, Eisenhower spoke emphatically about Lumumba:

---

26. *Hammarskjöld Papers*, Vol. 5, p. 142.

27. Church Committee Interim Report, p. 14.

The President said that the possibility that the UN would be forced out was simply inconceivable. We should keep the UN in the Congo even if we had to ask for European troops to do it. We should do so even if such action was used by the Soviets as the basis for starting a fight.... We were talking of one man forcing us out of the Congo; of Lumumba supported by the Soviets. There was no indication, the President stated, that the Congolese did not want UN support and the maintenance of order.

The decision recorded at the end of the meeting was "that a United Nations presence should be maintained in the Congo in the interests both of the Free World and the United Nations, despite Lumumba's efforts, supported by the Soviet bloc, to expel UN forces."[28]

Both Gordon Gray, the president's assistant for national security affairs, and DCI Dulles understood Eisenhower's words as authorizing the CIA to engage in covert action against Lumumba. When members of the NSC Special Group heard a senior CIA representative describe various standard covert action projects such as bribery, Gray said that "his associates had expressed extremely strong feelings on the necessity for very straightforward action in this situation, and he wondered whether the plans as outlined were sufficient to accomplish this." The minutes conclude: "it was finally agreed that planning for the Congo would not necessarily rule out 'consideration' of any particular kind of activity which might contribute to getting rid of Lumumba."[29] Dulles's operations chief, former Yale economics professor Richard Bissell, and others from CIA would later testify that they believed that Eisenhower's words, together with those of Gray, authorized the CIA to attempt to assassinate Lumumba.[30]

The next day, Dulles cabled Devlin:

In high quarters here it is the clear-cut conclusion that if [Lumumba] continues to hold high office, the inevitable result will at best be chaos and at worst pave the way to Communist takeover of the Congo with disastrous consequences for the prestige of the UN and for the interests of the free world generally. Consequently we conclude that his removal must be an urgent

---

28. NSC meeting, August 18, 1960, FRUS, 1958–1960, Vol. XIV, p. 424.

29. Church Committee Interim Report, p. 60.

30. The question of whether Eisenhower intended such an interpretation of his words has never been settled. See Church Committee Interim Report, pp. 9–70, and the discussion of this testimony and other evidence scattered through Kalb, *The Congo Cables*, and Kelly, *America's Tyrant*.

and prime objective and that under existing conditions this should be a high priority of our covert action.[31]

Bissell turned to his scientific adviser, Dr. Sidney Gottlieb. A month later Gottlieb would arrive in Léopoldville equipped with poisons to be inserted into Lumumba's food or possibly his toothpaste. Soon afterward, the CIA station in the Congo would be reinforced by other men prepared to kill Lumumba by other means.[32] In the meantime, however, political conditions in the Congo changed.

With UN troops having replaced Belgian troops in most parts of the Congo other than Katanga, and with Lumumba fulminating against Hammarskjöld, Kasavubu saw an opportunity to assert himself. On the evening of September 5, 1960, Kasavubu took to the radio to announce that he was removing Lumumba for having fomented an "atrocious civil war." He named as the new prime minister Joseph Ileo, the president of the Senate, who had been an early advocate of independence but who was known to believe that the Congo needed an extended period of Belgian tutelage.[33]

Kasavubu had given advance notice of his intentions to Andrew Cordier, an American acting as temporary UN representative in the Congo following the departure of Bunche. After Kasavubu's announcement, Cordier decided on his own to direct the UN forces to take over the radio station and the airport in Léopoldville. Cordier's decision, ostensibly intended only to minimize disorder, in fact put Lumumba at a disadvantage, for it prevented his using his oratorical skills to rally support. For this reason, nonaligned governments would later criticize Cordier's decision, question his neutrality, and press Hammarskjöld to replace him with someone not from a Western nation.

Lumumba took refuge in his official residence. Despite his criticisms of Cordier and the UN, he asked to be guarded by UN troops. Once safe behind their cordon, he fired off a response, declaring that Kasavubu had acted contrary to the *Loi Fondamentale* and had therefore forfeited his right to remain president. On September 7, the Congo's House of Representatives voted 60 to 19 to revoke both the attempted removal of Lumumba as prime minister by Kasavubu and of Kasavubu as president

31. FRUS, 1958–1960, Vol. XIV, p. 443.

32. Church Committee Interim Report, pp. 23–26.

33. U.S. Department of State, *An Analytical Chronology of the Congo Crisis*, March 9, 1961, p. 1, John F. Kennedy Presidential Library (JFKL), National Security File (NSF), Box 27, Congo General, hereafter referred to as *Analytical Chronology of the Congo Crisis*. See also Weissman, *American Foreign Policy in the Congo*, p. 82.

by Lumumba. The following day the Senate, too, voted overwhelmingly to cancel Kasavubu's action.[34] Since Kasavubu and Lumumba each stood fast in insisting that the other had no legitimate right to office, the Congo republic seemed for the time being to have no government at all.

Most of the ANC was still in south Kasai under the ANC commander, General Victor Lundula, Lumumba's uncle. The planned offensive against Katanga had gone no farther. Lundula's troops preoccupied themselves with robbing and murdering the Baluba tribesmen who worked Kasai's diamond mines. ANC troops around Léopoldville were under Lundula's deputy, Colonel Mobutu. On the evening of September 9, Mobutu encountered CIA station chief Devlin at Kasavubu's residence. Taking the American aside, Mobutu told him that he was considering temporarily seizing control from both Kasavubu and Lumumba. He asked whether the United States would support such a coup. After some hesitation, Devlin said, "I believe we would."[35]

On September 14, 1960, at 8:30 p.m., Radio Léopoldville broadcast an announcement by Mobutu that he was taking power. He declared that he was "neutralizing" the chief of state, the rival governments of Ileo and Lumumba, and Parliament until December 31.[36] He appointed a "College of Commissioners" made up of young Congolese who had been to Europe for higher education, and said that this group would monitor his interim rule. General Lundula having meanwhile returned to Léopoldville, Mobutu took the precaution of also removing him from office and placing him under house arrest. Mobutu became commander of the ANC.

Mobutu assembled an anti-Lumumbist group led by himself, Foreign Minister Justin-Marie Bomboko, and Victor Nendaka, the Sureté (police) chief. It came to be known as the "Binza group," after the Léopoldville suburb where most of them resided. By a decision to co-opt and reinstate Kasavubu, their junta gained a shred of legitimacy. In a press conference on September 16, Mobutu recognized Kasavubu as head of state and Kasavubu endorsed Mobutu's College of Commissioners (although he did not claim that the college was legal).[37] One of the first acts of Mobutu's new government was to close down the Soviet and Czech embassies and order all their personnel to leave the Congo.

Lumumba remained in the prime minister's residence, protected by UN troops. From there, he continued to wield influence. Rajeswar Dayal,

---

34. *Analytical Chronology of the Congo Crisis*, p. 33.
35. Ibid.
36. FRUS, 1958–1960, Vol. XIV, p. 490.
37. *Analytical Chronology of the Congo Crisis*, p. 38.

an Oxford-educated Indian diplomat sent by Hammarskjöld to replace Cordier, regarded the Mobutu government as unconstitutional. Dayal thought Lumumba the most legitimate leader in the Congo and, unlike Hammarskjöld, believed that Lumumba might cooperate with the UN. Dayal refused to deal with the College of Commissioners on the ground that the constitution required Parliament to approve any new government. This evidence of neutrality as between Mobutu and Lumumba displeased both Ambassador Timberlake and officials in Washington.[38]

Immediately after Mobutu's September 14 coup, the Security Council considered a resolution reaffirming the three previous resolutions, but also calling on all states to "refrain from direct or indirect provision of arms or other materials of war and military personnel…in the Congo during the temporary period of military assistance through the United Nations, except upon the request of the United Nations."[39] This time, the Soviet Union used its veto. Nonaligned and Western governments then joined in taking the resolution to the General Assembly, where it passed on September 20 by a vote of 70-0, with eleven abstentions (including the Soviet bloc, France, and South Africa).

The day before the General Assembly voted on this resolution, Khrushchev arrived in New York for a large UN-sponsored conference on disarmament. The Soviet Union had long claimed to want a world without armaments but to be frustrated by Western warmongers and war profiteers. Khrushchev planned to spend two weeks at the UN conference trumpeting this theme.

When Khrushchev set sail, he had had reason to gloat about events in the Congo, where Lumumba did indeed seem to be acting as Castro had earlier. By the time Khrushchev's ship docked in New York, however, the scene in the Congo had turned topsy-turvy. Lumumba was effectively under house arrest, Mobutu was in control, and Eastern bloc diplomats had been expelled. These developments prompted Khrushchev to add to his disarmament appeals an attack on Hammarskjöld and the UN Secretariat. "The colonialists," said Khrushchev on a September 23 speech to the UN, "have been doing their dirty work in the Congo through the Secretary-General of the United Nations and his staff."[40]

Khrushchev's attack on Hammarskjöld did not go down well with noncommunist Asian and African delegates at the UN. When Hammarskjöld

---

38. Conversation between Herter and Hammarskjöld, September 26, 1960, FRUS, 1958–1960, Vol. XIV, pp. 506–507.

39. *Hammarskjöld Papers*, Vol. 5, p. 191.

40. *Hammarskjöld Papers*, Vol. 5, p. 194.

responded by declaring that the UN existed not to serve the great powers but to protect the weak, he received a standing ovation.[41]

In November, faced with the question of whether to seat a delegation led by Kasavubu or an alternative delegation representing Lumumba, the General Assembly decided in favor of Kasavubu. Nervous about seeming thus to line up with the West, most Asian and African representatives justified their votes as simply acknowledging Kasavubu's status as head of state.

When Kasavubu returned from New York on November 27, his associates feted him with a boisterous all-night party. Heavy rain fell, during which both Lumumba's UN guards and the ANC troops cordoning the prime minister's residence lost their concentration. Concealing himself on the floor of a Chevrolet sedan that regularly transported servants to and from his quarters, Lumumba escaped. It was morning before a UN guard discovered his absence. By then Lumumba was in a three-car caravan bouncing over dirt roads in the direction of Stanleyville, some 1500 km away.[42]

Along the way, as villagers recognized Lumumba and hailed him, he could not resist the temptation to stop and make speeches. About 1,000 kilometers from Stanleyville, ANC troops caught up with him and took him captive. After beating him savagely, they flew him back to Léopoldville with his hands roped behind him. In Léopoldville, ANC soldiers again beat and kicked Lumumba, this time with U.S. newsreel cameras running. Timberlake, aghast, characterized this as a "gift of atomic bomb [to] Soviet bloc and friends."[43] Dayal demanded that the government treat Lumumba with "justice, dignity, and humanity." Foreign Minister Bomboko made the requested assurances, but in fact Lumumba was kept in close confinement in a military prison.

In the UN Security Council, ambassadors from Asia and Africa joined Soviet ambassador Valerian Zorin in condemning Hammarskjöld for not having protected Lumumba. On December 12, Lumumba's deputy, Antoine Gizenga, proclaimed a "Free Republic of the Congo" with its capital at Stanleyville. General Lundula, who had managed to escape from Léopoldville, appeared in Stanleyville, where Gizenga declared him still

---

41. To Dayal, Hammarskjöld would boast that the confrontation had strengthened the UN by showing it to be "the main obstacle to an expansion of empire into Africa." Kelly, *America's Tyrant*, p. 54.

42. A careful, detailed account of Lumumba's escape, recapture, and murder is Ludo de Witte, *The Assassination of Lumumba* (New York: Verso, 2001). There is also a good deal of authentic footage in the partially fictional film, "Lumumba," produced by Jacques Bidou and directed by Raoul Peck (Zeitgeist Films, 2002).

43. Kalb, *The Congo Cables*, p. 163.

the commander of the ANC. Before long, Gizenga had troops moving into Kivu and parts of Equateur and Kasai.

On December 17, the United States and the United Kingdom introduced a UN resolution implicitly backing the Kasavubu-Mobutu regime against Gizenga. This U.S.-UK initiative won not a single vote from an African delegation. The Western governments mustered enough votes to block an alternative resolution, which implicitly called on Kasavubu and Mobutu to release Lumumba, but their only African allies were Kasavubu's delegates and those from South Africa, then still a white-supremacy stronghold.

The Eisenhower administration had feared that the chaos in the Congo would enable the Soviets to make the country another Cuba. As Eisenhower's presidency neared its end, that fear persisted. In January 1961, the U.S. embassy in Léopoldville foresaw as the most likely future a Congo "pushed into the Communist camp under UN aegis."[44] The common front with nonaligned nations appeared to be in ruins.

JFK and "New Directions"

On January 20, 1961, John F. Kennedy succeeded Eisenhower as president. He had often accused the Eisenhower administration of indifference to the developing world. In a major campaign speech in October 1960 he had referred to Guinea as a nation that the Republicans had "lost" to communism, along with Cuba. "We must ally ourselves with the rising sea of nationalism in Africa," he said.

A number of Kennedy's appointees came to office determined that the United States should show more sympathy and support for new nations such as the Congo republic. Among them were Adlai E. Stevenson, the new U.S. ambassador to the UN; Chester Bowles, the new under secretary of state; and G. Mennen Williams and Harlan Cleveland, the assistant secretaries of state for, respectively, African Affairs and International Organization Affairs.

Stevenson had been the Democratic presidential nominee in 1952 and 1956; in 1960, he had been supported for a third nomination by Democrats who doubted the strength of Kennedy's idealism. Disappointed not to have been named secretary of state, Ambassador Stevenson would sometimes succumb to the lure of the limelight. Bowles, co-founder of one of America's biggest advertising agencies and ambassador to India under Truman, thought himself the Democratic party's expert on ways of wooing

---

44. January 10, 1961, FRUS, 1961–1963, Vol. XX, *Congo Crisis*, p. 13.

the Third World. In 1956 he had published a book entitled *Africa's Challenge to America*, saying that the United States had "a clear moral, ideological, and—one might say—historical responsibility to play a constructive role in Africa." He declared that: "America's role must be determined by her ability to shake loose from her present negative fascination with what *Moscow* is doing."[45]

Williams had been a two-term governor of Michigan, strongly supported by the state's African-Americans and by national African-American organizations. It was on this ground that Kennedy had offered him the assistant secretaryship for Africa and had announced his appointment before settling on Dean Rusk to be secretary of state. Williams thus had reason to regard himself as not necessarily subordinate to Rusk or to Bowles. Cleveland, as editor and publisher of the influential monthly *The Reporter*, had a well-established reputation as a spokesman for views similar to those of Stevenson and Bowles.

Stevenson, Bowles, Williams, and Cleveland would not have African policy all to themselves. Williams's African bureau had only been established in 1957. For the most part, African affairs had been a sideline for the Foreign Service officers in the European bureau, who were generally thought dominant in the department's bureaucracy. These officers tended to look at Africa much as did Europeans. In the words of one department veteran, they "were more aware of tribalism and backwardness" and leaned toward "slow independence, tutelage, schools."[46]

Stevenson, Bowles, and their colleagues would run into resistance not only from old-line Europeanists but also from other Kennedy appointees who had priorities different from theirs. George W. Ball, Rusk's under secretary for economic affairs, was Stevenson's former law partner and remained his close friend, but took much more interest in Europe and tended to think both Stevenson and Bowles men of words more than men of action. George C. McGhee, a geophysicist who had made a fortune in the oil business, had served in the Truman State Department and returned under his old friend, Rusk, as Counselor and chief of the policy planning staff. His views and attitudes were very similar to Ball's.

Policy toward the Congo during the Kennedy administration would be initially formed by debates between the Stevenson-Bowles group on one side and Ball and McGhee on the other. Rusk would intervene from time to time, but rarely tried to impose his own views. The Pentagon would .

---

45. Chester Bowles, *Africa's Challenge to America* (Berkeley: University of California Press, 1956), pp. 106, 134.

46. An anonymous interviewee in Weissman, *American Foreign Policy in the Congo*, pp. 47–48.

sometimes weigh in. Robert S. McNamara, who had left the presidency of the Ford Motor Company to become secretary of defense, was the strongest personality in Kennedy's inner circle; McNamara's assistant secretary for international security affairs was Paul H. Nitze, who had been chief of policy planning in the Truman State Department and was an extraordinarily articulate and artful manager of governmental processes.[47]

In the end, of course, decisions would be made in the White House. Kennedy had been critical not only of Eisenhower's policies but of his procedures for reaching decisions. Kennedy dismantled most of the NSC's boards and committees, preferring to rely on a very small staff under McGeorge Bundy, a former dean and professor of international politics at Harvard. Although Bundy attempted to act as honest broker among the president's advisers, his own views were unquestionably closer to those of Ball, McGhee, and Nitze than to those of the Stevenson-Bowles group.

Kennedy developed a practice of personally prodding cabinet and subcabinet officers for information and sometimes ringing up State Department desk officers or diplomats stationed abroad. He met with Dulles and Bissell to discuss details of covert action. Such direct intervention by the president had the effect of gingering up both the advisory process and action in the field. Sometimes, however, the price was late discovery of some consideration or implementation problem that the previous administration's processes had been designed to detect.

Soon, though not immediately, the change in administration would be accompanied by changes in the field. Timberlake, thought by Bowles and Williams to be too closely identified with the policies of their predecessors, was recalled at the end of April 1961. His eventual replacement would be Edmund Gullion, a foreign service officer who was a protégé of Bowles and who also had connections with Kennedy. Hammarskjöld, grateful to see the last of Timberlake, reciprocated by bringing Dayal home and appointing in his place a triumvirate led by Swedish businessman Stüre Linner.

Early in the new administration, the bureaucracy prepared two long background documents. The African bureau of the Department of State submitted a 73-page "Analytical Chronology" summarizing cables to and from the Congo. Probably intentionally, it highlighted the conservatism of Timberlake and the department's Europeanists, all of whom tended to deplore the departure of the Belgians. CIA's Office of National Estimates (ONE) submitted a Special National Intelligence Estimate (SNIE) on the Congo.[48] The ONE reported to Dulles, but otherwise had no connection

---

47. For one illustration of Nitze's skill, see Ernest R. May, ed., *American Cold War Strategy: Interpreting NSC 68* (Boston: Bedford Books, 1993).

48. SNIE 65-61, January 10, 1961, FRUS, 1961–1963, Vol. XX, pp. 2–11.

whatever with the part of CIA that maintained stations abroad, tried to recruit spies, and conducted covert action. At CIA headquarters, analysts were separated from operators by a solid wall. They used different elevators and had different meeting rooms and lunchrooms. Analysts were not supposed to learn the names or faces of officers in the clandestine service. While the authors of the SNIE may have had inklings of Devlin's reportage from Léopoldville, they can have had no direct knowledge of assassination or other schemes of Dulles, Bissell, and Devlin.

The anonymous authors of the SNIE said:

> In the Congo situation...we see little chance for signal improvement, and virtually none for a decisive outcome which would bring early stability.... There is no indication that the Congo is developing a national leader, a national party, or a national consciousness. Political instability on a grand scale...appears to be the most likely prospect for the Congo for some time to come.

While they said that the Congo had "become a battleground in the East-West struggle," they expressed doubt that any outside power could gain an enduring foothold. Regarding the UN, they wrote:

> The Congo operation represents by far the largest and most complex task yet undertaken by the UN and much of that body's standing is staked on its success. Yet the UN's present undertaking to maintain law and order without supporting any Congolese faction is almost impossible to carry through.

The new administration faced a forcing deadline, for the UN Security Council was scheduled to debate the Congo on February 1. On January 25, Rusk asked Williams and Cleveland to produce a review of Congo policy possibly pointing in "drastic new directions." Soon afterward, Kennedy himself asked Bundy, Rusk, and McNamara for advice on instructions to be given Stevenson for his role in the upcoming debate. These efforts fused in a paper put before Kennedy precisely on February 1, 1961.

The original draft prepared for Williams and Cleveland by the State Department's African Bureau had called for "a broadly based Congolese government," possibly including Lumumba. When the draft went to the Pentagon for review, however, Nitze questioned allowing for Lumumba's return and hence for a Congolese government that could "fall into the hands of individuals whose purposes are known to be inimical to Western interests." Nitze proposed that, against the possibility of UN failure, the United States prepare a "fall-back" plan for "a vigorous unilateral course of action." The document put before Kennedy compromised the two positions by recommending an effort to get Kasavubu to form "a middle-of-the-road cabinet." While it said that the United States should emphasize its "determination to make the United Nations succeed in the Congo," it also called for making clear "that we are determined that the Congo will not fall into Communist hands." Kennedy approved this language, thus leaving U.S. policy just about where Eisenhower had left it.[49]

THE DEATH OF LUMUMBA

While the new administration was conducting its policy review, rumors proliferated that Lumumba might no longer be alive. Just three days before Kennedy's inauguration, it was reported that Lumumba would be transferred from the military prison near Léopoldville to a place of confinement at Bakwanga, the diamond capital of Kasai, where the local strong man was one of Lumumba's mortal enemies. Two days later, on January 19, the CIA station in the Congo cabled that Lumumba had actually been transferred to Elisabethville, where he would be in the custody of Tshombe. Tshombe's spokesman said that Lumumba was alive and well and would be well-treated. Three weeks later, on February 10, however, the same spokesman said that Lumumba had escaped and fled into the countryside. On February 13, he announced that villagers at an unspecified location in Katanga had fallen upon Lumumba and his companions and killed them. No one believed this, but the spokesman did not seem to care: "We will be accused of having murdered them," he stated. "My reply is: prove it."[50]

---

49. February 1, 1961, FRUS, 1961–1963, Vol. XX, pp. 40–46. Allen Dulles wrote Kennedy subsequently that, if the CIA had officially commented on this policy document, it "might have suggested certain changes." Ibid., p. 46. Dulles would probably have put more emphasis on keeping control in the hands of the Binza group, which the CIA had been bankrolling.

50. *Hammarskjöld Papers*, Vol. 5, p. 340. Witte, *Assassination of Lumumba* and the Bidou-Peck film, "Lumumba," provide many details. The killing was personally overseen by Tshombe but carried out by Belgian mercenaries. They shot Lumumba and his companions and buried them in a shallow grave. Then, worrying that the remains might be chanced upon by humans or animals, they returned and, after difficulties, buried the bodies in another site. A senior Belgian officer, learning what had been done, ordered that the bodies be disinterred once again. Both to hide evidence of the murder and to make sure that fragments of Lumumba's body were not taken for talismanic uses, this officer ordered that the bones and teeth be reduced to powder and scattered to the wind. Although the evidence is imperfect, there is some reason to believe that Tshombe and his advisers decided to kill Lumumba because they feared that the new Kennedy administration might view him more tolerantly than had the Eisenhower administration. All the evidence so far unearthed on the U.S. side suggests that the CIA at the time knew no more about Lumumba's end than did news reporters. See especially Church Committee Interim Report; and Evan Thomas, *The Very Best Men—Four Who Dared: The Early Years of the CIA* (New York: Simon and Schuster, 1995), pp. 220–233.

The Soviet Union lost no time in blaming Lumumba's murder on the United Nations and on Hammarskjöld personally. A Soviet government statement of February 14, 1961, read:

> The murder of Patrice Lumumba and his comrades-in-arms in the dungeons of Katanga is the culmination of Hammarskjöld's criminal activities. It is clear to every honest person throughout the world that the blood of Patrice Lumumba is on the hands of this henchman of the colonialists and cannot be removed.[51]

Few governments outside the Soviet bloc joined in this condemnation of Hammarskjöld. Instead, the nations represented at the UN joined in trying to give Hammarskjöld a stronger hand. The Security Council voted on February 21, 9-0 with the Soviet Union and France abstaining, to invoke Chapter VII of the UN Charter, which prescribes that in event "of any threat to the peace, breach of the peace, or act of aggression," the Security Council may authorize "such action by air, sea or land forces as may be necessary." The new resolution directed that "the United Nations take immediately all appropriate measures to prevent the occurrence of civil war in the Congo" using "force, if necessary, in the last resort."[52]

Kennedy helped Hammarskjöld by persuading Indian Prime Minister Jawaharlal Nehru to send troops to replace the African troops pulled out in protest against the arrest and imprisonment of Lumumba. On March 12, as Indian troops were beginning to arrive in the Congo, Hammarskjöld wrote Kasavubu: "The Congo has to adjust itself to circumstances and accept the decisions of the Security Council in conformity with Chapter VII of the Charter."[53] On April 15, Hammarskjöld gained added authority when the General Assembly endorsed the February 21 Security Council resolution. Before the end of April, Hammarskjöld's words were backed by 4,000 men of what would eventually be a 5,800 man Indian brigade, composed mostly of battle-hardened Sikhs.

A NEW GOVERNMENT FOR THE CONGO?

Kasavubu apparently saw no good alternative other than to yield to the UN. On April 17, he signed an agreement in principle to observe the resolution, stipulating, however, that "the United Nations is to assist the President of the Republic so that all foreign personnel, whether civilian, military or paramilitary, and all mercenaries or political advisors who

---

51. *Hammarskjöld Papers*, Vol. 5, p. 342.

52. *Hammarskjöld Papers*, Vol. 5, p. 356.

53. *Hammarskjöld Papers*, Vol. 5, p. 407.

have not been recruited or recalled under the authority of the President, be repatriated from the Congo within the shortest possible period of time."[54]

On April 24, Kasavubu convened a conference at Coquilhatville, the capital of Equateur province. It included representatives from all the provinces, but none sent by Gizenga's "Free Republic." Tshombe did attend, but made plain that he was interested only in a federation loose enough to leave Katanga effectively independent. Kasavubu placed Tshombe under house arrest to prevent him from walking out. On May 28, the Coquilhatville conference ended by endorsing the principle of a federal system under a strong central government. Parliament was to come back into session to implement the agreement and choose a new government. Tshombe, released from detention, signed the agreement on June 24 but immediately upon return to Elisabethville repudiated it, saying he had signed under duress.[55]

The parliament assembled on July 15 at Lovanium University outside Léopoldville. Blue-helmeted Indian and Ghanaian troops guarded every access. Now, all provinces except Katanga were represented.[56] Though Gizenga himself did not attend, he sent a "Free Republic" delegation headed by Christophe Gbenye, his interior minister and the nominal successor to Lumumba as head of the MNC. The members of the lower house reelected as presiding officer the same man who had held that post in November 1960, when the parliament had last met. This seemed an omen that Lumumbists would be in control. The Senate, however, chose a presiding officer who was not a Lumumbist. The two houses then agreed to relegitimize Kasavubu in spite of his having governed unconstitutionally for the past eight months. The open question was whether Kasavubu would be forced to name a Lumumbist as prime minister. A vote was scheduled for August 1.

U.S. COVERT ACTION

In spite of the initial search for "drastic new directions," Kennedy had found himself following the course of his predecessor in part because his concerns were similar to Eisenhower's. Both presidents wanted the good will of nonaligned nations. Both hoped that UN action could prevent the Congo from becoming an arena of direct conflict with the Soviet Union. At the same time, both men assigned high importance to ensuring that the Congo did not become "another Cuba."

---

54. *Hammarskjöld Papers*, Vol. 5, p. 451.

55. *Hammarskjöld Papers*, Vol. 5, p. 497.

56. *Hammarskjöld Papers*, Vol. 5, p. 538.

For Kennedy, the last consideration always weighed heavily, and it gained still greater weight after mid-April 1961, when a CIA-sponsored invasion of Cuba came completely apart at the Bay of Pigs. Kennedy was forced to acknowledge U.S. responsibility for the invasion; its total failure, and the fact that thousands of Cuban exiles participating in the invasion ended up in Castro's prisons. For the remaining thirty-one months of his life, Kennedy would be fighting a charge that, while he had criticized Eisenhower for "losing" Cuba, he had not been man enough to carry out Eisenhower's plan for ridding Cuba of its communist government.

In mid-1961 Kennedy and his aides watched the maneuvers and controversies anxiously as Congolese politicians gathered on the Lovanium campus. They feared that Gizenga or another Lumumbist might emerge as prime minister. On June 8, members of the NSC Special Group worried that "if Gizenga decided to participate in a new Léopoldville Government or Parliament, he had ample resources and a chance eventually to win control of the government."[57]

In view of this presumption, Kennedy found himself doing almost exactly what Eisenhower had done: asking for covert action by the CIA to tilt the political scales within the Congo. The Bay of Pigs affair had caused the resignations of both Dulles and Bissell. The new DCI was former utilities executive and Atomic Energy Commission chairman John McCone. Kennedy had already asked Bundy for a report on "all of our clandestine activities in support of political leaders and parties"; Bundy had promised in particular "a proposal for action in the Congo which has the support of our Ambassador and our Department of State." While the full report and details of the proposal remain classified, we know that, in the interim, Bundy transferred $23,000 to the CIA "in support of particular activities designed to strengthen the moderate camp in the Congo." He assured Kennedy that "very much larger sums have been spent in the past in the same direction, through the same channels and without embarrassment."[58]

Although Rusk usually left African affairs to Williams or Cleveland, now he stepped in temporarily as, in effect, the desk officer for the Congo. Gullion, the new ambassador, was still deep in nuclear armaments negotiations and not yet on post. A newly arrived chargé d'affaires, G. McMurtrie Godley, manned the embassy in Léopoldville. In view of what

---

57. JFKL, National Security File, Box 319, Special Group (CI), memorandum of meeting of June 8, 1961, p. 1. Although this document is found in the files of the Special Group (CI), the meeting is of the Special Group 5412 dealing with covert action, whose members were the National Security Adviser (Bundy), the No. 2 at State (Bowles), the No. 2 at Defense (Roswell Gilpatric) and the Director of Central Intelligence (Dulles).

58. FRUS, 1961–1963, Vol. XX, p. 144.

had been said in the Special Group meeting and of news media reportage that seemed to confirm the Lumumbist tendency at Lovanium, Rusk directed Godley to get Kasavubu to slow down the process of choosing a prime minister.

To Rusk's surprise, Godley said "no." From Frank Carlucci, then a young but very perceptive foreign service officer on duty in Stanleyville, Godley had reports of confusion and disarray in Gizenga's immediate circle. Gizenga himself, probably from fear of being arrested or killed, was pretending to be too ill to come to Lovanium, and Godley understood that this was costing him support. In addition, Godley may have known details unknown to Rusk of efforts by the CIA and other Western secret services to influence the Congolese parliamentarians.

After failing to sway Godley, Rusk fired off a cable that said, in effect, "on your head be it." The cable read:

> Secretary desires emphasize for your guidance that Gizenga as Prime Minister not only question prestige abroad and reaction at home but involves our most vital interests in Africa and our future ability support UN in such situations. As you are aware from previous instructions, blocking Gizenga from controlling government is a specific object of policy for which your full attention and imaginative effort are required. Secretary considers you are doing excellent job in difficult circumstances but he wanted to underline gravity this matter.[59]

Fortunately for his future career, Godley proved to be right in predicting that Gizenga would not carry the day. On August 1, Kasavubu asked Cyrille Adoula to form a government. A member of the Senate who had also served on the Congolese delegation at the UN, Adoula had been praised by Timberlake and would later be described by Hammarskjöld as "the most purposeful, energetic and capable African he knew."[60] On August 2, the parliament gave Adoula an almost unanimous vote of confidence. Gizenga was named first deputy prime minister but, since it was clear that he was to have no power, he refused to assume the post unless and until the Katanga secession ended.

Without providing details about Godley's initiative, Rusk sent Kennedy a gratulatory report. With Adoula's victory, wrote Rusk, Gizenga

---

59. FRUS, 1961–1963, Vol. XX, pp. 178–179.

60. Timberlake, November 15, 1960, FRUS, 1958–1960, Vol. XIV, pp. 586–588; *Hammarskjöld*, September 15, 1961; FRUS, 1961–1963, Vol. XX, p. 215.

lost any basis for asking recognition of his Free Republic: "It is the second Soviet defeat in the Congo."[61]

Whether justly or not, the *New York Times* would later credit the result to CIA covert action. Looking back at developments in the Congo in the early 1960s, a team of *Times* reporters wrote of the outcome at Lovanium:

Money and shiny American automobiles, furnished through the logistic wizardry of [the CIA at] Langley are said to have been the deciding factors in the vote…. Russian, Czechoslovak, Egyptian and Ghanaian agents were simply outbid, where they could not be outmaneuvered.[62]

Bringing Tshombe to Heel

The Congo seemed now to be more nearly unified and more competently led than at any time since independence. In these circumstances, the United States and the UN could turn their attention once again to Katanga. An end to its quasi-independence would complete the unification of the Congo and would greatly strengthen the economic position of the government in Léopoldville.

Although Hammarskjöld and his agents in the Congo, as well as Stevenson and the others in Washington, favored moving immediately to end Katanga's autonomy, they faced opposition both internationally and within the United States. Katanga's autonomy enabled the Union Minière to continue operations, exporting ore through Rhodesia or Angola. The roughly 15,000 whites still in Katanga, mostly Belgian or French, thought that their safety depended on Katanga's remaining independent. The company and the whites looked to Tshombe's Katanga gendarmerie for protection against both Léopoldville and the UN, which they saw as Léopoldville's ally.

All along, the Belgian, British, and French governments had favored allowing Katanga to retain a large measure of autonomy. They had not pressed this case vigorously while Eisenhower was president; his credentials as a friend of Europe were too strong. But Europeans felt fewer qualms about speaking up to Kennedy. Moreover, Kennedy had handed them new bargaining chips by announcing that he wanted to move away from Eisenhower's strategy of defending Europe by a threat of nuclear "massive retaliation." Kennedy's proposal to substitute a strategy of "flexible response" depended for its success on Europeans agreeing to increase their non-nuclear forces.

---

61. FRUS, 1961–1963, Vol. XX, p. 185.
62. *New York Times*, April 26, 1966, p. 30.

Solidarity within the Western alliance became all the more important to the Kennedy administration because of Khrushchev's stepped-up pressure on the question of West Berlin. Meeting Kennedy at Vienna in June 1961, Khrushchev had said categorically that he intended to end the special status of West Berlin and would not be deterred by Western threats of nuclear war. On August 13, as a stopgap means of halting illegal emigration from East Germany via West Berlin, the Soviets and East Germans hurriedly erected a huge wall cutting East Berlin off from West Berlin. For more than a year thereafter—until the Cuban missile crisis of October 1962—the prospect of a showdown over Berlin preoccupied planners in Washington and at NATO headquarters. This made it harder for Kennedy and his top advisers to disregard European pleas to go slow regarding Katanga.

In addition, Kennedy and his advisers heard words of caution from within the administration and from Congress and the public. Even Charles Yost, one of Stevenson's closest aides at the UN, warned that the Adoula regime might not last, in which case the United States might welcome having Tshombe as a "conservative counterweight."[63] Tshombe, like Chiang Kai-shek, had ties to American missionaries. He had been educated in a Methodist school. He had active supporters on Capitol Hill, among them powerful Southern Democrats, such as Richard Russell of Georgia, who were worried about how U.S. diplomatic concern regarding Africa was giving encouragement to African-American opponents of segregation at home.

The administration had, however, committed itself by allowing Stevenson to vote for the Security Council resolution that called on Katanga to submit to UN control. Kennedy himself was partly responsible for the presence in the Congo of the Sikhs who comprised much of the UN force stationed in Elisabethville. When UN managers on the ground decided to use this force to carry out the Security Council resolution, the Kennedy administration faced a dilemma. Keeping faith with Hammarskjöld would anger European allies and Tshombe's supporters in the United States. Deserting Hammarskjöld, on the other hand, could undo all that had been accomplished in the Congo and perhaps even cripple the UN.

"RUMPUNCH," "MORTHOR," AND THE DEATH OF HAMMARSKJÖLD

The individuals who forced this dilemma on Kennedy and his aides were members of the team sent by Hammarskjöld to substitute for Dayal. While Linner had the title of officer-in-charge, the Irish writer Conor Cruise

---

63.   September 6, 1961, FRUS, 1961–1963, Vol. XX, p. 204.

O'Brien, stationed in Elisabethville, regarded himself as at least Linner's equal, and so did Mahmoud Khiary, who had the assignment of mediating between Léopoldville and Elisabethville.

On a theory that Tshombe would have to come to terms with Adoula and the central government if he could not call on his white mercenaries, the UN team mounted on August 28 a surprise operation, codenamed "Rumpunch," aimed at rounding up these mercenaries and deporting them. The operation netted only 81 men. The UN force, however, suffered not a single casualty. When O'Brien obtained from Tshombe a promise to expel the remaining mercenaries, he sent the UN troops back to their barracks.

When Tshombe reneged on his promise, O'Brien and Khiary, with authorization from Linner but probably not from Hammarskjöld, ordered a second round-up. This time they planned not only to break up Tshombe's mercenary force but to take Tshombe himself into custody along with his key ministers.

On September 13, UN forces carried out Operation "Morthor" (from an Indian term for "smash.") The mercenaries, their native troops, and anti-UN Europeans in Katanga had resolved not to be taken by surprise again. They deployed to block the UN troops. Though at a cost of fifty of their own, they killed eleven UN soldiers. This was enough to induce the UN commander to retreat empty-handed. Tshombe meanwhile slipped away to refuge at Ndola in Rhodesia.

Hammarskjöld was at the time en route to Léopoldville, hoping to foster a settlement between Adoula and Tshombe. Gizenga had finally taken up his post as deputy prime minister, and Tshombe already had delegates in Léopoldville; Hammarskjöld thus hoped to be able to complete the reconciliation of Congolese factions and announce his success before September 19, when the General Assembly was to convene.[64]

Learning to his dismay of the "Morthor" fiasco, but learning also that Tshombe had invited O'Brien to meet him at Ndola, Hammarskjöld decided to go himself, talk with Tshombe and, as he said, "end the senseless killing."[65] Hammarskjöld left Léopoldville on the afternoon of September 17, 1961, in a plane with a Swedish crew. A few hours later, the plane crashed in a night approach to Ndola airport. Hammarskjöld, along with everyone else on board, was killed. Despite many rumors of foul play, the crash appears to have been an accident, as a UN inquiry concluded, resulting from an approach "a few feet too low to clear the trees on rising

---

64. *Hammarskjöld Papers*, Vol. 5, p. 567.

65. Charles Cogan interview with, and letter from, Bengt Rösiö, who was Swedish consul in Léopoldville at the time and who met with Hammarskjöld before the latter's departure for Ndola.

ground beneath it."[66] The crash at Ndola immediately transformed Hammarskjöld into a martyr, and that fact made it still more difficult for the Kennedy administration to manage its dilemma concerning Katanga.

On September 20, three days after Hammarskjöld's death, Khiary, on behalf of the UN, signed a cease-fire with Tshombe at Ndola. It was not a settlement. Tshombe returned to Elisabethville still presiding over a quasi-sovereign state. On November 24, the Security Council passed its fifth resolution on the Congo.[67] Supported only reluctantly by the United States, because it focused only on Katanga and said nothing about other secessionist movements such as that of Gizenga, the resolution passed by a vote of 9-0 with two abstentions (Britain and France). It expanded the authority of the acting secretary general, Burmese diplomat U Thant, to use force to apprehend and deport foreign mercenaries.[68] However, the failure of Operation Morthor had shown the weakness of the UN force in Katanga, and since no member states showed eagerness to send in new troops or support elements, the situation on the ground remained, for the time being, unaltered.

TOWARD DEEPER U.S. ENGAGEMENT

In 1961, the Kennedy administration began to revise its view of the Congo. It formed an action plan that in some degree accommodated the concerns of Europeans without visibly lessening U.S. support for the UN. The key figure was George Ball, who had moved into the number-two spot under Rusk after Kennedy and Rusk had eased Bowles into a powerless ambassador-ship-at-large. Bundy teased Ball about becoming "local Commander-in-Chief of Congo Affairs." When Ball complained that the African bureau produced nothing but "a lot of mush," Bundy said, "to put it another way it is one sector of the Department which is being run by the preceding Under Secretary." Ball replied that, "the spirit [of Bowles] certainly hovered."[69]

During World War II, Ball had helped select targets for strategic bombing and had become expert at identifying choke points in Nazi Germany's supply chains. Applying this skill, Ball identified the weaknesses, both military and economic, in Tshombe's position. On the military side, Ball calculated that the balance of power between UN forces and those of Katanga would be markedly altered if the UN gained clear air superiority—not a great challenge given that Katangan air power during Operation

---

66. *Hammarskjöld Papers*, Vol. 5, p. 573.

67. Kalb, *The Congo Cables*, p. 311.

68. FRUS, 1961–1963, Vol. XX, pp. 278–279.

69. Bundy to Ball, December 17, 1961, FRUS, 1961–1963, Vol. XX, p. 324; notes on a Bundy-Ball telephone conversation, August 14, 1962, ibid., p. 551.

Morthor had consisted of a single French-built Fouga Magister jet trainer mounting two machine guns. On the economic side, Ball calculated that the best way of attacking Tshombe was to persuade the Union Minière to cut off some of his money. For this end, Ball had the advantage of generally close relations with Europeans and a personal relationship with Paul-Henri Spaak, the socialist who had become deputy prime minister and foreign minister of Belgium as a result of elections in April 1961.

Kennedy accepted Ball's analysis to the extent of authorizing more U.S. airlift for UN forces in the Congo. He preferred, however, that any combat aircraft be provided by others; therefore Ball and his allies sought to obtain fighter aircraft for the UN from Ethiopia, Sweden, and India. Even this limited show of support for the UN drew furious criticism not only from Tshombe's spokesmen in Elisabethville but from his partisans in the United States, the United Kingdom, and Belgium.

There already existed a well-publicized U.S. committee supporting the "Katangan Freedom Fighters." Conservative journals such as William Buckley's *National Review* lionized Tshombe as a resolute anti-Communist. Toward the end of 1961, conservative students at Buckley's alma mater, Yale University, announced an effort to recruit an International Brigade for Katanga. Full-page ads appeared in major U.S. newspapers with the headline, "Katanga, the Hungary of 1961." In London, Tory backbenchers forced their Prime Minister, Harold Macmillan, to withdraw an offer to provide bombs for UN aircraft.

Pro-Tshombe agitation in the United States created particular difficulty for Kennedy because he needed to get $100 million from Congress to help finance the UN effort in the Congo.[70] Kennedy put the request to Congress soon after the beginning of 1962. Hearings and deliberations in the Senate in the spring and in the House in the late summer and early fall provided innumerable opportunities for criticism of UN policy regarding Katanga. In September 1962 Kennedy would finally get the requested funds, but with strings attached. All the while, the administration would be constrained by the need not unduly to inflame the friends of Tshombe.

Luckily, during much of this period there were negotiations going on between Adoula and Tshombe, which the administration could periodically describe to the press as "promising." Gullion had brought the two men together at the heavily guarded military base at Kitona. There, in the early hours of December 21, 1961, they had inked an eight-point accord that promised reconciliation. As soon as he returned to Elisabethville, however,

---

70. Recognizing that the UN was running out of money, the United States and other governments had agreed to a $200 million bond issue for the UN. The American commitment was to put up half.

Tshombe began to insist that Katangan "authorities" could not ratify all elements of the accord. Gullion acted as intermediary to work out differences. Whenever he heard of pessimistic predictions that the accord would never work, he protested to Washington that they were the work of troublemakers.

A Special National Intelligence Estimate (SNIE) of mid-May 1962 challenged Gullion's optimism. "Negotiations between Adoula and Tshombe," it said, "are unlikely to achieve any early accommodation unless both sides are subjected to stepped up pressures and inducements by outside forces." The estimate's authors also called into question Ball's judgment that Tshombe could be brought to terms by impressing him with the potential military threat posed by the UN: "We do not believe that any attempt to subdue Katanga militarily by either UN or Congolese Army forces would be promising."[71] On June 26, 1962, the analysis in this SNIE was confirmed. Adoula and Tshombe met for a final time but were not even able to agree on a joint communiqué.

Kennedy periodically pressed his advisers for an action plan that might break the logjam. On August 3, 1962, Ball recommended a four-phase approach. In phase one, Adoula would be pressed to agree in principle to replace the *Loi Fondamentale* with a federal constitution assuring Katanga of some limited autonomy. In phase two, Tshombe would be pressed to give up his flag, share tax revenues with the central government, and agree to integrate the Katanga gendarmerie with the ANC. If Tshombe resisted, Katanga would be threatened with a variety of economic sanctions, beginning with an international boycott of Katangan copper. If this proved inadequate, phase three would see implementation of the rest of the sanctions. If Tshombe still held out, phase four would see the UN take "more stringent measures."[72]

Kennedy gave cautious and partial approval to this plan. Recognizing that the president was anxious not to be seen as leading an effort sure to be resented by Tshombe, Ball and Stevenson persuaded U Thant to let this four-phase approach be labeled "the U Thant Plan," and representatives of the secretary general led in laying it out before both Adoula and Tshombe.[73]

Kennedy said candidly to Stevenson, "At least George Ball's becoming more active in this Congo thing now. I don't think it's been handled particularly well, even though it's very complicated."[74] Talking late in August

---

71. May 16, 1962, FRUS, 1961–1963, Vol. XX, pp. 450–451.

72. FRUS, 1961–1963, Vol. XX, pp. 527–532.

73. FRUS, 1961–1963, Vol. XX, pp. 549, 554–557.

74. Taped conversation, August 21, 1961, in Philip D. Zelikow, Ernest R. May, and Timothy Naftali, eds., *The Presidential Recordings: John F. Kennedy, The Great Crises*, 3 vols.

with Rusk, Ball, Williams, and Bundy, Kennedy described his sense of the administration's predicament: "we don't want to have the U.N. lose face. We don't want to lose face. We don't want to have a situation where everything goes flat and Tshombe really thinks we're a bag of wind. So…we're going to have to keep these negotiations going." He complained, however, that "until we get this bond thing by, there's not much we can do."[75]

Judgments within the administration as to whether anything could come of negotiations varied widely. Confidence in Adoula had dwindled. He had gained strength against Gizenga, but this was largely because of Gizenga's own bad management and bad luck. After a mutiny among Gizenga's troops, General Lundula had abandoned him and returned to Léopoldville to serve under his former deputy, Mobutu. Accusing Gizenga of having fomented a civil war, Adoula obtained approval of parliament for arresting and imprisoning him. But Adoula also worried Washington by seeming to flirt with the Soviets. Americans in Léopoldville speculated that Adoula might turn against the UN and the United States if he feared he might be unseated by Lumumbists in the parliament. Some of Gullion's reports raised questions about Adoula's emotional stability. For example, he cabled on one occasion that a brief vacation seemed to have given Adoula a "somewhat better grip on himself."[76]

Regarding Tshombe, U.S. officials held widely different opinions. Gullion, who felt he had been deceived in the Kitona negotiations, took the view that Tshombe was never to be trusted and that the only solution for Katanga was for the UN to crush him and his gendarmerie. Ambassador-at-Large W. Averell Harriman, in whose judgment Kennedy had considerable confidence, viewed Tshombe quite differently. Harriman had met Tshombe before Congolese independence and had favorable memories of him. To Kennedy, Harriman praised Tshombe as an anti-Communist and "a very determined young man."[77] When Tshombe made a brief visit to Switzerland in early November 1962, Harriman flew over for a quiet private talk. Afterward, Harriman reported that he had found Tshombe accommodating and that, as a result of the talk, Tshombe had "gained confidence in [the] good will of our approach."[78]

(New York: W.W. Norton, 2001), Vol. I, pp. 564–565 (hereafter: *Presidential Recordings: Kennedy*).

75. Taped conversation, August 29, 1962, Presidential Recordings: Kennedy, Vol. I, pp. 647–650.

76. May 5, 1962, FRUS, 1961–1963, Vol. XX, p. 441.

77. Taped conversation, August 8, 1961, *Presidential Recordings: Kennedy*, Vol. I, pp. 284–285.

78. Harriman cable, November 5, 1961, FRUS, 1961–1963, Vol. XX, p. 264.

In between Gullion on one hand and Harriman on the other was McGhee, whom Kennedy had commissioned in late September to visit both Léopoldville and Elisabethville. Talking at length with both Adoula and Tshombe, McGhee was impressed by the constraints under which each man labored. According to McGhee, Adoula himself spoke of the Congolese parliament as "incredibly corrupt" and worried lest "all sorts of disparate elements...combine against him."[79] As for Tshombe, McGhee cabled: "His position in Katanga is to considerable extent result of his skill as a consummate politician in promising all things to all people. Almost any decision he takes in fulfillment of plan runs counter to strong forces on whom he must rely." These forces included Europeans resident in Katanga who were "interested only in making a killing while they can"; Katangans who had discovered a nationalism of their own; and a young Katangan elite whom Tshombe had put in power. A "close balancing of the rights and wrongs as between Tshombe and Adoula," McGhee concluded, "is as impossible as it is perhaps irrelevant." The United States had decided it wanted a united Congo. Therefore it had to give both Adoula and Tshombe incentives to come to terms.[80]

A MUCH COLDER COLD WAR

During the summer and autumn of 1962, the Congo was only one focus of Kennedy's attention. At home he was campaigning hard in hope that the November elections would preserve or possibly even enlarge the narrow Democratic majorities in the House and Senate. Abroad, he had to prepare for confrontations with Khrushchev. One was already in progress: ignoring an earlier promise to maintain a tacit ban on tests of new nuclear weapons, Khrushchev in late August had not only commenced a series of tests but had talked openly of trying thermonuclear blasts of unprecedented scale, perhaps equivalent to a hundred million tons of TNT. Meanwhile, through various channels, Khrushchev told Kennedy that he would bide his time until the U.S. elections were over but that, in November, he would demand a change in the status of West Berlin. When Kennedy met with the Earl of Home, the British foreign secretary, at the end of September, he complained that "the Congo is diverting Western energies and weakening [the] solidarity of the West at a time of increasing bloc pressures."[81]

79. McGhee cable from Léopoldville, October 4, 1962, FRUS, 1961–1963, Vol. XX, pp. 600–603.

80. McGhee cable from Elisabethville, October 8, 1962, FRUS, 1961–1963, Vol. XX, pp. 617–619; McGhee to Kennedy, October 22, 1962, ibid., pp. 635–638.

81. September 29, 1962, FRUS, 1961–1963, Vol. XX, p. 595.

On October 14, 1962, Bundy brought to the president's bedroom in the White House U-2 photographs that showed the Soviets urgently and secretly installing nuclear-armed missiles in Cuba. For the next thirteen days Kennedy and his top advisers, including Stevenson, were almost totally engaged in the duel of wills with the Soviet Union that ended finally with Khrushchev agreeing to withdraw the missiles and, as events soon showed, abandoning his dangerous campaign to take over West Berlin.

Although Kennedy and his aides were conscious of having won the test of wills, they hardly emerged free from concern. In the first place, it would be weeks before they would know for sure that the Soviets were keeping their end of the bargain. In the second place, they were dealing with another huge crisis that had erupted just in the middle of the crisis over missiles in Cuba. On October 20, thirty thousand Chinese Communist troops invaded India at two widely separated points along the Chinese-Indian border. Nehru compromised his nonaligned status by appealing to the United States for military supplies and other aid, which Kennedy promptly supplied. This war in South Asia would rage until late November when, with equal suddenness, the Chinese Communist dictator, Mao Zedong, announced a cease-fire.

Get Out or Get In Deeper

In these circumstances, Kennedy had little appetite for becoming more deeply engaged in the Congo. On October 31, he met with McGhee, Williams, Cleveland, and some others and said flatly that, in view of world conditions, "there could not be any consideration at this time of military action in the Congo on the part of the United Nations forces."[82] During the missile crisis, Bundy had transferred the handling of most other matters to his deputy, former Harvard economics professor Carl Kaysen. On November 1, Kaysen wrote Rusk that Kennedy thought "we are near or at a decisive point in the Congo situation." The president's view, said Kaysen, was that, unless Adoula and Tshombe came to terms soon, "our further interference and support seems useless." Hence, the president wanted Rusk and others to develop "alternative courses of action, including, if necessary, paths of withdrawal from the Congo."[83]

By the end of November 1962, there was an increasing sense in Washington that time was running out in the Congo. Adoula was reported to be under more and more pressure to turn to the Soviets or to supposed

---

82. October 31, 1962, FRUS, 1961–1963, Vol. XX, pp. 641–643.
83. Kaysen to Rusk, November 1, 1962, FRUS, 1961–1963, Vol. XX, pp. 646–647.

Soviet surrogates such as the United Arab Republic. Although McGhee and Spaak had made some headway with the management of Union Minière, inducing them to shift some tax payments to the government in Léopoldville, Tshombe seemed obdurate. He spoke darkly of destroying Katanga's resources before turning them over to his enemies—leaving the province "scorched earth."[84] Meanwhile, U Thant warned that, even with the new bond issue, the UN would soon be out of money. The Indian troops would be on their way home, and he could foresee having to report to the Security Council that the Congo operation was a failure. In that case, as Stevenson described his views, the "UN would probably have no recourse but to withdraw from Congo and leave solution to Africans, with U.S. and Sovs each backing its own horse."[85]

It was clear to everyone around Kennedy that he was not going to temporize much longer. Kaysen and Ralph Dungan, an all-purpose White Houses aide, favored a decision to leave the Congolese to themselves. They—and Ball—thought that this was also Kennedy's inclination. Before making his choice, however, Kennedy listened to some comparatively new voices. Spaak visited him and made clear how much of his own political capital had been committed to the effort to bring Tshombe and Adoula together. Chester Bowles also came to the White House, having just returned from a swing through West Africa. Bowles emphasized to Kennedy how many new problems were likely to come crowding in on the United States if failure in the Congo were to cost the UN its capacity to act as peacemaker.[86]

Ball also brought the State Department's intelligence analysts to speak to Kennedy. The department had a small Bureau of Intelligence and Research (INR) headed by Roger Hilsman, a Columbia University political scientist who had run guerrilla operations in Burma during World War II. Ball asked Hilsman to take a new, hard look at Congo policy. While a career intelligence officer might have been reluctant to respond with more than an assessment of relevant facts and suppositions, Hilsman relished involvement in the debate about what to do. Working day and night, Hilsman and his chief Africa specialist, Robert C. Good, came up with a recommendation that the United States threaten military action of its own if Tshombe refused to knuckle under to the UN. The

---

84. Cable from Elisabethville, November 30, 1962, FRUS, 1961–1963, Vol. XX, pp. 704–705.

85. Stevenson telegram, November 26, 1962, FRUS, 1961–1963, Vol. XX, p. 685.

86. Spaak meeting with the president, November 27, 1962, FRUS, 1961–1963, Vol. XX, pp. 686–690; Bowles to Kennedy, December 12, 1962, in Chester Bowles, *Promises to Keep: My Years in Public Life*, 1941–1969 (New York: Harper and Row, 1971), pp. 425–427.

alternative, they said, was to surrender Africa to the Soviets and at the same time to cripple the UN.[87]

On December 14, Kennedy had a long meeting with Ball, McGhee, Bowles, and a number of others, including Admiral George W. Anderson, the chief of naval operations, and Bronson Tweedy, the head of the Africa division in CIA's operational arm. The whole focus of the meeting was on how to strengthen UN forces so that they would impress both Adoula and Tshombe. Admiral Anderson said that the military forces themselves could come from almost any nation: "It was the political part that required U.S. force." Kennedy agreed, but noted that this course of action involved political difficulty for him at home. The minutes record his saying, "The sense that the alternatives to Tshombe and Adoula were sufficiently adverse to U.S. interests to justify American military intervention did not exist," and then asking, "What could we do to create it?" At another point, Kennedy is recorded as raising "the question of how we make it into an anti-Communist effort since this was the only way we could justify these movements publicly in the U.S."[88]

On the following day, Kennedy ordered that a U.S. military mission go to the Congo to assess the needs both of the UN force and of the ANC. The previous such mission in July 1962 had been headed by a colonel. This one was to be headed by a three-star general, Lewis W. Truman. Moreover, Kennedy himself arranged for reporters to receive a background briefing in Bermuda, where he had gone to confer with British Prime Minister Harold Macmillan; the briefing stressed the importance of this mission and the extent to which it indicated willingness of the United States to commit its own forces. The reporters were given encouragement to say that the mission would "also seek to assess ability of Congo to resist any Soviet attempt to take advantage of growing tension in Congo."[89]

To Macmillan, who had often expressed doubts about the wisdom of supporting the UN against Tshombe, Kennedy said that he feared the Adoula government would collapse. In that event, "chaos would ensue, thus providing an opportunity for the Soviets." Kennedy said that he intended to back the UN to the hilt even though he realized that "it may bring on a military clash." Ball, who was also present, explained that, "in order to exert any effective pressure on Tshombe and Adoula we must

---

87. Kaysen to Kennedy, December 13, 1962, FRUS, 1961–1963, Vol. XX, pp. 727–728, summarizes Hilsman's memorandum. Roger Hilsman, *To Move a Nation: The Politics of Foreign Policy in the Administration of John F. Kennedy* (Garden City, N.Y.: Doubleday, 1967), pp. 263–266, describes its composition.

88. Meeting, December 14, 1962, FRUS, 1961–1963, Vol. XX, pp. 734–737.

89. December 18, 1962, FRUS, 1961–1963, Vol. XX, p. 755.

make it clear to Tshombe that he is dealing with the United States as well as with the UN."[90]

As initial proposals began to filter in from General Truman, some of Kennedy's advisers thought that he might—or should—have second thoughts. Bundy and Kaysen understood the president to believe that he had committed himself to having the U.S. air force provide transport and, if necessary, a fighter squadron. Minutes of a White House staff meeting shortly after Christmas describe the two of them as saying that "the reinforcing operation as conceived by the UN and General Truman is so enormously complex as to approach the adjective Bundy used: 'feckless'."[91]

THE END OF KATANGA'S SECESSION

In fact, there proved to be no need for the president to revisit his decision. The announcement of the military mission; dispatch to the Congo of some U.S. trucks, armored personnel carriers, and transport aircraft; and evident preparations for bringing in U.S. fighter planes and helicopters proved enough to melt what remained of Tshombe's resolve. A skirmish in Elisabethville provoked by the Katangan gendarmerie ended with the UN's Sikh troops marching into the streets and the gendarmerie retreating pell-mell. The UN troops cautiously fanned out toward the military bases at Kamina, Jadotville, and Kolwezi. They met no resistance. UN forces then began to move freely throughout the province. On January 17, 1963, Assistant Secretary Cleveland declared that, "The Congo is about to be free and whole again. It is moving toward law and order."[92]

For some time, Kennedy and his advisers had been looking hopefully toward a day when both the UN and the United States could disengage from the Congo. All along, they had seen a stronger ANC as the key. Cleveland and Williams were convinced of this, as were Ball and McGhee. From the spring of 1963 onward, U.S. thinking about the Congo almost exclusively concerned arrangements for helping the ANC to obtain equipment and training.

In May 1963 Mobutu, the commander of the ANC, visited Washington and met with Kennedy at the White House. He presented a three-year plan for U.S. military aid. Kennedy agreed in principle, saying to Mobutu at one point: "General, if it hadn't been for you, the whole thing would have collapsed and the Communists would have taken over." Mobutu replied modestly, "I do what I am able to do."[93]

---

90. Meeting, December 19, 1962, FRUS, 1961–1963, Vol. XX, pp. 760–764.

91. December 28, 1962, FRUS, 1961–1963, Vol. XX, pp. 787–788.

92. Weissman, *American Foreign Policy in the Congo, 1960–1964* (Ithaca, N.Y.: Cornell University Press, 1974), p. 191.

93. Memorandum of conversation, Kennedy and Mobutu, May 31, 1963, FRUS, 1961–1963, Vol. XX, pp. 858–862.

The Congo did not cease to be a crisis zone. During Johnson's presidency, civil war erupted in several provinces. The ANC fought against guerrillas who thought that a mysterious force protected them from enemy bullets. Mobutu went in person to the front, denounced his troops for firing from too great a distance, and demonstrated to the guerrillas that ANC fire from a shorter range was indeed lethal to them. In another incident, a group of guerrillas who professed admiration of Lumumba seized control of a large part of the country. They killed a number of Europeans and took others hostage, including an American consul and some of his staff. But a Belgian-led force, with U.S. air support, managed to rescue most of the hostages and, in the process, to demolish the guerrillas. Mobutu continued to build up the ANC. In November 1965, after giving brief advance notice to Washington, Mobutu removed Kasavubu and made himself head of state and head of government. Spaak commented at the time that Mobutu's coup was "the best thing that could possibly have happened; it remains to be seen whether it is also a good thing."[94]

---

94.   Cable from Léopoldville, November 25, 1965, Lyndon Baines Johnson Library, National Security File, Congo, Box 82. *Office of Current Intelligence (OCI) Weekly Report,* "The Situation in the Congo," February 24, 1966, p. 1.

Chapter 3

Nicaragua, 1977–1979:
Losing *"Our* Son-of-a-Bitch"

Robert D. Johnson, with assistance from
Kirsten Lundberg

Franklin Roosevelt is often quoted as saying of a Caribbean dictator, "He's a son-of-a-bitch, but he's *our* son-of-a-bitch." The particular dictator is sometimes said to have been Anastasio (Tacho) Somoza Garcia of Nicaragua.

On July 17, 1979, Tacho's son, Nicaraguan President Anastasio (Tachito) Somoza Debayle, flew to exile in Miami, ending a dozen years as a successor "son-of-a-bitch." Two days later, the leftist Sandinista National Liberation Front (FSLN, its acronym in Spanish) entered Managua and assumed power. The United States had spent the better part of the previous year trying to prevent this outcome. But a combination of bureaucratic divisions at home, faulty intelligence abroad, and the unintended effects of President Jimmy Carter's human rights rhetoric handicapped U.S. efforts to prevent the Sandinistas from sweeping to power.

Background

Somoza's overthrow ended one of the longest-running family dynasties in Latin American history. Tacho had first come to prominence during the 1920s, when he assisted U.S. forces then occupying the country. At American urging, he was named head of the nominally nonpartisan National Guard. However, Somoza had little intention of staying out of politics. After ordering the assassination of his key rival, Augusto Sandino, he took over the nation's presidency in 1937 and ruled until his own assassination in 1956 by a young poet and printer from the minuscule anti-Somoza underground. Tacho was succeeded by his eldest son, Luis Somoza Debayle; Luis's younger brother, Tachito, assumed the office in 1967 after Luis died of a heart attack.[1]

---

1. Knut Walter, *The Regime of Anastasio Somoza, 1936–1956* (Chapel Hill: University of North Carolina Press, 1993).

Like his predecessors, Tachito Somoza relied on four pillars to support his regime: the National Guard, the Liberal Party, the family's widespread economic interests, and a close relationship with the United States. He retained the loyalty of the officer corps with generous budgets, opportunities for enrichment, and tight control over the command structure. His Liberal Party, which routinely won rigged elections, provided sinecures for allies. The family's varied businesses—manufacturing concerns, commercial farms, a shipping company, and the national airline—generated revenues and jobs for family loyalists. He had attended LaSalle Military Academy in New York and gone from there to West Point, where he graduated in 1946. It was said that he was "the only West Pointer to have received an army as a graduation present."[2] Continued cordial relations with the United States helped give legitimacy to his regime.

Despite the assassination of Tacho, domestic challenges to the Somozas were rare. In the 1960s, however, a modest opposition began to materialize. In July 1961, at a meeting in Honduras, three Nicaraguan student activists founded the Sandinista National Liberation Front (FSLN), which was named after the assassinated Sandino, and whose members would therefore become known as Sandinistas. Energized by the Cuban revolution, the FSLN embraced a strategy of armed struggle as the most appropriate path for overthrowing the Somoza regime. One of the group's founders, Carlos Fonseca, had already participated in an unsuccessful Cuban-backed revolt in northwestern Nicaragua in 1959. In Sandino, the FSLN had a martyr of impeccable nationalist credentials, although his ideology had been an eclectic blend of nationalism and socialism rather than the more doctrinaire Marxism-Leninism the Sandinistas would embrace.[3]

Differences over strategy soon divided the FSLN and, over time, the movement split into three groups. By 1977, however, the moderate Terceristas emerged predominant. Led by brothers Humberto and Daniel Ortega, the Terceristas favored a combined urban-rural insurrection in cooperation with middle-class anti-Somoza groups. They advocated immediate action to create a revolutionary climate, rather than wasting time in long-range organizing efforts. The Terceristas' beliefs were reflected in the FSLN's "General Political-Military Platform" of May 1977. This outlined a strategy for seizing power via a broad front of all anti-regime groups, including the "opposition bourgeoisie," without compromising

---

2. Lawrence Pezzullo and Ralph Pezzullo, *At the Fall of Somoza* (Pittsburgh: University of Pittsburgh Press, 1993), p. 17.

3. David Nolan, *The Ideology of the Sandinistas and the Nicaraguan Revolution* (Miami: University of Miami Press, 1984), pp. 12–24; Donald Hodges, *Intellectual Foundations of the Nicaraguan Revolution* (Austin: University of Texas Press, 1986), pp. 161–196.

the hegemony of the "Marxist-Leninist vanguard organization," the FSLN. Utilizing this blueprint, the Sandinistas hoped to ignite a national insurrection that would topple the Somoza dynasty.[4]

The FSLN's growth coincided with broader developments that undermined Somoza's long-term stability. In December 1972, a series of earthquakes devastated Managua. While thousands of Nicaraguans went hungry and homeless, the National Guard pilfered international relief supplies. Instead of rebuilding downtown Managua, Somoza arranged the construction of new shopping areas along a peripheral highway through lands owned by himself and his associates. Moreover, the Somoza circle began to move into new areas of the economy formerly dominated by the country's upper and middle classes. The regime's growing rapacity, combined with Somoza's decision to stand for reelection in 1974 to a seven-year term, alienated wide sectors of Nicaraguan society. The shift included groups that had previously cooperated with the regime, such as businessmen, the hierarchy of the Catholic Church (headed by Archbishop Mauricio Obando y Bravo), and the Conservative Party, Somoza's token opposition for the previous four decades.[5]

In March 1974, in the first public break between Somoza and private business, an umbrella organization of entrepreneurs accused the regime of misusing relief funds. Many children of the elite, radicalized by student activism and the powerful new doctrines of liberation theology, began to join the Sandinistas. The guerrillas' prestige rose after a band of FSLN members captured and held hostage the celebrants at a wealthy businessman's 1974 Christmas party. They forced Somoza to free fourteen imprisoned Sandinistas, pay $1 million in ransom, publish an FSLN communiqué, and grant the kidnappers safe passage to Cuba. In mid-1977, the FSLN leadership persuaded a group of upper- and middle-class Nicaraguans to form the "Group of 12," the first time the Sandinistas were able to make common cause with more moderate anti-Somoza elements.

Then an assassination united Somoza's opposition. On January 10, 1978, several gunmen shot Pedro Joaquín Chamorro, head of the Conservative Party and editor of the country's major newspaper, *La Prensa*. After years of support for the Somoza government, for which the party was rewarded with patronage posts, Chamorro's Conservatives had begun in the mid-1970s to criticize the dictator openly and, in Chamorro's newspaper, to expose the regime's corruption and human rights abuses. Although Somoza claimed that Cuban agents had killed the editor, Nicaraguans almost universally blamed Somoza. This incident sparked

---

4. Hodges, *Intellectual Foundations*, pp. 218–244.

5. Walter, *Regime of Anastasio Somoza*, pp. 236–249.

street riots, a national strike organized by employers with the support of some labor organizations, and uprisings in several communities.[6]

For five decades, the Somozas had counted on support from the United States to sustain the dynasty. More than perhaps any other foreign government, the Somoza regime understood how to exert influence in the U.S. political system. Each Somoza in power positioned his nation as an unswerving supporter of the United States in the international arena. During World War II, Tacho had lined up Nicaragua unequivocally with the Allies; Nicaragua actually declared war against Japan before the U.S. Congress did. After the war, Nicaragua became a reliable U.S. ally in the Cold War, and provided key assistance in the CIA's 1954 overthrow of Jacobo Arbenz's left-leaning Guatemalan regime. Nicaragua almost never failed to vote with the United States in international organizations such as the United Nations and the Organization of American States.[7]

But the Somozas did more than support U.S. foreign policy: they actively cultivated the U.S. military. Luis as well as Tachito had attended West Point, and members of the National Guard regularly went to the United States for training. In addition, the Somozas courted members of Congress, building up a network of allies, notably Republican Charles Wilson, a Texan known for his hard-line Cold War views; John Murphy, a Staten Island Democrat who chaired the House Merchant Marine Committee; and other Republicans and Democrats who sometimes called themselves "the dirty thirty."[8]

By the mid-1970s, however, conditions in the United States had begun to change in ways ominous for Somoza's hope of a continued comfortable relationship. The domestic and international effects of the conflict in Vietnam, together with the Sino-Soviet split, undermined presumptions commonly held earlier in the Cold War. The Watergate crisis meanwhile weakened the executive branch and opened the way for independent-minded liberals in the Senate, often using foreign aid riders, to begin advancing an alternative ideology. They charged that policymakers in the executive branch had subordinated traditional American ideals, such as support for democracy, human rights, and self-determination, to the anti-Communism of the Cold War. They argued secondly that the Cold War had given the military an excessive voice in foreign policy.

6. Shirley Christian, *Nicaragua: Revolution in the Family* (New York: Random House, 1985), pp. 30–33, 36–43, 46–49.

7. Piero Gleijeses, *Shattered Hope: The Guatemalan Revolution and the United States, 1944–1954* (Princeton: Princeton University Press, 1991), pp. 203–208; Charles Ameringer, *The Democratic Left in Exile: The Antidictatorial Left in the Caribbean, 1945–1949* (Coral Gables: University of Miami Press, 1974), pp. 83–96.

8. Pezzullo and Pezzullo, *At the Fall of Somoza*, p. 175.

Third, they contended that democracy required openness and, as a corollary, a larger role for Congress in policymaking.

Each tenet in this alternative ideology implied a decrease in U.S. friendliness toward right-wing regimes, whether in Latin America or elsewhere. After Augusto Pinochet's military government assumed power in Chile in 1973, Representative Donald Fraser (D-Minn.) and Senator Edward Kennedy (D-Mass.) opened hearings on Pinochet's human rights abuses. Congress then enacted a series of measures to wind down U.S. assistance to the regime. When Turkey invaded Cyprus in 1974, Thomas Eagleton (D-Mo.) pushed through the Senate an amendment cutting off foreign aid to the Ankara government. In 1976, Congress passed an amendment sponsored by Representative Ed Koch (D-N.Y.) to terminate assistance to the military government in Uruguay.[9]

Following these successes, several liberals in the House of Representatives turned their attention to Nicaragua. Koch proposed an amendment to suspend military credits to Nicaragua, while Fraser convened hearings on Nicaraguan human rights abuses. Although the Ford administration attempted to protect Somoza, the national news media gave considerable play to the liberals' allegations of human rights abuses in Nicaragua.

The Carter Era and Human Rights

With the election of Jimmy Carter in 1976, elements of the human rights agenda were adopted by the executive branch. Carter had featured human rights diplomacy prominently in his campaign for the presidency. In March 1976, he told the Chicago Council on Foreign Relations that U.S. foreign policy needed to reflect the principles outlined in the Helsinki Accords, as well as the basic idealism inherent in the nation's founding documents. By the fall, the Democratic nominee was promising that his administration would make the United States "a beacon light for human rights throughout the world." In his inaugural address, the new president declared: "Our moral sense dictates a clear preference for those societies which share with us an abiding respect for individual human rights." After his inauguration, Carter appointed Patricia Derian the first assistant secretary of state for human rights.[10]

9. Lars Schoultz, *Human Rights and United States Foreign Policy toward Latin America* (Princeton: Princeton University Press, 1981), pp. 63–91.

10. Burton Kaufman, *The Presidency of James Earl Carter, Jr.* (Lawrence: University of Kansas Press, 1993), pp. 37–39.

Nicaragua received scant attention from Carter during his first year in office. Without direct White House involvement, U.S. policy toward Nicaragua devolved into a battle between the State Department's Bureau of Inter-American Affairs (ARA) and State's newly created Bureau of Human Rights and Humanitarian Affairs (HA). The two bureaus had radically different visions of the proper U.S. role in Central America. Carter's first head of ARA, Terence Todman, believed that the United States needed to concentrate on strategic and economic concerns and avoid alienating potential allies in Central America. Derian and the Bureau of Human Rights, on the other hand, thought human rights considerations should dominate any decision on whether a foreign government would receive U.S. assistance. Derian accused ARA of "overstating the extent of U.S. interests at stake in particular cases, and the damage that could possibly result from failure to approve proposed security assistance." Disputes between the two bureaus generally were referred to a committee chaired by Undersecretary of State Warren Christopher, who often sided with Derian and HA.[11]

From Christopher's decisions, Somoza was quick to pick up signals that the bases of U.S. decisions were changing. Accordingly, throughout 1977, he made cosmetic changes designed to respond to Carter's pressure. He ordered the National Guard to curb its brutality; he broadened his cabinet, ended censorship, and lifted the state of emergency that had been in place since December 1974. But he also sought to influence the emerging U.S. debate over human rights policies. After some rather mild criticism from Washington on the issue, Somoza "pointedly" advised U.S. ambassador Mauricio Solaun that the Carter administration should show more "political sophistication" in which regimes it targeted for human rights critiques. If the United States did not stop "picking" on him, he would appeal to his "influential 'friends' in Congress who would embarrass the Administration."[12]

The United States was not the only country applying pressure on Somoza's government. Frosty relations between the Somoza regime and several nations in the region long predated the 1970s. In the 1920s, Mexico had been the foremost international supporter of Augusto Sandino, and the

---

11. Schoultz, *Human Rights and United States Foreign Policy toward Latin America*, p. 118; Morris Morley, *Washington, Somoza, and the Sandinistas: State and Regime in U.S. Policy toward Nicaragua, 1969–1981* (New York: Cambridge University Press, 1994), pp. 93–97; Stephen Cohen, "Conditioning U.S. Security Assistance on Human Rights Practices," *American Journal of International Law*, Vol. 76 (April 1982), p. 260.

12. American Embassy Managua to Secretary of State, May 22, 1978, Digital National Security Archive, "Nicaragua, the Making of U.S. Policy, 1978–1990" (hereafter DNSA "Nicaragua"), document no. 112.

Mexican government never reconciled itself to normal relations with the government that had murdered him. In the 1940s, Nicaragua had earned the enmity of Costa Rica and Venezuela when it supported dictatorial forces against democratic uprisings. At the outset of the FSLN revolt, two Latin American nations led in lending it support. One, not surprisingly, was Fidel Castro's Cuba. The other was Panama, where President Omar Torrijos, though himself a dictator, was also an opponent of U.S. hegemony.

By early 1978, Secretary of State Cyrus Vance acknowledged that "Nicaragua may well present a crucial test for our Latin American policy, affecting not only Nicaragua but our interest in the promotion of human rights and political independence as well as the avoidance of instability in the Central American nation." But, as Vance conceded, balancing these goals was not easy. On the one hand, there were arguments for "strict neutrality" between Somoza and his opponents—a position that Vance himself preferred. On the other hand, both the HA in Washington and opponents of Somoza forces in Nicaragua argued that human rights principles required the United States openly to distance itself from the Somoza regime. From Managua, Ambassador Solaun described the "blandness" in U.S. policy as playing to Somoza's advantage.

In the end, it was not Somoza's human rights abuses but the growing strength of the Sandinista insurgency and the resulting possibility of a Marxist regime in Central America that focused policymakers' attention on Nicaragua. A sudden surge of Sandinista attacks produced a remarkably widespread consensus—in a Washington skittish after Vietnam but struggling to cope with mounting evidence that popular protest might topple the Shah of Iran—that Somoza had little chance of retaining power in the long term. Though President Carter's national security advisor, Zbigniew Brzezinski, was often at odds with Vance, they and their top subordinates agreed that the United States should not promote a "premature" regime change, for the result "could be worse than what we have now." Though terming Somoza's defeat all but certain, Frank Church (D-Idaho), the ranking Democrat on the Senate Foreign Relations Committee, also agreed. Church urged Carter to do everything possible to block the "extremists" who could produce "another Castro-type government." Framers of U.S. policy at both ends of Pennsylvania Avenue saw a need to try to find in the complex maze of Nicaraguan politics an alternative to Somoza other than the radical Sandinistas.[13]

What emerged was a carrot-and-stick approach by which the United States sought to distance itself from Somoza without condemning his

---

13. Administration policymakers quoted in *U.S. News and World Report*, September 11, 1978; 124 *Congressional Record*, 95th Cong., 2nd sess., p. S15379 (September 22, 1978).

regime outright. It was a policy of "Somocismo sin Somoza": retaining the vestiges of the Somocista state, especially the National Guard, while pressuring Somoza himself to resign. This approach, it was hoped, would encourage the creation of a power base other than the FSLN in post-Somoza Nicaragua.

Despite this shift, enforcing human rights remained key to U.S. Central American policy. In July 1978, for example, Carter sent Somoza a letter congratulating him on taking measures to improve his regime's human rights practices. Carter hoped that the missive, sent at the urging of NSC staff and over fierce objections from most of the State Department, would offer a public reminder of the importance the United States attached to human rights issues without alienating the Nicaraguan dictator. Instead, virtually all sides attacked Carter's move as evidence of administration confusion. Somoza publicly equated the letter with U.S. intervention in internal Nicaraguan affairs. The Nicaraguan opposition attacked the president for having said anything positive about Somoza's conduct. In the United States, there was a similar split between liberals and conservatives. Historian William LeoGrande terms the letter "arguably the worst policy error made by the United States in the Nicaraguan crisis."[14]

In September, the administration again struggled to split the difference between its stated commitment to human rights and its increasing fear that breaking with Somoza would create a vacuum for the Sandinistas to fill. The administration announced that it would delay further military assistance to Nicaragua, but at the same time, the United States signed the annual military assistance agreement, so as to maintain the option of restoring aid quickly in the future.[15]

Conditions in Nicaragua, meanwhile, continued to deteriorate. On August 23, 1978, the Sandinistas staged their most spectacular operation to date, when a group of guerrillas commanded by Edén Pastora seized the National Palace in Managua. The rebels took more than 1,500 hostages, including dozens of members of the Chamber of Deputies. Two days later the guerrillas, having negotiated concessions similar to those obtained in 1974, departed the country with fifty-nine released prisoners under Somoza's guarantee of safe conduct. The cheering crowds that lined their

14. William LeoGrande, *Our Own Backyard: The United States and Central America, 1977–1992* (Chapel Hill: University of North Carolina Press, 1997), p. 20. See also Robert Pastor, *Condemned to Repetition: The United States and Nicaragua* (Princeton: Princeton University Press, 1987), pp. 50–71. Pastor, a political scientist specializing on Latin America, served on the NSC staff at this time.

15. Anthony Lake, *Somoza Falling* (Boston: Houghton Mifflin, 1989), pp. 69–90.

departure route to the airport demonstrated the extent to which the regime had alienated the populace.

The rebel success gave courage to a newly formed coalition known as the Broad Opposition Front (Frente Amplio de Oposición, or FAO), which united independent political parties, labor confederations, and the "Group of 12" (including the FSLN). Within days of the National Palace seizure, the FAO called for a national strike. On September 9, the FSLN launched a major offensive, attacking National Guard units in six major cities.[16]

Somoza chose to blame the United States for the instability. The United States had "made its point" on human rights, said Somoza, and now it was time to "mend its fences." The first step would be a public statement of support for his government. Otherwise, Carter's "excessive idealism" could have the "distasteful" effect of intensifying regional instability.[17]

In Washington, Assistant Secretary of State for Latin American Affairs Todman had essentially shared Somoza's view, which was one reason why Vance decided to replace him. His successor, Viron Peter Vaky, formerly U.S. ambassador to Venezuela, had followed Nicaraguan developments closely, prompted by Venezuelan President Carlos Andres Perez's outspoken opposition to Somoza. Vaky returned to Washington believing that only the immediate ouster of Somoza would prevent hard-line forces from coming to power in Nicaragua. Convinced that the human rights question had "faded out of the picture," the new assistant secretary considered the issue "a question of political succession with geostrategic dimensions and ramifications." Within the administration, however, Vaky was in the minority. On one side, officials at HA still opposed any policy that compromised human rights principles. The NSC staff, while agreeing with Vaky that the United States needed to "prevent the Sandinistas from winning a military victory, without defending Somoza," worried that the State Department's approach was overly interventionist and could backfire.[18]

The U.S. intelligence community was ill prepared for a crisis in Central America. For military officers, as for foreign service officers, a tour in a Central American country seldom seemed career-enhancing; the post of defense attaché in Managua did not therefore attract high-fliers. In any case, Somoza's tight control over the officer corps constrained the ability of

---

16. John Booth, *The End and the Beginning: The Nicaraguan Revolution* (Boulder, Colo.: Westview Press, 1982), pp. 161–164. The FAO had formed after Carter's July letter to Somoza, when the moderate opposition concluded that relying on the United States to help remove Somoza had little prospect of long-term success.

17. Solaun to Secretary of State, September 6, 1978, DNSA "Nicaragua," document no. 205.

18. James Worthen interview with Viron Peter Vaky. All further quotations from Vaky, unless otherwise attributed, are from this interview.

U.S. defense attachés to develop independent contacts within Nicaragua's National Guard. One defense attaché was warned that, if he talked to a Guardia officer without Somoza's advance approval, the officer might meet with "an accident." As for seeking contacts among the opposition, defense attachés had to bear in mind prevailing Pentagon doubts whether, anywhere in the world, "we should be speaking to our enemies."[19] As for the CIA, government-wide cost-cutting efforts in the mid-1970s had resulted in its sharply scaling back staff in Central America. For most of the decade prior to 1979, the CIA station in Managua was staffed by a single officer. Senior figures from the State Department and the NSC staff who have written memoir-histories assert that, regarding the Somoza regime, human intelligence was sparse and, regarding the opposition, it was almost non-existent. Although the National Security Agency (NSA) vacuumed up communications in all parts of the globe, its standard procedures called for disseminating intercepts only on priority subjects. Neither the lone Nicaragua analyst in CIA's Directorate of Intelligence nor James Buchanan, the general purpose Latin Americanist in State's Bureau of Intelligence and Research, stood high in the chain of NSA's customers. Though the writers of these memoir-histories commend these analysts as individuals, they rate their performance in this case as "failure."[20]

Even had there been more ambitious collection and analysis of intelligence, it is doubtful that the results would have reached top decision-makers. In the second half of 1978, the Carter administration had other urgent matters to address: the search for peace in the Middle East in the Camp David process; multiple issues involving the Soviet Union, including negotiations for the SALT II Treaty, Soviet meddling in Afghanistan, and Cuban military intervention in Africa; normalization of diplomatic relations with Communist China, which included revising all U.S. treaties with Taiwan; an interagency review of policy toward Mexico preparatory to a presidential visit to Mexico City in early 1979; the possible disintegration of the shah's rule in Iran; and efforts to obtain Senate approval of the Panama Canal Treaties.[21]

In addition to distracting policymakers from events in Central America, the Iran and Panama Canal issues directly affected the administration's policy on Nicaragua. The situation in Iran bore a resemblance to

---

19. Pezzullo and Pezzullo, *At the Fall of Somoza*, pp. 71, 127.

20. Lake, *Somoza Falling*, pp. 216–217; Pastor, *Condemned to Repetition*, pp. 140–174; Pezzullo and Pezzullo, *At the Fall of Somoza*, pp. 70–72. See also Morley, *Washington, Somoza, and the Sandinistas*, pp. 182–183. "Human intelligence" or "humint" is intelligence from agents or other human sources, in contrast to "sigint" or intelligence derived from intercepted communications.

21. Kaufman, *The Presidency of James Earl Carter, Jr.*, pp. 125–142.

Nicaragua: both countries were run by reliably pro-U.S. dictators being challenged by popular revolts that involved powerful anti-American factions. The administration had criticized both regimes for human rights abuses, although in both cases, its emphasis on human rights was only sporadic. Most important, Iran was already being cited by some conservatives as an example of how diplomacy that linked improvements in human rights to military and other aid could weaken a pro-U.S. government even when the opposition had equally poor human rights credentials. This line of attack would reach a crescendo late in 1979 with an influential article by Jeane J. Kirkpatrick, "Dictatorships and Double Standards." If the administration forcefully opposed Somoza, only to see the Sandinistas come to power, domestic criticism of its foreign policy would intensify.[22]

The relationship between the Panama Canal treaties and Nicaraguan affairs was more subtle, but probably more important for several reasons. First, since Senate conservatives had already questioned the reliability of Panama's President Torrijos as a treaty partner, Carter wanted to avoid high-profile diplomacy in Nicaragua until the treaties cleared the Senate, lest the full extent of Torrijos's support for the Sandinistas come out. Second, once the treaties were ratified, they still would require legislation to implement the transfer of territory in the Canal Zone from the United States to Panama. This gave the House a voice in the implementation stage and, as it happened, the House Merchant Marine and Fisheries Committee, which would handle the matter, was headed by Somoza's most devoted ally in the lower chamber, Representative Murphy. Although administration officials made no public comments connecting the treaties with Nicaraguan policy, privately they ruled out a complete break with Somoza until Murphy's committee had finished with the implementation legislation.

Throughout late 1978, day-to-day management of Nicaraguan policy fell to Vaky at State and Robert Pastor at the NSC. (The Defense Department played a relatively minor role in discussions on Nicaragua.) President Carter, however, made the policy judgments. Typically, his decisions were guided by memoranda summarizing the discussions of two NSC committees: the Policy Review Committee, chaired by a cabinet secretary, coordinated foreign, defense, and international economic policy, while the Special Coordination Committee, chaired by the national security advisor, handled intelligence policy, arms control, and crisis management.[23]

---

22. Jeane J. Kirkpatrick, "Dictatorships and Double Standards," *Commentary*, Vol. 68 (November 1979), pp. 34–45. See John Ehrman, *The Rise of Neoconservatism: Intellectuals and Foreign Affairs, 1945–1992* (New Haven: Yale University Press, 1995).

23. Pastor, *Condemned to Repetition*, pp. 80–82; Lake, *Somoza Falling*, pp. 150–151.

What to Do?

Policy discussions increasingly revealed a difference of opinion between the State Department and the National Security Council. On August 29, 1978, at the first interagency meeting to address the Nicaraguan situation, State's Vaky argued that, as he later recalled, "we couldn't escape responsibility; we were involved in Nicaragua. On a question of intervening or not intervening, we were an actor in the scenes, so whether we didn't do anything or did something, it had an effect. And I thought the thing to do was to work out something that would get Somoza out while you had a moderate center that could take over—that if you didn't, you were likely to end up with a radicalization.... We had to make it clear to Somoza that we wanted him to go, and we probably would have to do that by being severe, by the use of sanctions of some kind, until he understood it."

Vaky's prescription was resisted by Pastor at the NSC and others in the administration, including National Security Advisor Zbigniew Brzezinski as well as Undersecretary of State Christopher and President Carter himself. They "felt that taking steps to overthrow regimes like Somoza's would be both inappropriate and also likely to fail [and] therefore put us in a difficult, awkward, and apparently impotent position we should try to avoid." For lessons of the past, Pastor and his supporters looked back to the Vietnam of November 1963, when the United States had orchestrated a coup against Ngo Dinh Diem in the hopes of bolstering the war against local communists. Instead, the coup had destabilized the South Vietnamese political system, drawing the United States further into the conflict and ultimately leading to U.S. military intervention. Most administration policymakers, especially Brzezinski, also worried that Somoza's departure would create so much instability that only the Sandinistas would have sufficient organization to assume power.[24]

The administration's emphasis on human rights only compounded the policy paralysis caused by this split between State and the NSC. In Congress, Somoza's allies blamed the dictator's difficulties on an unwise application of Carter's idealism. Seventy-eight members of the House, led by Representatives Murphy, Wilson, and the newly elected Larry McDonald (a Georgia Democrat affiliated with the John Birch Society), published an open letter to Carter demanding that the administration do its "utmost" to demonstrate support for Somoza, "a long and consistent ally of the United States" who was threatened by a "revolutionary group

---

24. Worthen interview with Robert Pastor. All further quotations from Pastor, unless otherwise attributed, are from this interview. See also LeoGrande, *Our Own Backyard*, pp. 20–21.

whose leaders have been trained in Havana and Moscow and whose goal is to make Nicaragua the new Cuba of the Western Hemisphere."[25]

Their influence was considerable. Murphy's ability to hold the Panama Canal Treaty hostage was matched by Wilson's willingness to use his clout on the Appropriations Committee, where his was one of the few swing votes. One Carter official recalled that, "Wilson was in all the time at the operational level," threatening to hold the foreign aid bill hostage unless the administration increased aid to Somoza. Moreover, a host of mid-level officials, ranging from Robert Pastor of the NSC to State Department spokesman Hodding Carter, worried about the threat of a domestic backlash if there were an official U.S. call for Somoza to step down.[26]

Somoza also used the administration's human rights rhetoric as a tool to frustrate U.S. policy. He complained privately to Ambassador Solaun that, "because of your human rights policy, a bunch of imbeciles have thought that you are going to overthrow me. Do not," he warned, "contribute more to the tragedy of this country." Although he said that "Latins don't know how to compromise or understand free elections," Somoza expressed willingness to hold a snap plebiscite on whether he should remain in power, probably expecting that the opposition would reject the gambit. Solaun conceded that "it will be hard for us to resist the constitutional/free election arguments." Indeed, at the end of September, the *Washington Post* termed the development of Nicaraguan policy a perfect example of the "limits on U.S. clout abroad."[27]

After the flurry of activity in the summer of 1978, conditions in Nicaragua seemed to grow more stable in September, strengthening the hand of those in the administration who were arguing for a cautious approach. From Managua, Solaun reported that the decision whether to resign "appears to be totally in Somoza's hands," with the United States only able to influence events on the margins. The FAO, he lamented, was too divided ideologically to pose an immediate threat to the dictator's position. Sensing his renewed strength, Somoza delivered a blustery address ridiculing the "dreamers" who thought he would leave the presidency before the conclusion of his term. Secretary of State Vance termed

25. *New York Times*, September 23, 1978.

26. Cynthia Arnson, *Crossroads: Congress, the President, and Central America* (State College: Pennsylvania State University Press, 1993), pp. 16, 21; LeoGrande, *Our Own Backyard*, pp. 21–22.

27. Solaun to Secretary of State, October 5, 1978, DNSA "Nicaragua," document no. 351; *Washington Post*, September 30, 1978.

the speech a signal "that he has no intention of leaving and is going to hang tough."[28]

The Nicaraguan leader then enjoyed some successes against his domestic opponents, which changed U.S. estimates of his chances. After the National Guard successfully suppressed an FAO strike, CIA analysts reversed an earlier assessment and seconded Solaun's analysis, predicting that Somoza would most likely survive until the end of his term in 1981. A CIA officer whom we will call "Tom Fiske," who took over the Nicaragua portfolio at CIA's Directorate of Intelligence in the spring of 1978, later recalled that, "from what we knew about Sandinista strength at the time, and what we knew about National Guard strength, purely in terms of a one-on-one match-up, we didn't see that the Sandinistas had the capability to overthrow the government. The uncertainty was whether the public outcry could develop enough of a life of its own that it could be a determining factor."[29]

With U.S. policy frozen, other nations in the hemisphere seized the initiative. On September 23, 1978, following up on a Costa Rican proposal, the Organization of American States passed a resolution urging mediation, but without assuming responsibility for it or proposing a mechanism under which it would occur. Eventually, the OAS set up a three-nation mediation panel on which the United States was represented along with Guatemala and the Dominican Republic, two countries whose right-wing governments were hardly eager for a Sandinista triumph. As U.S. representative on the panel, Vance chose William Bowdler, a career Foreign Service officer then serving as director of the State Department's Bureau of Intelligence and Research (INR).[30]

The mediators hoped to negotiate an agreement spelling out the conditions for Somoza's departure. Instead, the effort only exposed the weakness of the moderate opposition. Upon Bowdler's arrival in Managua, recalls Vaky, the moderates sat back saying, "OK, he's going to come in like Henry Stimson in the '20s, and he's going to take over and turn it over to us."[31] Solaun, too, was disturbed by the moderates' attitude, commenting to Vance that their program consisted of little beyond hope that the United

---

28. Morley, *Washington, Somoza, and the Sandinistas*, p. 138; *New York Times*, October 15, 1978.

29. Worthen interview with Tom Fiske (pseudonym). All further quotations from Fiske, unless otherwise attributed, are from this interview.

30. Lake, *Somoza Falling*, pp. 192–210; Morley, *Washington, Somoza, and the Sandinistas*, p. 143. Bowdler was second choice; Somoza had rejected Carter's first choice.

31. In 1927, Calvin Coolidge had sent former secretary of war Stimson (later to be secretary of state) to Nicaragua to mediate the nation's civil war, and the eventual result had been to vest power in the Somozas. See Richard Salisbury, *Anti-Imperialism and*

States would apply pressure on Somoza to depart. "They apparently have not considered," Solaun noted, "or are unwilling to contemplate, the possibility that despite all possible external pressure Somoza may have sufficient holding power to continue in control." The ambassador complained that the FAO structure was "inherently unstable."[32]

On October 25, 1978, however, the FAO submitted a detailed plan for the immediate resignation and departure of Somoza and his family, the installation of a Government of National Unity, the reorganization of the National Guard, and the scheduling of elections for a new Constituent Assembly.[33] This suited neither Somoza nor the Sandinistas. The Sandinistas, understanding that they had the most to lose from mediation, decided to scuttle it with a dramatic gesture. On orders from the FSLN national directorate, Sergio Ramirez, who was a "Group of 12" representative on the FAO negotiating team and a secret FSLN member, denounced mediation as an effort to perpetuate the old order and then asked for asylum at the Mexican embassy in Managua.[34] Somoza, meanwhile, was playing for time. Throughout late 1978, he responded with counter-offers that he knew the FAO would reject, while strengthening the National Guard. Bowdler, believing that Somoza intended to reject the FAO proposal, joined Vaky in pushing for strong measures, such as economic sanctions, to force the dictator from office. In Managua, Solaun seconded the recommendation.

But Washington preferred to wait until after the pending U.S. midterm elections. Dramatic gains by conservatives in both houses of Congress then further constrained the administration's options. Reflecting the new consensus, Brzezinski argued that the United States could not afford to contemplate forcing Somoza out of office until it had some assurance that the moderate opposition would assume power. "The one thing we don't want to happen," the national security advisor cautioned, "is a Sandinista victory." As a result, the United States began trying to find a National Guard officer not tainted by visible participation in the recent repression who might be able to take command of a reconstituted Guard and head a transitional regime. To some, this represented an abandonment of the

International Competition in Central America, 1920–1929 (Wilmington, Del.: Scholarly Resources Press, 1989), pp. 73–78.

32.   Managua cable, January 5, 1979, DNSA Nicaragua, document no. 617; also quoted in Morley, *Washington, Somoza, and the Sandinistas*, pp. 164–165; Vaky interview.

33.   Pastor, *Condemned to Repetition*, pp. 101–102.

34.   Interview with Sergio Ramirez, published in Pilar Arias, *Nicaragua: Revolución* (Mexico: Siglo Veintiuno Editores, 1980), pp. 170–171.

human rights principles upon which Carter's foreign policy was theoretically based.[35]

Somoza, meanwhile, continued his efforts to divide his opponents. He did reject the FAO proposal, although the mediation effort dragged on until January 1979. In early November, just as Solaun had warned, the Nicaraguan dictator proposed a snap plebiscite as an up-or-down vote on his rule. Both Vaky and Bowdler, who was summoned back from Managua for consultations, termed the proposal "mud in our eye" and recommended a public rejection by the United States. However, as Pastor notes, "if you put an issue before a political administration, and it says that you either overthrow these people or you propose an election to determine whether they have support or not, 99.9 times out of 100, they're going to pick the second" option. As Somoza had hoped, the proposed plebiscite further fractured his domestic opposition: the FAO, after some internal debate, agreed to a plebiscite and opened direct negotiations with the Liberal Party, while the Sandinistas firmly rejected the plan. The moderates thus were badly compromised, having abandoned their call for an immediate resignation by Somoza without receiving anything tangible in return. This fit with Somoza's intentions. As Vaky recalled, the dictator felt that "if he could polarize [the situation] and make it…Somoza versus the Marxists, that the United States and everybody else would rally to him." Somoza had thus maneuvered himself back into a commanding position in Nicaragua.[36]

By early 1979, says Vaky, "Washington was in disarray" with regard to Nicaragua. On January 26, Director of Central Intelligence Stansfield Turner told the NSC's Policy Review Committee that the CIA gave Somoza a better-than-even chance of completing his term in 1981. With that appraisal—and with the legislation implementing the Panama Canal Treaty safely through the House—the administration enacted a program of mild political and military sanctions, holding economic sanctions in reserve. This initiative aimed less to persuade Somoza to negotiate with his rivals than to bolster the morale of the moderate opposition and prevent widespread defection to the Sandinistas.

CIA analysts, meanwhile, remained reluctant to make a definitive call as to Somoza's chances of serving out his term. Fiske recalls that, while the agency believed that "time and history" were against Somoza, a prediction as to when the "doomed" leader would fall "was a tougher call." Analysts

---

35. Pastor, *Condemned to Repetition*, pp. 124–128.

36. LeoGrande, *Our Own Backyard*, pp. 22–23; Vaky quoted in Christopher Dickey, *With the Contras: A Reporter in the Wilds of Nicaragua* (New York: Simon and Schuster, 1985), p. 44.

alternated between periods in which they believed Somoza would tough it out and times "when things were in flames and it didn't look like he would." When pressed, however, the CIA predicted that Somoza would remain president of Nicaragua until the scheduled expiration of his term in 1981. Given this view, U.S. representatives reversed an earlier policy and backed a $65 million loan from the International Monetary Fund to Nicaragua.[37]

The CIA failed, however, to recognize or report accurately on outside support for the FSLN. Panama, Costa Rica, and Venezuela, says Vaky, "lied" to the United States about the extent of their assistance to the Sandinistas, and the CIA remained ignorant of the truth. "It was only in retrospect that we saw what they were doing," says Vaky, namely, establishing a logistical system by which arms were flown from Venezuela and Cuba to Panama and thence into Nicaragua through northern Costa Rica, where the Sandinistas had several sanctuaries. To Pastor, the intelligence community's lack of reporting on this assistance represented the most serious intelligence failure of the crisis. The "stuff would have been available," he noted, "by a good, enterprising single officer leaving [Costa Rican capital] San José and going north to the border and looking around."[38]

The decision by Cuba, Panama, Costa Rica, and Venezuela to help the FSLN reflected a broader shift of power in Nicaragua, where momentum again favored the Sandinistas. In March 1979, FSLN officials met in Havana to iron out their internal differences, and while they were there, Cuban leader Castro promised them a substantial increase in military assistance. The next month, the Sandinistas launched guerrilla operations in northern and western Nicaragua. Meanwhile, the U.S. sanctions, while welcomed by the moderates, had proved too little and too late to preserve the moderates' freedom of action.

In April 1979, the FSLN succeeded in winning over to its ranks the more moderate FAO coalition. The two merged to form the National Patriotic Front. Alfonso Robelo, a key moderate leader, fled to Costa Rica, where he began helping the Sandinistas organize a government-in-exile. The Sandinistas then launched what they termed their "final offensive" which, while not final, did put the National Guard on the defensive. Internationally, Somoza suffered a setback when, on May 20, the Mexican government severed relations with Managua and urged other Latin American nations to do the same.[39]

---

37. Pastor, *Condemned to Repetition*, pp. 115–120; *Washington Post*, May 11, 1979.

38. Vaky interview; Pastor, *Condemned to Repetition*, pp. 125–128; Morley, *Washington, Somoza, and the Sandinistas*, pp. 185–190.

39. *Washington Post*, April 17–18, 1979. This broke with the tradition under which

In April, the State Department decided to replace Ambassador Solaun (who had been recalled to the United States in February as part of the sanctions package) with Lawrence Pezzullo, then serving as U.S. ambassador to Uruguay. Pezzullo was stunned to find most U.S. policymakers still convinced "that the Sandinistas had some force but not enough to matter, that the real question [was] how to convince Somoza in '81 to accept retirement."[40] Other than to maintain some rhetorical distance from Somoza, the Carter administration had done little after announcing sanctions in February. In Pezzullo's view, at the time of his appointment, "there was no policy." Pastor agrees that policymakers tried to avoid dealing with Nicaragua because "we didn't have any new answers."

The new fighting, however, galvanized the administration. At a Policy Review Committee meeting on June 11, 1979, Nicaragua dominated the discussion, especially after the CIA reversed its earlier estimates and predicted that Somoza would not last out his term. Those who earlier had opposed direct U.S. involvement now agreed that the situation called for urgent action. The meeting adopted a proposal by Brzezinski to try to create an inter-American peacekeeping force to maintain order in Nicaragua following Somoza's resignation. The goal, as before, was to avert an outright Sandinista victory, described by the administration now as creating the "potential for a Castroite takeover of Nicaragua."[41] Secretary of State Vance listed the preconditions for a successful resolution of the crisis: a transitional government; preservation of existing institutions, "especially" the National Guard; and negotiations with "all elements" of the Nicaraguan government and the opposition for a "formula leading to democratic elections."

Just when it seemed that the administration had arrived at a coordinated Nicaragua policy, the human rights issue reemerged. In a blistering memorandum to Vance, Assistant Secretary of State for Human Rights Derian dismissed the new approach as unrealistic and inconsistent with stated administration policy. She accused the Policy Review Committee of equating a government of national reconciliation with something that was merely "Somocismo without Somoza." Any such regime, she maintained, needed to have "legitimate" representation from the FAO, Group of 12, and FSLN. Secondly, she strongly opposed Brzezinski's inter-American peace force idea, noting that "for historical reasons, for political reasons,

---

Mexico City had extended diplomatic recognition to any de facto government (with the sole exception of Franco's regime in Spain).

40. Worthen interview with Lawrence Pezzullo. All further quotations from Pezzullo, unless otherwise attributed, are from this interview.

41. Morley, *Washington, Somoza, and the Sandinistas*, pp. 184–185; Secretary of State to All American Diplomatic Posts, June 15, 1979, DNSA "Nicaragua," document no. 765.

and for the very desire to set in motion a process that will not mean a continuation of the current prolonged battle," the concept was highly unlikely to win support outside the United States. Derian urged Vance to renounce publicly any possibility of unilateral U.S. military intervention, "even if the worst scenario played itself out and an FSLN military victory appeared imminent." She also strongly criticized the increasingly hardline public posture of both the NSC and the Defense Department. She disparaged comparisons between the developing situation in Nicaragua and that in Cuba two decades before, contending that basing policy on this assumption would only make it a self-fulfilling prophesy.[42]

Between Derian's forceful objections and international developments, the newly adopted Policy Review Committee plan was not implemented. Indeed, Washington had all it could do to stay abreast of events. On June 12, 1979, the CIA estimated that Somoza's regime might last only a short time, prompting the U.S. embassy to begin evacuating personnel. Four days later, the members of the Andean Pact—Venezuela, Colombia, Ecuador, Peru, and Bolivia—broke relations with Managua and granted to the Sandinistas the status of "belligerent," which was the next thing to recognizing them as a government. In San José, Costa Rica, a five-person junta representing both the FSLN and the moderate opposition announced itself to be the provisional government that would succeed Somoza. By June 19, CIA analysts were assessing Somoza's chances on a week-by-week basis, while a Pentagon briefing paper described the National Guard as stretched "to the breaking point." In its most aggressive position so far, the Defense Department suggested that an "active, forceful U.S. role" was the only way to "prevent a hard left, Marxist-Leninist government from coming to power."[43]

That approach, however, swiftly became politically impossible. On June 20, 1979, ABC News correspondent Bill Stewart was ordered out of his van by a contingent of National Guard soldiers who forced him down on the ground and shot him in the head, killing him instantly; they then killed his interpreter. Stewart's cameraman, hidden in the news crew's van, captured the event. Pastor recalls the outpouring of public emotion in response to broadcast of the film as "unlike anything I had seen since I had been in the White House." The murder by Somoza's National Guard intensified pressure on the administration to do something to resolve the crisis. Brzezinski floated the notion of unilateral military intervention, but Carter

---

42. Derian to the Secretary, June 20, 1979, DNSA "Nicaragua," document no. 791.

43. Secretary of State to All American Diplomatic Posts, June 15, 1979, DNSA "Nicaragua," document no. 765; Fiske interview; *New York Times*, June 23, 1979; *Washington Star*, June 30, 1979.

rejected it out of hand. On June 23, an OAS resolution endorsing "constructive actions" by member countries provided a multilateral umbrella under which the United States could try to resolve the Nicaraguan situation.[44]

At a June 25 meeting of the NSC's Special Coordination Committee, policymakers agreed to pursue two tracks, both designed to diminish Sandinista influence in post-Somoza Nicaragua. On the one hand, the administration would work to place additional moderates in the junta dominated by the FSLN. Simultaneously, Washington would try to convene an executive committee of prominent Nicaraguan moderates which, bolstered by a purged National Guard, could negotiate with the junta over the shape of a new government. Both tracks, however, depended on Somoza's willingness to step aside.

Events Take the Saddle

On June 27, 1979, Ambassador Pezzullo arrived in Managua to assume his post, guided by three principal instructions: persuade Somoza to resign, recruit moderate leaders to form an executive committee, and negotiate a restructuring of the National Guard under a new commander acceptable to both the Guard and the moderates. He found Somoza ready to leave if Washington would guarantee certain conditions of exile as well as the preservation of the Guard and the Liberal Party. The new ambassador wondered if this move alone might solve the U.S. dilemma, and optimistically predicted that "the transitional president would ride a wave of public joy occasioned by Somoza's departure, win over an unknown, though perhaps considerable, amount of FSLN support and thereby permit moderates to play a bigger role in forming [a] transition government."[45]

Pezzullo quickly set about implementing his instructions. As a first step toward restructuring the National Guard, Pezzullo persuaded both Somoza and the FSLN junta in San Jose to approve Colonel Federico Mejia as head of a reconstituted National Guard. Recruiting moderates to an executive committee proved more difficult; from the start, Vaky had argued against the idea, predicting that "it isn't going to work, because there's no one there." Nonetheless, supporters within the NSC kept this effort alive until July 2. At that point, Carter approved a framework incorporating the other track of expanding the number of moderates within the junta. Panama's leader, General Omar Torrijos, agreed to broker an agreement between the

---

44. Pastor, *Condemned to Repetition*, pp. 134–150.

45. American Embassy Managua to Secretary of State, July 6, 1979, DNSA "Nicaragua," document no. 871; Pezzullo interview; Lake, *Somoza Falling*, pp. 229–236.

Sandinistas and the junta. This plan, however, proved unacceptable to the two existing moderate members of the junta, who worried about diluting their power and seeming to act at Washington's behest.

Pezzullo did succeed in persuading Somoza to agree to resign. He then won junta agreement to an arrangement under which, after Somoza's departure, an interim president, Francisco Urcuyo, speaker of the lower house of Congress, would take office, but would cede power to the junta within 72 hours. All senior officers would resign and a cease-fire would go into effect. On July 12, 1979, the Carter administration reinforced Pezzullo's efforts with what Vance termed a diplomatic "full court press" to "contain extremist power" in Nicaragua. But that initiative failed to produce any results.

On July 17, 1979, Somoza departed Managua for Miami, but the scheme for an orderly transfer of power unraveled almost immediately. With no independent relationships between U.S. officials and members of the National Guard, the administration had to rely on Somoza's word that the dictator had informed his army officers of the outlines of the transition deal. Instead—fearing they would kill him otherwise—he had told them that the U.S. military would intervene on their side once he left the country. Urcuyo, meanwhile, called on the guerrillas to lay down their arms, and gave no sign that he intended to hand the presidency over to the junta. The FSLN then declared the transfer-of-power agreement void. The last vestiges of the Somocista state dissolved. Within 48 hours, Nicaragua's National Guard had ceased to exist. Its leading officers, Mejia, and Urcuyo all fled to Honduras and Guatemala.[46] On July 19, 1979, the junta returned to Managua from San José to fill the power vacuum. The Sandinistas were the only military and political power left in the country.

---

46. Pezzullo interview; State 179849, Secretary of State to All American Republic Diplomatic Posts, July 12, 1979, Subject: "Nicaragua—Status Report," DNSA "Nicaragua," document no. 914; also quoted in Morley, *Washington, Somoza, and the Sandinistas*, p. 204.

Chapter 4

Iran, 1978–1979: Coping with the Unthinkable

Gregory F. Treverton, with assistance from James Klocke

The fall of the shah of Iran at the end of 1978 was a foreign policy disaster for the United States. A man on whom successive American administrations had relied as a pillar of strength in his region was suddenly swept away by currents that officials in Washington were hard pressed to fathom. President Jimmy Carter's administration was handicapped in its efforts to interpret events by divisions and rivalries among the State Department, the U.S. Embassy in Teheran, and the National Security Council. In addition, U.S. intelligence capabilities in the region were minimal. The shah's regime collapsed despite intensive U.S. diplomatic efforts to negotiate with the Iranian government and its domestic opposition, including the Ayatollah Ruhollah Khomeini.

Background

When Jimmy Carter became president on January 20, 1977, he inherited a unique relationship with Iran and its ruler established by former President Richard Nixon. Nixon and the shah had known each other as far back as 1953, when then–Vice President Nixon visited the young Iranian leader in the wake of the coup sponsored by the U.S. Central Intelligence Agency (CIA) that returned the shah to the throne. Two decades later Nixon, in the aftermath of the Vietnam War, sought in what became known as the "Nixon Doctrine" to reduce U.S. military commitments in far-flung areas. Iran fulfilled the crucial role of protecting U.S. and Western interests in the Persian Gulf. In return, Nixon and the shah agreed in 1972 that Iran would receive U.S. military advisers, technicians, and weaponry, including the most sophisticated conventional arms then in the U.S. arsenal.

Henry Kissinger, Nixon's Assistant for National Security Affairs, outlined the rationale for the deal with the shah:

Under the shah's leadership, the land bridge between Asia and Europe, so often the hinge of world history, was pro-American and pro-West beyond any challenge. Alone among the countries of the region—Israel aside—Iran made friendship with the United States the starting point of its policy. That it was based on a cold-eyed assessment that a threat to Iran would mostly likely come from the Soviet Union, in combination with radical Arab states, is only another way of saying that the shah's view of the realities of world politics paralleled our own.[1]

At the end of those remarkable 1972 meetings, Nixon said to the shah across the table: "Protect me."[2] Following up on his part of the deal, Nixon instructed his top foreign policymakers that future Iranian arms requests "should not be second-guessed."[3] What the shah wanted, he would get. He wanted a lot, especially after the oil crisis of 1973 multiplied his government's revenues. In the four years after Nixon's visit, Iran ordered more than $9 billion worth of American weaponry, more than half of all U.S. foreign arms sales.

American deference to the shah spread beyond weapons to intelligence. The CIA dismantled many of its own operations in Iran, making it ever more reliant on SAVAK, the shah's feared secret police, for information on Iranian internal affairs. When U.S. officials from the Department of State or the CIA did hazard contacts with the opposition, they often bumped into SAVAK or the court ministry. Henry Precht, the Iran desk officer in the State Department in 1977–1978, recalled one time when "one of our political officers went to talk to a mullah, [and] we got word back that the shah's court ministry learned of this and didn't think it was a good idea."[4]

In these circumstances, the quality of American intelligence on Iran—both covert and open—declined steadily. A later appraisal called State Department reporting on the Iranian opposition "rare and sometimes contemptuous."[5] For its part, the CIA from 1975–1977 provided not a single

---

1. Henry Kissinger, *White House Years* (Boston: Little, Brown, 1979), p. 1262.

2. Quoted by Gary Sick in a presentation at the American Enterprise Institute, January 20, 1985 (hereafter cited as AEI conference). Unless otherwise indicated, this and other quotations from Sick and from William Sullivan are from this conference.

3. Kissinger, *White House Years*, p. 1264.

4. Gregory F. Treverton interview with Henry Precht. All further quotations from Precht not otherwise attributed are from this interview.

5. House of Representatives, Permanent Select Committee on Intelligence, Subcommittee on Evaluation, *Iran: Evaluation of U.S. Intelligence Performance prior to November 1978* (1978).

report based on sources within the religious opposition. "That veil was hard to pierce," commented Harold Saunders, assistant secretary of state for the Near East and Asia during that period.[6]

The transformation of the U.S.-Iranian relationship in the mid-1970s was dramatic. In the summer of 1976, the Inspector General of the American Foreign Service reported that "the government of Iran exerts the determining influence" in relations with the United States. The preponderance of funding for joint efforts was Iranian, and "he who pays the piper calls the tune."[7] As early as 1969, Kissinger had canceled the U.S. government's annual review of Iran as an unnecessary intrusion into internal Iranian politics.

In office, President Carter quickly came to share the view that Iran was vital to American security interests in southwest Asia. The oil crisis had driven home the extent of American dependence on Persian Gulf oil, and Carter needed stability in that region to have a chance of pursuing a comprehensive settlement of the Arab-Israeli conflict. Carter's campaign promises to reduce American sales of offensive weapons abroad meant that his administration gave closer scrutiny to Iran's requests, but sales did not sharply diminish.

Yet it was these campaign promises—to reduce arms sales and to emphasize human rights—that dominated Washington's relations with Teheran during the first year of the Carter administration. An Iranian request for ground-based radar stations was pending at the beginning of 1977, but Carter decided instead to offer the sophisticated Airborne Warning and Control System (AWACS) aircraft then coming into the U.S. Air Force. The $1.23 billion offer was meant to betoken both support for the shah and restraint in arms sales, as Iran's request for ten AWACS planes was pared to seven.

However, in July 1977, the House of Representatives Foreign Affairs Committee rejected the sale as contrary to the president's own promise to reduce arms sales. Congress was also concerned because the AWACS was far more than a warning system; it was an air warfare management instrument that could be used, for example, against Israel. The rejection stung the shah's pride and his confidence in the relationship with the United States; he considered withdrawing the request altogether. The White House made a major effort to allay congressional concerns over AWACS capability and security in the hands of Iran and, in October 1977, Congress

---

6. Treverton interview with Harold Saunders. All further quotations from Saunders not otherwise attributed are from this interview.

7. Gary Sick, *All Fall Down: America's Tragic Encounter with Iran* (New York: Random House, 1985), p. 20.

relented and approved the sale of seven AWACS aircraft. Congress also protested against but did not stop other sales of sophisticated fighter planes.

Carter's campaign pledge to emphasize human rights in American foreign policy was greeted with apprehension by the shah, who had made little secret of his hope that Gerald Ford would be re-elected instead in 1976. According to the Iranian ambassador in London, the shah feared that Carter might press for reform, as Kennedy had in the early 1960s.[8] The shah's concerns seemed warranted; in his inaugural address, Carter announced, "Our moral sense dictates a clear preference for those societies which share with us an abiding respect for individual human rights."[9] Carter seemed committed to exerting pressure on regimes, even those friendly to the United States, in which torture, political imprisonment, and other violations of basic human rights were common practice.[10]

Yet in the first year of the administration, the human rights issue lay dormant. When Secretary of State Cyrus Vance visited Teheran in May 1977, he reassured his hosts that Washington viewed favorably a limited reform package the shah had introduced in 1976, and that sanctions against Iran were not under consideration. "We decided early on," noted Vance, "that it was in our national interest to support the shah." One embassy official recalled that Vance considered that "there were many more important issues [than human rights] to be discussed."[11]

Opponents of the shah were, however, encouraged by Carter's support of human rights, taking it as a sign that international support for the shah was waning. Demonstrations against his rule stepped up, both inside and outside Iran. In the United States, those demonstrations reached a peak during a November 1977 state visit by the shah to Washington. Some 60,000 Iranian student demonstrators, pro- and anti-shah, clashed outside the White House; many of the "antis" wore masks to prevent identification by the SAVAK officers they presumed to be filming the demonstration. During the arrival ceremonies, police used tear gas to separate the battling groups. When winds carried the tear gas over the ceremonies, the world was treated to the televised sight of the president, the shah, and

---

8. Ibid., p. 22

9. James Bill, *The Eagle and the Lion: The Tragedy of American-Iranian Relations* (New Haven: Yale University Press, 1988), p. 226.

10. As the shah arrived on the South Lawn of the White House for his first visit during the Carter administration, Treverton heard a young speechwriter who had written fulsome praise of the shah for the president's welcome say, "You'll recognize the shah. He's the one with blood under his fingernails."

11. Bill, *The Eagle and the Lion*, p. 227, fn. 18.

other senior officials wiping tears from their eyes. At a state dinner that night, Carter broke the tension by quipping: "There is one thing I can say about the shah—he knows how to draw a crowd." He went on to deliver a toast celebrating Iranian-American relations.

Both the toast and the reassuring words were repeated at year's end when the president stopped in Teheran at the end of a hop-skip-and-jump tour of Europe and western Asia. Carter and the shah reached a verbal understanding on non-proliferation arrangements to accompany the sale of American nuclear power plants to Iran, and they discussed Iran's future military needs. In his toast, Carter described Iran as an "island of stability."

The Shah Loses Ground

Under the surface, politics in Iran were becoming increasingly turbulent. Opposition to the shah's repressive government had been building steadily. In 1978, his opponents took to the streets. On January 7, the government-sponsored newspaper *Ettelaat* had ridiculed the Islamic fundamentalist opposition leader, the Ayatollah Khomeini. The next day, police fired on demonstrators marching in protest in the religious city of Qom; twenty were killed. As stipulated by Islam, the dead were commemorated at forty-day intervals, offering occasions for ever larger demonstrations.[12] The government responded to the demonstrations with increased repression; opposition leaders' houses were bombed and the leaders beaten up by vigilante groups widely believed to be connected with SAVAK.

For his part, the shah displayed no public doubts that he would prevail over the opposition. In a June 1978 interview headlined "Nobody Can Overthrow Me—I Have the Power," the shah blamed the demonstrations on religious reaction to his reform measures and on external subversion:

> In some cases, it is a matter of personal vengeance against me. There is the religious reaction of some of the Moslem priests against our programs of modernization. The Communists are also active, and we have the strange phenomenon here of the reactionary groups and the leftists working together.... Nobody can overthrow me. I have the support of 700,000 troops, all the workers and most of the people. Wherever I go, there are fantastic demonstrations of support. I have the power, and the opposition

---

12. Sick, *All Fall Down*, p. 35. The cycle was later dubbed, by an official of the Khomeini government who had taken part in them, "doing the 40-40." The ayatollah, meanwhile, denounced Carter for using the "logic of bandits" in his foreign policy. Bill, The Eagle and the Lion, fn. 36.

cannot be compared in strength with the government in any way.[13]

However, the shah had a secret, although its influence on his actions can only be guessed at: he had cancer. In the words of Gary Sick, the National Security Council officer most directly responsible for Iran:

> We were unaware that the shah had cancer and even that he was ill. Not only were we not aware of it, but the French intelligence was not aware of it, although his two doctors were French.... His twin sister did not know it...and I believe it is true to say that his wife did not know it. As a matter of fact, despite the rumor mill in Teheran, after the news of the shah's illness came out...the revolutionaries said they had heard every rumor in the world except that one. They had never heard even a rumor in Teheran that the shah had cancer.

For the time being, however, the shah's illness played no part in Iranian politics. Most foreign assessments, including those of the CIA and State Department, judged that the shah's chances of weathering the current wave of opposition were favorable.

By the summer of 1978, although some foreign analysts noted signs of breakdown in Iran's internal stability, few predicted that the shah would fall. A junior French diplomat expressed the view that the shah would not survive, and a senior Israeli representative in Iran, Uri Lubrani, cabled Tel Aviv in June 1978 that the shah might not last as long as two or three years. Lubrani later indicated that he had discussed his assessment with U.S. Ambassador William Sullivan. But Sullivan's June cable to Washington included neither Lubrani's conclusions nor the French officer's. Later that summer, as Sullivan returned to Washington for home leave, he was still expressing confidence in the shah.

The turbulence in Iran made any confident prediction difficult. For U.S. officials, a natural reluctance to "make the call" against the shah was reinforced by a pattern of almost reflexive American support for him. U.S. reliance on the shah had eliminated incentives to maintain independent sources of information, and it had also made his downfall too unpleasant to contemplate. In August 1977, for instance, the CIA produced a 60-page estimate concluding that "the Shah will be an active participant in Iranian life well into the 1980s" and that there would "be no radical change in Iranian political behavior in the near future."[14] The State Department's

---

13. *U.S. News and World Report*, June 26, 1978, p. 37.

14. Bill, *The Eagle and the Lion*, fn. 85.

Iran desk officer, Henry Precht, described the attitude of National Security Advisor Zbigniew Brzezinski: "Brzezinski simply wanted to see the shah's regime remain, wanted to see us support him, and wasn't going to hear anything that contradicted that position." Precht said that Brzezinski's order was: "Tell me how to make it work."

Washington was not alone in its immobility: no other Western nation, including Israel, made a dramatic change in its policy toward Iran until late 1978. History supported caution in predicting an end to the shah's regime. Old Iran hands remembered the troubles of the 1960s. Then, the shah had been able to "jump ahead of the opposition," as Saunders put it, so why not now? Moreover, those events and the early 1970s had led Washington to believe, in Ambassador Sullivan's words, "that he was a hard-nosed fellow. [This was] the first myth I learned in Washington." However:

> During my first meeting with the shah after presenting my cre-
> dentials, it became quite clear to me that he was not. He was a
> rather indecisive man, a rather gentle person, a man who was con-
> fused about what to do, about how, over the next few years, he
> would turn over the realm to his son.

William Colby, who had been Director of Central Intelligence during the Ford administration, also recalled that a CIA profile of the shah portrayed him as a weak man.[15] However, that was not the shah's image in official Washington.

The shah's position unraveled precipitously during the second half of 1978. August 5 marked the beginning of the holy month of Ramadan, devoted to fasting and religious observances. During the month, another wave of demonstrations swept Iranian cities; strikes interrupted oil production; and some universities were closed because of student violence. As tensions rose, a fatal fire fueled the stand-off between the shah and Muslim clerics: on August 19, a fire swept through a movie theater in Abadan, killing 477 because exit doors were locked. The government and opposition each charged the other with setting the fire, and the perpetrators were never caught. The incident incited more violence.

At the end of August, the shah turned to a new government, a "reform" cabinet headed by Prime Minister Ja'far Sharif-Emani, who had held the same post in the early 1960s. Then, he had promised political participation to the opposition, favored the Islamic calendar, and moved

---

15. Treverton interview with William Colby. All further quotations from Colby not otherwise attributed are from this interview.

against corrupt "Western" practices and institutions such as casinos. He had been viewed, however, as ineffectual and too tied to the monarchy. Ambassador Sullivan considered him "personally corrupt."[16] His second tenure as prime minister was no more successful than his first: after two months in office, universities remained closed and strikes continued in oilfields and refineries.[17]

Opposition groups marked the end of Ramadan with large demonstrations in Teheran on September 4 and 5. The success of those demonstrations prompted calls for a general strike, to which the government responded by declaring martial law, announced on the evening of September 7. The next morning 20,000 people congregated in Teheran's Jaleh Square for a rally against the shah. When the crowd ignored orders to disperse, government troops opened fire. The shooting went on all day. Casualty estimates varied wildly: the government estimated 122 killed and 2,000–3,000 wounded, while the opposition claimed 1,000 killed. Doctors attending the wounded put casualties at 300–400 killed and several thousand wounded. The NSC's Sick later identified the massacre as "the turning point from sporadic acts of popular rebellion to genuine revolution."[18]

Washington Rouses

U.S. officials recognized that the growing violence in Iran could pose difficulties for U.S. policy. They doubted, however, the shah's rule would be threatened, so long as he retained control of the military and security organizations, which seemed likely. But events made it even more important that the United States not allow human rights concerns to cloud its pro-shah policy. As Assistant Secretary of State for the Near East and Asia Harold Saunders put it in an August 17 memo to Vance: "Rejection of an arms sale or a human rights gesture would carry extra—and unintended—weight" in the charged climate.[19]

But Carter's attention at the time was elsewhere. Word of the September 8 killings reached the president at Camp David, where Carter

---

16. Bill, *The Eagle and the Lion*, p. 229.

17. Barry M. Rubin, *Paved with Good Intentions: The American Experience and Iran* (New York: Oxford University Press, 1980), pp. 210–213.

18. Sick, *All Fall Down*, p. 51.

19. Harold Saunders to Cyrus Vance, August 17, 1978, Digital National Security Archive, "Iran: The Making of U.S. Policy, 1977–1984" (hereafter DNSA "Iran"), document no. 1476.

and his senior foreign policy aides were spending 24 hours a day on Middle East peace negotiations between Israeli Prime Minister Menachem Begin and Egyptian President Anwar Sadat. Assistant Secretary of State Saunders later said he "couldn't claim I gave Iran top priority attention," and indeed Iran Desk Officer Precht was unable to schedule a meeting with Saunders following the massacre. John Stempel, who had been chief U.S. political officer in Iran since 1975, likewise concluded that, "America did not realize what was happening in Iran." As a result, U.S. policymakers consistently underestimated the strength of the Iranian opposition; Vance asserted, in October 1978, that "we hear that security agencies believe [the] opposition can be quelled by only 400 key arrests."[20]

Nonetheless, both Sadat and then Carter—who throughout the period was generally reluctant to contact the shah—took time to telephone the shah to express their support for him. Carter also encouraged the shah not to let his liberalization program flag. The shah agreed and asked the president to reiterate his public support. Shortly after, the White House released a statement describing the telephone conversation and reaffirming the close ties between Iran and the United States, a statement that was read on Teheran Radio. Under the circumstances, however, the statement—intended to strengthen the shah's hand—probably operated instead to identify the United States with the Jaleh Square massacre.

The increasing turmoil in Iran did not set off alarm bells in the American intelligence community. An effort to produce the government's premier coordinated assessment on Iran, a National Intelligence Estimate (NIE), ran into the sand over the summer. Samuel Huntington, a Harvard political science professor and long-time friend of Brzezinski, was serving on the National Security Council during 1977 and 1978. He recalled that, after the Jaleh Square massacre, he asked the CIA for an assessment of prospects for a post-shah Iran. What he received was a discussion of the Iranian constitution and the chances of creating a regency council for a transition within the Pahlevi dynasty. There was no mention of potential successor regimes.

Within Iran, the pace of events continued to quicken. Pilgrims returning from the Iraqi holy city of Najaf, where Ayatollah Khomeini was in exile, brought back cassette recordings of his sermons attacking the shah; these were played in mosques across Iran. The shah responded by putting pressure on Iraq to curtail Khomeini's activities. Iraq agreed, and within two weeks Khomeini left Iraq for Paris.

---

20. Bill, *The Eagle and the Lion*, fn. 52; Secretary of State to American Embassy, Tehran, October 28, 1978, reproduced in A.H.H. Abidi, ed., *The Tehran Documents* (New Delhi: Patriot Publishers, 1988).

The Iranian government expected that distance would mute the force of Khomeini's anti-shah efforts. However, like almost everyone else, it failed to anticipate how modern technology had changed the politics of revolution. Simply by using the direct-dial telephone, Khomeini continued to guide his lieutenants in Iran. Moreover the Ayatollah, although well into his seventies and a medievalist with no previous experience outside Shi'a Islam, became a cynosure for Western journalists, who had a much larger presence in Paris than in either Iraq or Iran. Street demonstrations increased in Iran rather than abated after Khomeini moved to Paris, as the forty-day mourning date for the Jaleh Square dead approached.

By mid-October, Precht and his colleagues at the working level of the State Department were worried enough to put their concerns in writing. Their paper acknowledged the worsening violence and ineffective response, and found no evidence that the existing policy of U.S. support for the shah had helped him. It concluded that the shah had to reestablish his authority "within a few weeks." It ruled out a military government, however, as likely only to incite the shah's opponents.[21] The paper took a small step away from the prevailing mind-set in Washington, which held in essence that U.S. destiny was to work with the shah. It found almost no support.

Asked to comment on Precht's paper, Ambassador Sullivan argued against any dramatic change in policy. Quiet reassurance, he believed, was more important than expressions of high-level support for the shah. On October 22, Sullivan said that while it was too early to make a "definitive prediction," he detected "encouraging" signs, most notably in the firmness of the military.[22] As Sullivan later recalled:

> The embassy tended toward the presumption that the shah would use force and that he would put the rebellion down. We did not get any instructions from Washington suggesting that we recommend the use of force. The Carter administration, given its stand on human rights, would never have put that on paper. But some encouragement was coming in one form or another.

In comments dated five days later, Sullivan outlined his own efforts to persuade moderates to participate in the political process. Given Sullivan's objections, Precht's document was quietly interred in the State Department.

By late October, however, the shah himself seemed to be having doubts about whether he could manage the turmoil. Perhaps sensing this

---

21. Sick, *All Fall Down*, p. 59.
22. Sullivan to Vance, October 22, 1978, DNSA "Iran," document no. 1608.

indecision, Sullivan suddenly reversed his appraisal of events in Iran, reporting on a "significant" change in Iran, where some members of the elite were for the first time "thinking the unthinkable"—Iran without the shah. Sullivan continued, however, to worry about the "visceral reaction" of some Iranian military officers to U.S. human rights policies, what he saw as a suddenly burgeoning "underground organization of Tudeh" Communist activists, and the danger that large numbers of Iranians had come to see strikes and demonstrations as a legitimate expression of effective political action.[23]

In a November 1 meeting with Ambassador Sullivan and British Ambassador Anthony Parsons, the shah said he would rather leave Iran than submit to a referendum on the monarchy, which was one of the demands presented by the National Front, a broad secular reform movement of the moderate left. Sullivan reported on the meeting to Washington the next day, drawing particular attention to the shah's remark hinting at abdication. He expected the shah to seek American advice about whether to abdicate or impose a military government. Sullivan added his belief that a military government of some sort was likely.[24]

Making the Call

Ambassador Sullivan's memo finally stirred senior Washington foreign policy officials to pay attention to Iran. Their inattention had reflected not just a natural inclination to disregard bad news that threatened to undermine the basic premise of U.S.-Iran policy. It was also due to the sheer weight of business at the time, including not only the Middle East peace negotiations but talks about a second round of limitations on strategic nuclear armaments and progress toward normalization of relations with China. All of these came to a head within a short period and, for two full weeks in October, senior policymakers were literally out of town, at Camp David.

But in the evening of November 2, 1978, the National Security Council's Special Coordination Committee (SCC) finally met at the White House to respond to Sullivan's request for instructions. National Security Advisor Brzezinski chaired the meeting, whose other participants included Deputy Secretary of State Warren Christopher, Secretary of Defense Harold Brown, Chairman of the Joint Chiefs of Staff General David Jones,

---

23. American Embassy to Secretary of State, October 31, 1978, reproduced in Abidi, *The Tehran Documents*.

24. Sullivan to Vance, November 2, 1978, DNSA "Iran," document no. 1659.

and Stansfield Turner, the Director of Central Intelligence. Brzezinski reported on conversations with Carter and with the shah's ambassador to Washington (and former son-in-law), Ardeshir Zahedi. He presented a draft message for Sullivan to take to the shah.

The message reflected Brzezinski's view that the chaos in Iran called for strong action, perhaps even military rule. It expressed unconditional American support for the shah, noted the need for "decisive action" to restore order, and encouraged the resumption of liberalization once order had been restored.[25] After some discussion and modification, the Special Coordinating Committee approved the message. Brzezinski telephoned the shah the next day to assure him of Washington's firm support, and Vance stressed the same point publicly at a news conference.[26]

Brzezinski dismissed the possibility of conciliation, which he characterized as "a quaint notion favored by American lawyers of liberal bent." He conceded that it might have worked in 1976, but not by the time of acute crisis in 1978. His advocacy of a tough response was influenced, he later wrote, by a historian of revolutions, Crane Brinton, who had argued that in the English, American, French, and Russian revolutions, the turning point to violence had come when those in power started to make concessions:[27]

> I felt strongly that successful revolutions were historical rarities, that they were inevitable only after they happened, and that an established leadership, by demonstrating both will and reason, could disarm the opposition through a timely combination of repression and concession.[28]

Brzezinski's views were reinforced in his contacts with Iranian Ambassador Zahedi, which became more frequent during 1978. Like Brzezinski, Zahedi thought Iran's turmoil required a military clampdown. Zahedi's father had helped restore the shah to his throne in 1953. He himself was a figure to be reckoned with in Iranian politics; many in the shah's inner circle believed that he coveted the prime minister's post. Through Zahedi—whom Brzezinski described as "a useful source of information"—Brzezinski was able to ensure that the shah heard his views during late 1978. Zahedi in turn used the contact to his advantage, leaving

---

25. Sick, *All Fall Down*, p. 67.

26. *Washington Post*, November 3–4, 1978.

27. Crane Brinton, *The Anatomy of Revolution* (New York: W.W. Norton, 1938).

28. Zbigniew Brzezinski, *Power and Principle: Memoirs of the National Security Advisor* (New York: Farrar, Straus, Giroux, 1983), p. 355.

many in Iran uncertain whether he spoke for himself or reflected White House views.

While Brzezinski thus underlined his commitment to the shah, the State Department's Bureau of Intelligence and Research (INR) began to move in the opposite direction. In a lengthy briefing memo of November 2, INR Acting Director David Mark concluded that "only drastic measures by the shah hold any promise for staving off a descent into chaos," but the shah himself "cannot see beyond half-measures designed to defer hard decisions." Given Khomeini's "almost mystical sway over current Iranian protesters," Mark argued that the shah would "have to offer the moderates a deal they cannot refuse that would leave Khomeini out in the cold." Even this approach, he conceded, might fail, since "the ordinary Iranian has learned that, even without guns, he can exercise strong military power."[29]

The divergence between National Security Advisor Brzezinski and the State Department, including Secretary of State Vance, was initially less about ends than means, for both Brzezinski and Vance wanted the shah to remain on his throne. As the situation in Iran deteriorated, however, the agreement on ends became less critical than the disagreement over means. An early sign of this pattern came in a cable from Ambassador Sullivan that arrived on November 2, in which he stated that "a military takeover is feasible, but at heavy long-term cost for U.S. interests as well as for Iran." Most notably, he worried, "the international outcry from the United States and elsewhere would reach new decibel levels." Moreover, given U.S. identification with the Iranian regime, policymakers needed to consider "the effect on USG [U.S. Government] image and policy" of any military government.[30]

Belatedly, as official Washington began to realize that the scale of dissent in Iran was running well beyond expectations, the quality of intelligence became an issue. On November 6, National Security Council official Gary Sick wrote Brzezinski that "the most fundamental problem at the moment is the astonishing lack of hard information we are getting about developments in Iran."[31] Carter had raised the issue of intelligence with Secretary of State Vance just before Sick's note, and raised it again with CIA Director Turner at a Policy Review Committee meeting. Turner acknowledged the problem but said there was little in the short term he could do about it because of the draw-down of American intelligence

---

29. David Mark to Vance, November 2, 1978, DNSA "Iran," document no. 1661.

30. American Embassy to Secretary of State, November 2, 1978, reproduced in Abidi, *The Tehran Documents*.

31. Sick, *All Fall Down*, p. 90.

capabilities in Iran during the 1970s. A few days later, on November 20, Turner's unhappy assessment was confirmed when a tentatively phrased CIA report speculated that junior officers and enlisted men in the Iranian army "presumably are more responsive to Khomeini's Shi'a message," but offered no hard numbers or analysis of the implications of this development. As to Khomeini's political leanings, the CIA considered the cleric anti-Communist, but reasoned, again without providing evidence, that his movement "may be susceptible to Communist and radical penetration."[32]

Brzezinski composed a directive requesting a joint State-CIA review of U.S. political reporting on Iran, and at the same time sent a memo to Carter complaining about the quality of political intelligence more generally. On November 11, Carter replied in a handwritten note to "Cy, Zbig and Stan" (Vance, Brzezinski, and Turner), directing them to improve political intelligence capabilities. The note leaked to the press, embarrassing the administration and turning the government's debate over the quality of its intelligence into a public one.[33]

While Washington debated the quality of intelligence, tensions rose in Iran. By early November, strikes in the petroleum industry and by civil servants were costing the country $60 million a day. Prime Minister Sharif-Emani's reconciliation efforts came to nothing, and he resigned on November 5 after anti-shah demonstrators rampaged through Teheran setting fire to buildings. The shah ordered the military to restore order, and placed the country under military rule. An eleven-member cabinet headed by the armed forces chief, General Gholam Riza Azhari, quickly arrested several prominent public figures and business leaders, and ordered striking oil workers to return to their jobs. Most did return, but the calm was brief. Late in November, workers in major cities heeded a call by Shi'a leaders for a one-day strike. From Paris, Khomeini then called for an indefinite strike.

By November 9, Ambassador Sullivan had finally accepted that the shah might have to go. In a long cable entitled "Thinking the Unthinkable," he argued that this was the last chance for the shah. If the military government failed, the United States should anticipate the collapse of the shah and begin "to examine some options which we have never before considered relevant."[34] He identified the integrity of the armed forces as the key factor

---

32. Intelligence Memorandum, "The Politics of Ayatollah Ruholla Khomeini," November 20, 1978, DNSA "Iran," document no. 1778.

33. *Washington Post*, November 12, 1978; Vance to William Sullivan, November 17, 1978, DNSA "Iran," document no. 1754.

34. For Sullivan's account of this message, see Sullivan, "Dateline Iran: The Road Not Taken," *Foreign Policy* (Fall 1980), pp. 179ff. The passages quoted from the cable are from Sick, *All Fall Down*, pp. 81 and 83, respectively.

in post-shah arrangements, but otherwise his cable had more questions than suggestions. In the short run, the United States had no choice but to continue trusting the shah and the military, but "if it should fail and if the shah should abdicate, we need to think the unthinkable at this time in order to give our thoughts some precision should the unthinkable contingency arise."

Precht and his colleagues at the State Department were coming to a similar view about the shah. Their willingness to contemplate what Precht called "a soft landing, using the shah to effect some kind of transition," gained them a reputation as "anti-shah." They differed from their colleagues in the embassy, however, by placing some faith in the moderate-left National Front to mount a credible government. As Sullivan puts it, "we in the embassy did not agree. We did not think they had any constituency. We thought they would be rolled over by the revolution."

Precht and his colleagues had "no one to carry their arguments from the State Department to the White House," according to Sick. "They became frustrated and angry and were reduced to a form of guerrilla warfare to try to get the word out." At one point in early November, for instance, Precht and his colleagues, concerned over Zahedi's growing influence, sought to discredit him in Brzezinski's eyes. In a cable to the U.S. embassy in Teheran, they said that Zahedi favored military action by the shah. Ambassador Sullivan responded predictably that the shah had rejected Zahedi's advice. However, the exchange of messages had little evident effect on Brzezinski.[35] This state of affairs continued even after late November, when the SCC created—as it had done for other crises—a "mini-SCC," chaired by Brzezinski deputy David Aaron, to serve as the focal point for policymaking at the senior staff level.

Precht reflected on the difficulty at the State Department of knowing what was afoot at the White House:

> The White House got copies of all our cables and reports, but we never got copies of NSC reports or the little notes they'd put on top of the president's copies. We never got to see what they said. I guess that's the privilege of the president's staff...but I never saw any of them. So you don't know what's going into the White House decisionmaking apparatus, you don't know how what you're saying is being perceived, which makes it very difficult.

In December 1978, the administration turned to the first of a series of high-level "outsiders" for help—George Ball, a lawyer and investment

---

35. Sick, *All Fall Down*, p. 72.

banker who had been undersecretary of state for Kennedy and Johnson and who was famous for having opposed escalation in Vietnam. Suggested to Carter by Secretary of the Treasury Michael Blumenthal, Ball had "reluctantly concluded that the shah was on the way to a great fall and that, like Humpty-Dumpty, his regime could not be put together again." He had expressed that view to private New York gatherings in September and October.[36]

Sick, assigned by Brzezinski to serve as Ball's aide, first met Ball on December 1. Ball's incisive questions over four hours convinced Sick that "Ball would produce some fresh insights about the situation but that they would not be what Brzezinski wanted to hear."[37] Indeed, Brzezinski would later observe: "One should never obtain the services of an 'impartial' outside consultant regarding an issue that one feels strongly about without first making certain in advance that one knows the likely contents of his advice."[38] Ball conducted his review from Washington, having "learned from our Vietnam experience how dangerous it can be when travel is substituted for thought.... My sudden appearance in Teheran would merely provide new documentation for those attacking the shah as subservient to America."[39]

Meanwhile, events in Teheran began to unfold with alarming speed. December 2 marked the beginning of the holy month of Moharram, watched with apprehension in both Teheran and Washington. Demonstrations involved hundreds of thousands, and several times ran out of control; in Teheran and Isfahan, demonstrators were killed. Strikes by oil workers reduced production to record low levels and fed the flight of capital from Iranian banks.

In these circumstances, casual remarks by Carter at a breakfast meeting with reporters caused a sensation in the world press, and plunged the shah into deep depression. When asked if the shah could ride out the crisis, Carter replied:

> I don't know. I hope so. This is something that is in the hands of the people of Iran.... We personally prefer that the shah maintain a major role in the government, but that is a decision for the Iranian people to make.[40]

---

36. George W. Ball, *The Past Has Another Pattern: Memoirs* (New York: Norton, 1982), p. 456.

37. Sick, *All Fall Down*, p. 104.

38. Bill, *The Eagle and the Lion*, fn. 64.

39. Ball's report, his meeting with the president, and his worries about the state of U.S. policymaking are described in his memoirs, *The Past Has Another Pattern*, pp. 458–462.

40. *New York Times*, December 9, 1978.

For Carter, the remark may have been little more than a statement of American principles. But to Iranians, both government and opposition, who were accustomed to examining any official remarks out of Washington for hints of a change in policy, it was taken as an indication that the United States intended to dump the shah. A stream of clarifications and restatements issued over the following days in Washington could not change that reading.

Ambassador Sullivan saw more and more of the shah as the shah debated how to restore order. On December 12, the shah told Sullivan that, in view of Khomeini's popularity, he saw three options: form a national coalition; surrender to the opposition, leaving a regency council in charge; or form a military junta to put down the opposition with force. The shah was pessimistic about all three options. Sullivan held to the lines of his cable a month earlier, urging the shah to continue negotiations with the moderate opposition, especially the National Front. Sullivan resisted State Department suggestions that he play a more visible political role in Teheran; he still believed that maneuvering behind the scenes would be more effective, and he feared that activism would only make the United States more of a target.

On the same day—December 12—that Sullivan met with the shah, Ball submitted his report to the president. The report concluded that the shah's regime "is on the verge of collapse." It argued:

We must make clear that, in our view, his only chance to save his dynasty (if indeed that is still possible) and retain our support is for him to transfer his power to a government responsive to the people.

In view of "growing discontent, particularly among junior officers," any attempt to use the army to restore order was doomed to fail; the army would disintegrate. The challenge was to provide a mechanism for the shah to transfer power without discrediting the recipient as the shah's own creature. To that end, Ball suggested a "Council of Notables," perhaps fifty Iranians carefully chosen to represent all opposition groups except the extreme left. The council would not be a government, but it would choose one. The SCC met to discuss the Ball report on December 13, and the next day Ball met with Carter. Although the president agreed with much of Ball's diagnosis, he said he could not accept the proposal for a council: "I cannot tell another head of state what to do."

In the meantime, another experienced official had weighed in. Energy Secretary James Schlesinger was a former secretary of defense and director of the CIA who had known the shah for some time. He shared Brzezinski's view that the collapse of the shah would be a strategic disaster for the

United States. He had lobbied the president's closest advisers—Chief of Staff Hamilton Jordan, Press Secretary Jody Powell, and White House Counsel Charles Kirbo—to send a high-level emissary to Teheran to buck up the shah and underscore U.S. support.

At Ball's December 14 meeting with the president, Carter raised this idea, and proposed sending Brzezinski as an emissary. Ball was strongly opposed, for the same reasons he himself had decided not to go to Iran: an emissary would immobilize the shah entirely and make all his subsequent actions appear to be results of instructions from the United States. Ball denounced the idea of sending a special emissary to the shah as the "dumbest" foreign policy idea he had ever encountered in government service.[41] Carter heeded Ball's advice.

Ball was distressed by the state of policymaking in Washington, and he confided his worries to Secretary of State Vance, an old friend. He found:

> ...a shockingly unhealthy situation in the National Security Council, with Brzezinski doing everything possible to exclude the State Department from participation in, or even knowledge of, our developing relations with Iran, communicating directly with Zahedi to the exclusion of our embassy, and using so-called back channel [CIA] telegrams of which the State Department was unaware.

Vance replied that Brzezinski had promised to stop using the back channel and said angrily that he would again try to put a stop to it.

Ball's report did convince the president that the Iranian crisis was acute. On December 16, Carter sent Ambassador Sullivan a message of concern and listed questions about conditions in Iran to raise with the shah. When Sullivan met with the shah two days later, the shah said he hoped to install a government of national unity—headed by Gholam Hussein Sadiqi, with whom he had just met—within two weeks. To Sick, reading the account of the meeting in Washington, the plan reflected the shah's ignorance of what was going on in his country. A nationwide strike was underway and the military was visibly coming apart, yet the shah was bargaining as he had for months, making marginal concessions but unwilling to share real power.

In the week before Christmas 1978, Precht at State and Sick at the NSC each reached the conclusion that the shah's collapse was imminent. At the time neither knew of the other's thinking: such was the lack of cooperation

---

41. Ball, *The Past Has Another Pattern*, pp. 436–440.

between State and the NSC. On December 19, Precht sent a lengthy memorandum to Ambassador Sullivan and Assistant Secretary of State Saunders. The chances of the shah surviving, he wrote, were minimal, and the United States should take steps to protect its interests in the transition to an Iran without the shah. He, like Ball, suggested a council of notables, although he had not known of the Ball proposal. Precht's cover letter candidly reflected his own frustration: "I have probably confided more than I should to a piece of paper, but I doubt I have much of a future anyway."[42]

Two days later Sick pulled his boss, Brzezinski, out of a White House Christmas party to tell him that the embassy in Iran had just cabled: Iranian Cabinet Chief General Azhari had been relieved of his military command after suffering a heart attack. That, Sick believed, marked a critical turning point. He returned to his office to put his thoughts on paper. Unless an effective government was established within two weeks, he wrote, "the shah and his dynasty are going to be swept away." The talks with Hussein Sadiqi were a waste of time; the United States should press the shah to make a dramatic move quickly. A military regime would not work, Sick reckoned, because the military was too divided and because there was no political framework for military action.

Neither Precht's warnings nor Sick's produced a change in policy. At the White House, Brzezinski did not share Sick's view that Iran was at the point of crisis. On December 21, Sullivan was instructed to continue supporting the shah's negotiations with Sadiqi.

Events soon validated the warnings. A wave of strikes shut down the oil industry entirely by December 27. With only one week's reserves of gasoline and heating oil, the government announced rationing plans. Street demonstrations reached a crescendo the same day: cars burned, merchants abandoned their stores, and tear gas filled the air. Conditions in Iran produced front-page headlines in the *New York Times* on December 28 and 30. The second *Times* story reported tellingly that "there was no air of crisis in the Administration." The administration did, however, order a carrier task force to leave the Philippines for possible deployment to the Persian Gulf.

On December 29, the shah named opposition leader Shahpour Bakhtiar to head a new civilian government, and on the first day of 1979 Bakhtiar announced an ambitious reform program aiming at a "socially democratic society." U.S. officials watched especially closely whom Bakhtiar would appoint as minister of war. He asked General Fereidoun Jam, who had lived in exile for years after a dispute with the shah over

---

42. Sick, *All Fall Down*, p. 121. Sick's own conclusions are described in the footnote, ibid., p. 119.

using the military to repress domestic dissent and who had the respect of the Iranian military. But after a meeting with the shah, Jam refused the job.

The refusal was a severe blow for Bakhtiar, for it suggested that his government was merely a front for the shah. Ensuing events only confirmed that image. For example, Jam had refused to become the minister of war because the shah refused to relinquish full control over the military; had concluded that the Bakhtiar government would not have enough real authority to govern.

By New Year's Day 1979, even Brzezinski acknowledged what now looked inevitable, that the shah would have to leave Iran if the new government were to have any hope. The United States pressed the shah to agree to a plan of Bakhtiar whereby the Shah would depart as soon as a new government was installed, but the shah demurred. On January 2, he told Ambassador Sullivan that he would leave for a rest but only after law and order had been restored, in words implying that he expected the Bakhtiar government to fail at that task. The shah then debated aloud his two remaining options—the "iron fist" or a regency council—but vacillated visibly. Sullivan left the meeting convinced that the United States would have to apply strong pressure to force a decision by the shah.

The National Security Council met the next day, January 3, in Washington. Its participants, who had earlier been reluctant to conclude that the shah was on the way out, now were reluctant to push him. Some feared that his departure would alarm neighboring states; others that it would plunge Iran into civil war. Charles Duncan, the acting secretary of defense, suggested sending General Robert Huyser, deputy commander of U.S. forces in Europe, to Iran with the mission of trying to keep the Iranian military together and assuring them that American assistance would continue as planned. Huyser's qualifications for the assignment were open to question: he admitted that he had never heard of Khomeini before April 1978, and he believed that "if Iran becomes an Islamic Republic, it would eventually end up in the Communist camp."[43] Nevertheless, he agreed to go to Teheran.

In parallel, the president sent a message to the shah through Sullivan. Carter supported the Bakhtiar government and pledged continuing American support for stability in Iran. He also approved suggesting to the shah that he form a regency council and then leave Iran. Sullivan reported from Teheran that the shah would welcome an invitation to come to the United States, and Carter replied within twenty-four hours with a detailed

---

43. Bill, *The Eagle and the Lion*, fn. 71.

offer to have the shah and his entourage accommodated at an estate near Palm Springs, California.[44]

Several weeks earlier, with the shah's departure appearing imminent, Ambassador Sullivan had begun to take steps according to his "Thinking the Unthinkable" telegram of November 9. He took it that he had authorization to take these steps because the State Department had given him no contrary instructions. In his words, "through telephone intercepts, we learned that [Mehdi] Bazargan and the Ayatollah Beheshti enjoyed the support of the Ayatollah Khomeini and would probably emerge as the leaders of the new government" after the shah relinquished power. Accordingly, the embassy sought agreement with them about ground rules under which the Iranian military, purged of some of its members, might remain intact. Sullivan also thought it critical to discuss in advance with Khomeini the transition to Bakhtiar, which Sullivan regarded as no more than a fig-leaf covering the shah's departure.

Sullivan discussed this plan with Vance on a secure telephone, fearing that any classified cables he sent would, if the NSC staff disagreed with them, "appear, almost verbatim, in the *New York Times*."[45] Vance and Sullivan agreed on terms of reference for an emissary to Khomeini, and Vance chose as emissary Theodore Eliot, inspector general of the Foreign Service, a former ambassador to Afghanistan who was fluent in Farsi. They set January 6 as the date for the mission to Khomeini.

The White House first heard of the scheme on the eve of the president's departure for Guadeloupe on January 4 to attend a long-planned summit of Western leaders. Brzezinski, skeptical in any case, insisted that the plan be discussed first with the shah. When Sullivan did so, the shah listened "gravely and without enthusiasm," but voiced no objection.[46] Vance called Carter in Guadeloupe, who consulted Brzezinski and then decided to defer a decision until he returned to Washington. Sullivan, out on a perilous limb, recalled that his "anguish could not have been more complete" when he heard of the postponement.

Nearly a week later, on January 10 in Washington, the president rejected the plan after passionate argument among his senior advisers. Sullivan responded with a fervent plea for reconsideration, calling the decision "insane," an "irretrievable" error. This was too much for Carter, who asked Vance to "get Sullivan out of Iran." Vance convinced the president that changing ambassadors in mid-crisis would be a mistake, but Sullivan's credibility with the White House was gone.

---

44. William H. Sullivan, *Mission to Iran* (New York: Norton, 1981), p. 231.

45. Sullivan, *Mission to Iran*, p. 181.

46. Ibid., pp. 223–224.

On January 11, the "mini-SCC" met again. Taking notes, NSC official Sick observed a "remarkable consensus" develop that Khomeini would not pose a great threat, because the National Front and other moderates in the opposition, such as Bazargan's Liberation Movement, would actually lead the country. In any case, the U.S. foreign policymakers believed, Khomeini probably would not make major changes and surely would not undo the popular portions of the shah's modernization. The obstacles to stability were the shah and his designated prime minister, Bakhtiar.[47] Troubled by this analysis, Sick wrote a memo to Carter summarizing the meeting and questioning its conclusions. Sick saw the National Front as aging and divided. He believed Khomeini would create an Islamic republic that would "make the shah look very good indeed by comparison."

That same day, January 11, Ambassador Sullivan and General Huyser, who had arrived in Iran to coordinate strategy with the Iranian military, met with the shah to discuss his departure, which by now was presumed. After the meeting, Huyser reported to Defense Secretary Brown. His conversations with Iranian officers had left him with the impression that, while the military wanted Bakhtiar to succeed, they had prepared contingency plans for a coup if he failed. Huyser's impressions spurred administration officials, particularly in the Defense Department, to refine options referred to as "A, B, and C." "A" was simply U.S. support for the Bakhtiar government; "B" involved limited U.S. military action to help the Bakhtiar government stay in power; and "C" was to back a military coup if public order collapsed.

Three days later, Huyser encouraged the Iranian military to establish contact with the religious leadership in order to clarify its intentions. By this time, he estimated desertions from the military at 500 to 1,000 per day. Those numbers, he reckoned, would not cripple a force that totaled 500,000, but he feared that Khomeini and his colleagues would see such a rate of desertion as evidence that their own victory was near. Ayatollah Beheshti, a key associate of Khomeini, told a U.S. Embassy officer that he did not fear a confrontation with the military, "since we control everyone below the rank of major."[48]

Also on January 14, Carter authorized a meeting in Paris between Warren Zimmerman, the American political counselor there, and Ibrahim Yazdi, who had represented Khomeini in the United States. The meeting was brief and amicable, mostly consisting of an exchange of prepared statements. Yazdi, citing coup rumors in Teheran, warned that if a military coup occurred, Iranians would believe it was the work of the United

---

47. Sick, *All Fall Down*, p. 138.

48. Ibid., p. 140.

States.[49] For their part, administration officials, especially Brzezinski, were eager to see "Option C" remain alive, for they believed that the threat of a military coup would buy time for Bakhtiar to engineer a constitutional solution. Sullivan concurred and drafted language along that line for Zimmerman's next meeting with Yazdi.

On January 16, 1979, the shah left Iran. His departure prompted noisy demonstrations. "Crowds cheered as statues of the shah and his father, Reza Shah, were toppled."[50] The first stop on his "well-deserved rest" tour was Egypt, where his host was President Sadat. He then planned to go to the United States, but ten days later changed his mind and accepted King Hassan's invitation to Morocco.

Zimmerman and Yazdi met again as the shah was leaving his homeland. Huyser had reported that the Iranian military was nervous about the possibility of Khomeini's return to Iran, fearing it would split the armed forces. Thus, following instructions, Zimmerman cited the threat of a military coup as reason to forestall Khomeini's return. The military had discussed a coup, he told Yazdi, but had deferred, at Huyser's urging. However, were Khomeini to return suddenly to Iran, the military's reaction would be unpredictable. Khomeini should neither return nor try to push the Bakhtiar government toward a collapse; rather, he should support the nascent dialogue between the government and religious leaders. Yazdi said he knew of no plans for Khomeini's imminent return. The two men met three more times in the following week, their conversation ranging over U.S. policy, the goals of the opposition, and relations between Iran and the United States, but with no tangible result.

Large-scale marches took place without violence in Teheran on January 19, but the Bakhtiar government was coming unglued. On January 20, Bakhtiar said that he would turn Iran over to the military if he could not consolidate his government; the new military chief of staff, General Gharabaghi, then threatened to resign lest he be part of a military takeover. Bakhtiar and Sullivan persuaded him to stay on. But not only was the government further weakened, the coup threat was becoming threadbare. The next week five air force personnel were arrested after taking part in a pro-Khomeini demonstration in Teheran.

When Zimmerman and Yazdi met for the last time on January 27, Yazdi delivered the first personal message from Khomeini to Washington. It said that the actions of Bakhtiar and the senior Iranian military were damaging Iran, the U.S. government, and the future of Americans in Iran. It threatened "new orders" bringing "great disaster" if that state of affairs continued.

---

49. The sequence of meetings is described in Sick, *All Fall Down*, pp. 142–143, 147.

50. AP, "Cairo Marks Shah's Flight from Iran," January 15, 1999.

Bakhtiar proposed to meet with Khomeini in Paris to discuss a constitutional solution, but Khomeini replied that he would attend only if Bakhtiar first resigned. Khomeini would then appoint him to the provisional government. Talks between representatives of the two men broke off after two days, and Bakhtiar said that he would not go to Paris. However, he also announced that Iranian airports would be opened for Khomeini's return.

Khomeini flew from Paris to Teheran on February 1, ending fourteen years of exile. Over a million people gave him a tumultuous greeting, and he immediately took up residence in a small Teheran school building. Soon after arriving, he rejected a plan crafted by Bakhtiar and Bazargan, leader of the Liberation Movement who was, in Sullivan's description, a "benevolent social democrat," for a popular referendum to choose between the monarchy and an Islamic republic. Khomeini continued to insist that Bakhtiar resign first, regarding both him and the regency council as creatures of the shah.

General Huyser returned to the United States on February 3. Briefing the president and other senior officials, Huyser painted a bleak picture. Iran was unstable, he said, and a Khomeini takeover would bring catastrophe: a drift to the left and eventual Communist takeover.[51] About what to do, the president's advisers remained divided, particularly over the role of the Iranian military. Huyser felt that the military should unequivocally support the Bakhtiar government until a new constitution was written, while Sullivan thought it better for the military to remain on the sidelines while the political groups contended. He thought the political outcome would be an Islamic republic that was democratically inclined.[52]

The division distressed the president, who had already lost all confidence in Sullivan. The final straw for the president came when, after the meeting with Huyser, a *Washington Post* story quoted "State Department officials" who did not expect the Bakhtiar government to last more than a few days.[53] Angered, Carter called in senior officials of the State Department and "laid down the law to them as strongly as I knew how."[54] He asked them to resign if they could not support his decisions, and threatened firings if the leaks continued.

After Huyser left Iran, Washington remained in contact with the Iranian military through General Philip Gast, chief of the Military

---

51. Jimmy Carter, *Keeping Faith: Memoirs of the President* (New York: Bantam Books, 1982), p. 449.

52. Carter, *Keeping Faith*, p. 449; Sick, All Fall Down, p. 151.

53. Sick, *All Fall Down*, p. 153.

54. Carter, *Keeping Faith*, p. 449.

Assistance and Advisory Group. Gast, like Huyser, communicated with Defense Secretary Brown daily on a secure telephone line. On February 9, he reported that fighting had begun, touched off by a television broadcast of Khomeini's return, between air force *homafars* (civilian technicians, whom the shah's government had forced to stay in low-paying jobs after their contracts expired) and Imperial Guards still loyal to the shah, at an airbase on the outskirts of Teheran. The fighting was quelled within hours but broke out again the next morning. A curfew was imposed on Teheran. Demonstrations and fires spread throughout the city.

In Washington, Brzezinski convened an emergency session of the SCC on the morning of February 11 to assess American influence over events and the safety of Americans still in Iran. American influence seemed to be rapidly approaching zero. Reports from Teheran indicated that Bakhtiar's whereabouts were unknown and that the military had withdrawn to their barracks. Although everyone at the meeting believed the military would not act, Brzezinski insisted that support for a military coup be presented as an option to the president. "If the military had the will and the capacity to take control of the situation," Brzezinski later wrote, "we should [have been] prepared to act like a major power and support them."[55]

When Carter called from Camp David, Brzezinski discussed "Option C" with him. As they spoke, a call came from General Huyser, who said Option C would not work without a major American commitment. From Teheran, Ambassador Sullivan reported that the military was in the process of making an accommodation with Bazargan and could not be counted on.[56] Reluctantly, Brzezinski concluded that the coup option was dead: "It was clear to me that we were faced with a fait accompli."[57] On February 11, 1979, Bakhtiar and the members of the Majlis (parliament) resigned. With Khomeini's backing, power passed to Bazargan, the man whom Sullivan had earlier predicted would be the first leader to emerge from the revolution.

Revolutionary fervor and anti-American zeal became increasingly intertwined, culminating on November 4, 1979, when a crowd of young Iranians stormed and occupied the U.S. Embassy in Teheran. Fifty-two Americans were held hostage for 444 days. Though Khomeini ordered the release of the hostages the day Carter was succeeded by Ronald Reagan, Iran and the United States would remain enemies from presidency to presidency thereafter.[58]

---

55. Brzezinski, *Power and Principle*, p. 391.

56. Sick, *All Fall Down*, p. 156.

57. Brzezinski, *Power and Principle*, p. 393.

58. For a recent survey by a former CIA analyst, see Kenneth Pollack, *The Persian Puzzle: The Conflict between Iran and America* (New York: Random House, 2005).

Chapter 5

The Philippines, 1983–1986: Arranging a Divorce

William E. Kline and James Worthen, with assistance from Kirsten Lundberg and Robert D. Johnson

On February 25, 1986, President Ferdinand Marcos fell from power after twenty years as leader of the Philippines. Throughout his tenure, Marcos had—despite evidence of corruption and despotism—received strong support from five U.S. presidents; in return, he had consented to the presence of two strategically vital U.S. military bases in the Philippines. Although his economy had floundered and he crushed political opposition, Marcos was friendly to the United States, which saw him as a bulwark against the threat of Communism.

As Marcos's power waned in the 1980s under the pressure of mass opposition demonstrations, however, U.S. policy was forced to change. President Ronald Reagan considered Marcos a personal friend, which only complicated the challenge for policymakers. From 1983 to 1986, the White House, the U.S. foreign policy establishment, and the intelligence community struggled, first to weigh the benefits and dangers to U.S. interests of continued support to Marcos, and then to manage a peaceful exit from power for a longtime U.S. client.

Background

The United States had strong political, economic, and military interests in the Philippines dating back to 1898, when it acquired the Philippines from Spain. The U.S. colonization served the needs of U.S. businessmen, who wanted a stopping-off point on the way to China, and U.S. military officers, who wanted a naval base in the Far East. The country's constitution was modeled on the U.S. Constitution, with a bill of rights that included freedom of the press and of religion. The Philippine constitution differed, however, in that it allowed the president to place the country under martial law if necessary.

The Philippines gained independence from the United States on July 4, 1946, but the two nations retained close military and economic ties. As of 1985, U.S. economic interests in the Philippines included some $2 billion in direct investments and total annual trade of about $4 billion. Nearly half the Philippines' foreign debt, which ran to approximately $26 billion, was owed to U.S. banks.

After independence, the Philippines had remained home to two strategically important U.S. military bases. Clark Air Base was headquarters for the 13th Air Force, which directed air operations in the Western Pacific. Clark was also a logistics center for the Western Pacific and was regarded by the U.S. military as essential to operations in the Pacific and Indian Oceans. Subic Bay Naval Base was the largest U.S. naval installation outside the United States. It supported carrier battle groups and provided logistics for Seventh Fleet operations in the Pacific and Indian Oceans. Both to compensate for use of these bases and to equip the Philippine government to play the part of ally if called upon, the United States provided both economic and military aid.

During the 1980s, U.S. defense planners pointed out that it would cost several billion dollars to relocate Clark and Subic Bay bases, and that was just for the move; operating costs for bases like Clark and Subic Bay would be substantially higher almost anywhere else in the world. In the spring of 1983, U.S. Ambassador Michael Armacost and Philippine Ambassador to the United States Benjamin Romualdez negotiated a review of the U.S. base agreement, which resulted in creating a prospect that the United States could retain the bases indefinitely, with the Philippine government receiving increased amounts of both economic and military aid. Marcos could display this accord as evidence of his excellent standing in Washington.[1]

Marcos had begun his public career with election to the Philippine House of Representatives at the age of 32. He served continuously in the House and the Senate until he ran for president. Marcos was first elected president of the Philippines in 1965 and then again in 1969; he ruled under martial law from 1972 to 1980. In 1981 Marcos had the Philippine constitution amended to strengthen the presidency, by lengthening the term from four to six years and providing for multiple presidential terms. In June 1981, Marcos was elected to a six-year term by an implausible 86 percent of voters. U.S. Vice President George Bush attended Marcos's inauguration and received wide press coverage with his remark: "We love your adherence to democratic principles and to democratic processes."[2]

But Bush was not the first representative of a U.S. administration to be charmed by Ferdinand and Imelda Marcos. In 1969, then-Governor of

1. *New York Times*, June 1, 1983.
2. *Far Eastern Economic Review*, July 7, 1981, p. 15.

California Ronald Reagan attended the opening of a cultural center in Manila as President Nixon's special representative. From that point on, the Marcoses considered that they had a special personal relationship with the Reagans; Nancy Reagan is reported to have felt the same way. President Nixon made a visit to Manila in 1969; President Ford in 1975; and Vice President Mondale in 1978. Marcos's warm relations with Washington peaked in September 1982 when the Philippine president paid a state visit to the United States.

Marcos's long rule came, however, at a price. His regime's corruption and financial mismanagement contributed to enormous economic problems. To maintain his hold on power, Marcos dismantled political institutions and permitted no real opposition to develop. Moreover, Marcos used his political power to enrich himself. By the early 1980s, this record of abuses encouraged the growth of an insurgency. The New People's Army—the military wing of the outlawed Philippine Communist Party—gained strength and began to show signs of posing a real threat to Marcos and his regime.

As Marcos started to feel in jeopardy, he isolated himself. He came to rely on fewer and fewer advisers, until he relied on just three people: his wife Imelda, Chief of Staff General Fabian Ver, and his crony Eduardo "Danding" Cojuangco. Contributing to his sense of vulnerability, Marcos in the early 1980s felt the first symptoms of the illness that would eventually become a political concern as well: the constitution provided that, upon the president's death, power would pass to a fifteen-member executive committee, which Marcos himself had appointed. Imelda Marcos was a member of the committee, and she clearly wished to succeed her husband. That prospect frightened many, inside and outside the Philippines, who suspected Mrs. Marcos of plotting with General Ver to reimpose martial law.

Elections to the National Assembly scheduled for May 1984 were seen by many, therefore, as an opportunity. They hoped to curb the aspirations of Marcos's inner circle, and at the same time to stem the threat from the Communist insurgency, by electing a legislative body with a commitment to democracy and reform. One of those who determined to make the elections meaningful was a long-time Marcos opponent who had been in exile in the United States for the three previous years.

The Aquino Assassination

Liberal Party leader Benigno Aquino was Marcos's most credible political opponent. Aquino's opposition to Marcos was longstanding. In 1972, when Marcos had declared martial law, Aquino was a senator, party leader, and Marcos's chief rival for the Philippine presidency. Shortly after proclaiming martial law, Marcos arrested Aquino and other political opponents. Aquino spent most of the next eight years in detention, sometimes in solitary confinement. A military tribunal convicted him of providing arms to Communist guerrillas and plotting the murder of a local politician. Aquino was sentenced to death in November 1977, although the death sentence was a ploy, intended to intimidate others; Aquino instead went back to jail.[3] In May 1980, however, Marcos had commuted the sentence and allowed Aquino to go to the United States for medical treatment of a heart problem.[4]

Now, Aquino wanted to take part in the National Assembly elections. He knew his return was dangerous; Imelda Marcos herself had warned him, at her husband's request, that he risked assassination if he came back.[5] Aquino took these warnings seriously, putting on a bullet-proof vest as his flight touched down in Manila on August 21, 1983. Shortly after landing, Aquino was escorted from the plane by three uniformed Philippine soldiers, while all other passengers were told to remain in their seats. Seconds after Aquino left the plane, shots rang out. By the time the press got to the scene, Aquino's body and that of his alleged assassin lay on the tarmac near the stairway leading from the aircraft door. Aquino had been shot in the back of the head at close range.

The Philippine government announced that a gunman had killed Aquino and that the military had killed the assassin. Few Filipinos believed that: it was generally assumed that Marcos had ordered the murder, or that it had been carried out by the military in the belief that he would approve. At the time, the public knew that Marcos was ill, despite official explanations that he had disappeared from public view to write a book.[6] Speculation grew that Imelda Marcos and General Ver had arranged to kill Aquino while Marcos was incapacitated. In any event, the

---

3. During the period of his detention, Marcos and Aquino met more than once and Aquino was sometimes allowed to leave prison for up to three weeks at a time. Immediately after the sentencing, a Marcos aide assured U.S. officials that Aquino would not be killed. See Stanley Karnow, *In Our Image: America's Empire in the Philippines* (New York: Random House, 1989).

4. While in the United States, Aquino had undergone heart surgery; he also held fellowships at MIT and Harvard.

5. *Far Eastern Economic Review*, September 15, 1983, p. 15. The day after the assassination, Marcos said that his wife had warned Aquino not to return.

6. It was not generally known that two weeks earlier, Marcos had secretly undergone a kidney transplant. See Raymond Bonner, *Waltzing With a Dictator* (New York: Times Books, 1987), p. 340. Marcos had lupus erythematosus, a degenerative disease that appears in cycles and attacks kidneys, lungs, and heart. He kept his condition so secret, says Stanley Karnow, that "he stymied even the CIA, and a Filipino surgeon who dis-

assassination provoked an unprecedented demonstration of anti-Marcos sentiment. Aquino's body lay in state at his birthplace in the northern province of Tarlac, where during two days more than 50,000 mourners paid their respects. He was buried in Manila, and more than a million people lined the streets for the funeral.

The day after the assassination, in his first public appearance in three weeks, Marcos appeared on television to condemn it. Noting that Aquino had been warned not to return, he suggested that only the Communists would benefit from the killing. Marcos named a commission of his political allies to investigate the assassination, but two months later he was forced by protests from Filipinos and from the international community to disband it and name a second, more neutral, panel. Respected jurist Corazon Juliano-Agrava agreed to chair the investigation.

Aquino had taken pains to make preparations with U.S. diplomats for his return to the Philippines. Then-Ambassador Armacost described a "fascinating and well-written document" in which Aquino detailed the threat posed in the Philippines by the growing strength of the Communist New People's Army. Aquino had argued that "time is running out" on any chance that moderates could succeed Marcos; he had warned that political initiative would pass before long to the Communist rebels.[7] Aquino had asked for decisive U.S. action to head off this outcome, contending that "American officials tend to downplay the extent of America's leverage in influencing Philippine affairs." Aquino had also paid calls on several members of Congress, including Senator Sam Nunn (D-Ga.) and Representative Stephen Solarz (D-N.Y.), before embarking for Manila.

Immediately after the assassination, the U.S. State Department released a statement condemning the murder as a "cowardly and despicable act," adding:

> The U.S. government trusts that the government of the Philippines will swiftly and vigorously track down the perpetrators of this political assassination and bring them to justice and punish them to the fullest extent of the law.[8]

The term "political assassination" was a considered one; some of Marcos's henchmen were spreading the story that Aquino had been

---

cussed it with an American reporter was mysteriously murdered." Karnow, *In Our Image*, p. 402.

7. Embassy Manila to Secretary of State, March 11, 1983, Digital National Security Archive, "The Philippines, 1965–1986" (hereafter DNSA "Philippines"), document no. 2339; Embassy Manila to Secretary of State, March 14, 1983, ibid., document no. 2341.

8. *New York Times*, August 22, 1983.

murdered by a longtime personal enemy. Ambassador Armacost paid a condolence call on Aquino's widow, Corazon, and attended the funeral mass. Representative Solarz, chairman of the House Subcommittee on Asian and Pacific Affairs, was traveling in the Far East at the time, and he returned to the Philippines to visit the Aquino family.

Aquino's assassination galvanized both American diplomats and the intelligence community. Even before the assassination, the State Department had been referring to a "winter of discontent" in the Philippine islands. Now the embassy in Manila foresaw a "distinctly unfavorable" situation in which "the Communists are likely to be the chief gainers."[9]

Meanwhile, the intelligence community released a Special National Intelligence Estimate (SNIE) in September 1983 which judged that Aquino's death would "permanently change Philippine politics" and would leave the domestic political environment unsettled for some time. These new conditions, along with concerns about Marcos's health, led the estimate's drafters to give the Philippine president only a 60 percent chance of completing his term of office, which would expire in 1987.[10]

These were strong words from analysts who had believed Marcos to be, above all, a survivor. The Philippines had long suffered the conditions that elsewhere produced political upheaval: authoritarian rule, insurgent movements, skewed income distribution, government corruption, and a sagging economy beset with financial problems. Yet these factors had been insufficient to topple the Marcos government.

Intelligence analysts had, however, begun in 1982 to document the role Marcos played in the country's declining political stability. That year, an intelligence estimate cited growing opposition to the president and accumulating domestic problems. The drafter later recalled that the message was not a popular one in some quarters:

> Most of the U.S. mission in Manila took offense at the estimate. There was a feeling that the paper might complicate the [U.S. military] base negotiations that were coming up in 1983. So the desire to strike a deal [on the bases] might have gotten in the way of an objective assessment of the deteriorating conditions there. This

---

9. Embassy Manila to Secretary of State, April 4, 1983, DNSA "Philippines," document no. 2361; Embassy Manila to Secretary of State, August 22, 1983, ibid., document no. 2492.

10. William Kline was allowed to see various special national intelligence estimates and other intelligence community assessments, and excerpts were declassified for him. The documents themselves have not been declassified. Where reference is made in this case to an estimate or other product of the intelligence community, the reference, unless otherwise noted, comes from Kline.

was the beginning of a parting of the ways between most Philippines analysts and the Reagan Administration.[11]

At the time of Aquino's assassination, Marjorie Niehaus was an analyst for the Congressional Research Service.[12] Niehaus was convinced that the Philippine government had ordered the assassination.[13] She had numerous contacts among Philippines specialists in and out of the U.S. government, and in the Philippines embassy in Washington. Unlike the majority of intelligence community analysts, who were unable after Aquino's death to identify any viable opposition leaders, Niehaus argued that there were several, including Aquino's widow, Corazon. Niehaus was also early to state her belief, even before the assassination, that Marcos represented the principal obstacle to reform and development in the Philippines. She later said:

It was in April 1982, when I saw Marcos being interviewed on TV. Marcos was clearly dissembling. From then on, I felt it was not in our interest to have him as leader of the Philippines. Not that I was for pulling the rug out from under him then. But it was not in our interest to have a man who was so authoritarian, who was becoming more militaristic. That would be working against us in the long run, because he was creating a climate in which the [Communist] insurgency would thrive.

A senior manager from the CIA's Directorate of Intelligence (DI), which produces intelligence assessments, later noted that "we at CIA agreed with Marjorie about Marcos":

At issue was whether Marcos had already destroyed the viability of the opposition. We believed that the moderate opposition was cut from the same cloth as the Marcos inner circle, while Marjorie was a firm supporter of this group, and even had personal friends in it. She saw Marcos as black and the opposition as white; we felt the situation was grayer than that.[14]

---

11. Kline interview with a senior DI analyst. Later quotations or paraphrases attributed to "senior DI analyst," unless otherwise attributed, come from this interview. The person is not to be confused with "senior DI manager" or CIA "Philippines analyst"; these are three different interviewees.

12. A year later, Niehaus became the Philippines analyst in the State Department's Bureau of Intelligence and Research (INR).

13. Kline interview with Marjorie Niehaus. All further quotations from Niehaus not otherwise attributed are from this interview.

14. Kline interview with a senior DI manager. (See note 11 above.)

The September 1983 estimate began a period of intense analytic focus on the Philippines. From Aquino's death in August 1983 to early 1986, the intelligence community would disseminate thirty-six separate studies on political or military issues in the Philippines and twelve on economic issues to policymakers around Washington. Six of these were Special National Intelligence Estimates. The topics most frequently addressed during these months were the state of the insurgency, the Philippine debt crisis, and Marcos's health. All three were viewed as serious problems. For example, the agency reported that the Philippines owed far more to foreign creditors than it admitted, and questioned the ability of the Marcos government to continue debt repayments.

By and large, policymakers felt well-served by intelligence reporting on the Philippines in 1983–1986. One contributing factor was that key CIA officers in Washington enjoyed good contacts with policymakers at the assistant secretary level. The director of the CIA's Office of East Asia and the National Intelligence Officer (NIO) for East Asia both had productive working relationships with Paul Wolfowitz, assistant secretary of state for East Asian and Pacific Affairs, as well as with Assistant Secretary of Defense Richard Armitage and the National Security Council (NSC) staff.

The CIA was thus able to bring its intelligence judgments directly to policymakers at the assistant secretary level, while the assistant secretaries from time to time sought intelligence judgments from their CIA colleagues on pending policy issues. In addition, policymakers received official reports from the U.S. Embassy in Manila. Armitage later called Ambassador Stephen Bosworth's reporting "terrific," and also praised the defense attaché's "tactical reporting on the armed forces of the Philippines."[15]

The secretaries of state and defense read comparatively little intelligence on the Philippines, relying instead on oral briefings. Secretary of State George Shultz listened to former Ambassador Armacost, by then serving as under secretary of state, while Secretary of Defense Caspar Weinberger relied heavily on Armitage and on Admiral William Crowe, commander in chief of U.S. forces in the Pacific who, in 1985, became chairman of the Joint Chiefs of Staff.

Rigged Elections?

In the weeks following the Aquino assassination, the number of anti-Marcos demonstrations soared. Opposition leaders learned they could

---

15. Kline interview with Richard Armitage. All further Armitage quotations not otherwise attributed are from this interview.

challenge the dictator and he could not respond.[16] Thus emboldened, opposition to Marcos became more open. Anti-Marcos rallies were held even in Makati, the wealthy business district of Manila. The assassination was turning the Philippine middle class, which had strongly supported Marcos when he took office, against him. On September 21, the eleventh anniversary of the imposition of martial law, a large demonstration in Manila erupted into violence, leaving eleven dead. At that point Marcos threatened the reimposition of martial law. The Catholic Church, a focal point of the opposition, urged calm.

As the public demonstrations grew, Marcos turned more and more to the military, and particularly to Chief of Staff General Ver, for support. Ver was generally regarded by Filipinos, including many in the military, as a Marcos crony with few qualifications for the position he held. He and Marcos were cousins and came from the same hometown. As an enlisted man, Ver had served as a driver for Marcos when he was senator. Ver rose through the ranks and, as a captain, was Marcos's adviser on military affairs. Ver subsequently became commander of the National Intelligence and Security Authority and of the Presidential Security Command. In 1981, Marcos gave Ver his fourth star and named him chief of staff of the armed forces.

The Philippine military had become a Marcos stronghold. After imposing martial law, Marcos expanded the armed forces from 58,000 to over 200,000 and placed the Philippine constabulary under their control. Marcos increased the military budget, although much of the money went into the pockets of senior officers, many of whom acquired lucrative business contracts and some of whom were believed to be selling arms to the insurgents. This arrangement served Marcos, however, by purchasing their loyalty.

The public outrage in the Philippines during the fall of 1983 prompted the U.S. intelligence community to release in January 1984 an even more pessimistic review of the Philippine political situation. It announced that the Aquino assassination and ensuing developments had "fundamentally altered [the intelligence community's] assessment of prospects for the Marcos regime and political instability in the Philippines over the longer run." Marcos, it argued, would be increasingly vulnerable on a wide variety of issues as time passed, while his ability to control the debate over policy alternatives would decline. Still, it refused to rate his chances of staying in power through the end of his term at any worse than even.

---

16.   Kline interview with Stephen Bosworth. Bosworth became U.S. ambassador to the Philippines in June 1984. All quotations from Bosworth not otherwise attributed are from this interview.

The U.S. intelligence community concluded that while the assassination may not have been ordered by the incapacitated Marcos, it was probably carried out by the Philippine army on his behalf and almost certainly at the direction of Ver. Analysts believed Marcos must have been concerned about Aquino's return, while Imelda Marcos and Ver were probably fearful that the opposition leader would rally the many elements disenchanted with Marcos.

The January 1984 estimate rated the chances for an orderly and democratic transition as low. If the government could orchestrate the murder of the principal opposition leader, this suggested that there was little hope for less established political figures to succeed in a lawful election.

By the end of 1983, the number and size of Philippine public protests had decreased, although anti-Marcos sentiment remained high. In early 1984, attention turned to the National Assembly elections scheduled for May 14. All 183 elected seats (the other seventeen Assembly members were appointed by the president) were being contested by Marcos's New Society Movement (KBL) and by the opposition umbrella group, the United Nationalist Democratic Organization (UNIDO).

Marcos controlled most of the media and the government apparatus, and had a virtually unlimited supply of money. "Guns, goons, and gold," which had traditionally played a large role in Philippine elections, were no less present in the campaign for the May 1984 vote. Marcos was conscious, however, of the need to appear to be conducting the election in an impartial manner, if not for the sake of Filipinos, then at least to impress the avowedly watchful U.S. government. Marcos therefore permitted the National Citizen's Movement for Free Elections (NAMFREL), an independent group of poll watchers, to oversee the elections.

Pre-election forecasts were that UNIDO would win about twenty Assembly seats. The U.S. Embassy, however, thought that estimate was low. In its confidential report back to Washington, it noted that Marcos had failed to "rise above the careful calculation of a partisan politician determined to protect his personal power and the interests of his immediate and extended family."[17] The best the Embassy thought Marcos could hope for were results that, "like most things Filipino," reflected a "shade of gray."

Much to the surprise of the pollsters and of Marcos, UNIDO won fifty-nine seats, nearly one-third of those contested. The opposition's good showing was due in no small part to NAMFREL, whose presence substantially reduced cheating by the ruling party. The results represented a huge

---

17.   Embassy Manila to Secretary of State, March 3, 1984, DNSA "Philippines," document no. 2737.

defeat for Marcos and the KBL, even though it retained control of the Assembly. The election also sent a clear message to Marcos about just how unpopular the KBL and he himself had become. Seeking to salvage something from the elections, Marcos cited the opposition results as evidence of the fairness of Philippine elections. In fact, NAMFREL officials estimated that the opposition would have won a near-majority of the seats in a fair election.

Marcos quickly established, however, that compromise was not on his mind. On June 30, 1984, he named a new cabinet consisting entirely of Marcos loyalists. Imelda Marcos was named governor of Metro-Manila. On July 23, the new Assembly convened, with Marcos apparently in good health and prepared to conduct business as usual.

In October 1984, the Agrava Board investigating Aquino's assassination released its findings. The majority report (four of five members) said that a high-level military conspiracy was responsible for the murder. Ver, two other generals, six lower-ranking officers, sixteen enlisted men, and one civilian were cited as "indictable for the premeditated killing of Aquino."[18]

Immediately after the report was issued, Marcos named a special prosecutor to bring charges. General Ver was placed on leave of absence, and Lieutenant General Fidel Ramos, a competent officer respected by his peers and junior officers, was appointed chief of staff. The following January the special prosecutor filed charges against those blamed in the majority report.

Marcos's problems were not only political. The Philippine economy had deteriorated rapidly after the Aquino assassination, as political uncertainty provoked massive capital flight. In October 1983, the peso was devalued 21 percent against the dollar; in June 1984, it sank a further 22 percent. In late 1983, the Philippine government was forced to suspend principal payments on its foreign debt. Around the same time, the discovery that the Philippine Central Bank had been falsifying estimates of its foreign debt burden caused a loss of confidence in the Central Bank. In 1984, economic growth went down by 5.5 percent; in 1985, it declined another 4 percent. Real per-capita GNP was estimated to have declined more than 15 percent over those two years. Meanwhile, neighboring countries in the Pacific were experiencing substantial economic growth.

Political uncertainty was not the only cause of the economic deterioration. Marcos's policies were also to blame. After the imposition of martial

---

18. Justice Agrava issued a minority report which charged that Aquino had been killed in a military plot, but that only one general (not Ver) and six enlisted men were involved. Karnow, *In Our Image*, p. 404.

law in 1972, Marcos had centralized both political and economic decision-making. Sectors of the economy were placed under the control of various political loyalists, destroying incentive and leading to a decrease in productivity. That in turn resulted in fewer jobs and lower wages. Corruption was rife. Capital continued to flow out of the Philippines, as even Marcos himself deposited huge sums in foreign banks, where it was easier to hide wealth and interest rates were higher.

Under these conditions, the Communist-led New People's Army (NPA) grew dramatically. According to U.S. government estimates, the NPA surged from some 7,500 armed regulars in mid-1983 to approximately 16,500 by October 1985.[19] NPA regulars were operating in fifty-nine of the Philippines' seventy-three provinces, and battalion-sized units of approximately 500 men staged attacks against villages on Mindanao. Assistant Secretary of Defense Armitage told the House Subcommittee on Asian and Pacific Affairs that 20 percent of Philippine villages were "influenced or controlled by the CPP," the Communist Party–Philippines. In November 1985, Larry A. Niksch, an Asian specialist for the Congressional Research Service, concluded in a report for the Senate Foreign Relations Committee:

> At this stage of the insurgency, the Communist party is gaining strength and the Philippine government does not have an effective counter strategy. The CPP-led movement has developed to the point where it seems to have a credible chance of overthrowing the government within five to 10 years if present trends continue.[20]

In addition, since the 1960s the Moro National Liberation Front (MNLF) had led a Muslim rebellion in the southern Philippines, where one-third of the 12 million inhabitants of the southern island of Mindanao were Muslim. In 1983, the MNLF claimed 30,000 under arms and controlled 25 southern provinces.

Should Marcos Go?

Although the U.S. Congress was well aware of the strategic importance of the U.S.-Philippine relationship, the Aquino assassination triggered a

19. Larry A. Niksch, "Insurgency and Counterinsurgency in the Philippines," prepared by the Congressional Research Service for the U.S. Senate Foreign Relations Committee, S. Prt. 99–99 (Washington, D.C.: U.S. Government Printing Office [U.S. GPO], November 1988).

20. Ibid.

barrage of criticism of the Marcos regime. In the spring of 1984, the Senate Foreign Relations Committee, chaired by Senator Charles Percy (R-Ill.), began to take a critical look at the Philippines. In May, June, and July two Committee staffers, Frederick Z. Brown and Carl Ford, traveled extensively in the Philippines on a fact-finding mission. They reported to Percy that: "A disciplined, purposeful Communist insurgency with sophisticated political infrastructure and growing military capability countrywide has become a major threat to the Philippine democracy." Moreover, they found:

> There has been a profound loss of confidence in President Marcos and his ability to govern. The country's leadership is virtually bankrupt in terms of public confidence. There appears to be little popular expectation that the leadership will act for the good of the country as opposed to its own narrow interests.[21]

In the House, Congressmen Solarz's Subcommittee on Asian and Pacific Affairs recommended early in 1985 that military sales credits to the Philippines for that year be decreased from $50 million to $25 million and that economic aid be increased from the $95 million requested by the Reagan administration to $155 million. The subcommittee intended the changes to facilitate political, economic, and military reform and to demonstrate to the Filipinos that the aid was "not for the benefit of any particular leader or faction." The Senate Foreign Relations Committee added an amendment to the foreign aid bill to provide that future aid to the Philippines would depend on U.S. security interests and sufficient progress by the Philippine government in, among other things, guaranteeing free and fair elections and ensuring the prosecution of Aquino's assassin.

Meanwhile, the Executive Branch was conducting its own reassessment of the U.S.-Philippine relationship. The administration had already expressed its view about responsibility for the assassination: immediately after the Agrava Board findings were released in October 1984, the State Department had issued a statement urging Marcos to act on the majority report. In the fall and winter of 1984, the administration conducted a wholesale review of U.S. policy toward the Philippines.

The NSC staff issued the terms of reference of the 1984 policy reviews, but the State Department drafted the new policy paper (taking, as was usual, the lead in the formation of policy toward the Philippines). Assistant Secretary of State for East Asian and Pacific Affairs Wolfowitz coordinated U.S. policymaking on the Philippines at the time. He worked

---

21. *New York Times*, September 30, 1984.

closely with Assistant Secretary of Defense for International Security Affairs Armitage and with NSC Asian specialists Gaston Sigur and Richard Childress. The group, which also included Armitage deputy James Kelley, met regularly on Monday afternoons, according to Armitage, and the officials were unusually compatible.

> The reason was there was not a professional Foreign Service officer among us; we were all political appointees except Dick Childress, who was a military officer. We all had the same views about supporting the President…. By background, we were all Asian specialists…so you had people who were doing the policymaking who had experience, who knew the players personally, who had no bureaucratic conflicts.

As a rule, after a policy decision was agreed at the assistant secretary level, the director of the State Department's Office of Philippine Affairs was assigned to draft instructions to the embassy in Manila, or a public statement if one was involved. Those drafts then went for approval through the hierarchy at the State Department and the Department of Defense (DOD). If a major policy shift was involved, the draft was sent via the national security assistant for the president to endorse.

The policy review resulted in a January 1985 policy directive signed by President Reagan. An early draft of the directive had leaked to the press and was reported in the *Washington Post* and the *Far Eastern Economic Review*.[22] The directive identified Marcos as "part of the problem," but "also necessarily part of the solution." According to the directive, "we need to be able to work with [Marcos] and to try to influence him through a well-orchestrated policy of incentives and disincentives to set the stage for a peaceful and eventual transition to a successor government whenever that takes place." It was not the administration's intent, according to the directive, to remove Marcos or destabilize his government. Rather, the United States hoped to revitalize democratic institutions, to dismantle crony capitalism, and to restore professional, apolitical leadership to the Philippine military.

The intelligence community was not so sanguine about continued support of Marcos. In February 1985, Carl Ford became National Intelligence Officer for East Asia. As a Senate Foreign Relations Committee staffer, he had traveled to the Philippines the summer before, and had characterized the Marcos leadership as "virtually bankrupt." Now, as NIO, Ford questioned the generally positive tone of Reagan's policy direc-

---

22. *Far Eastern Economic Review*, March 21, 1985; *Washington Post*, March 12, 1985.

tive. The analyst who had then been chief of the CIA's Directorate of Intelligence branch handling the Philippines later recalled that:

> Ford early on wondered what kind of intelligence the administration could be getting if they thought so highly of Marcos. So right off he asked to see the stuff we had been publishing. I think he was persuaded that we had been properly pessimistic.[23]

Ford set out to put his mark on the next Special National Intelligence Estimate (SNIE) on the Philippines. "Ford had an 'in-your-face' style," the Philippine analyst recalled, "and he may have felt that this would be the time to take a more confrontational posture and send a tougher message downtown." Published in March 1985, the SNIE declared that "the end of the Marcos era in the Philippines is rapidly approaching." Because Marcos's survival in office seemed to guarantee that problems in the Philippines would worsen, the assessment suggested that "the best solution for both Philippine and U.S. interests would be for Marcos to voluntarily step down or announce his intention not to run again," an event the Estimate nevertheless rated as highly unlikely. It expressed the view that the succession, however it played out, would be fraught with difficulties for the United States.

The State Department's Bureau of Intelligence and Research (INR) took a somewhat more optimistic view of a post-Marcos environment and felt strongly enough to dissent formally by appending a footnote to the March estimate. Perhaps reflecting Marjorie Niehaus's views, it assessed the Philippine moderate opposition as stronger than did the rest of the intelligence community. If Marcos were to leave the scene under existing succession arrangements, INR judged, the next government would probably be a popular and broad-based regime with a significant chance of instituting reforms, restoring legitimacy to Philippine political institutions, and gaining control over the insurgency.

Not only were there differences of opinion between the intelligence and policy bureaucracies about the deteriorating situation in the Philippines, there were also unresolved disagreements within the Executive Branch agencies. Some State Department officers believed the new January 1985 policy directive did not go far enough: that Marcos was the problem and could not be part of any solution. Morton Abramowitz became assistant secretary of state for intelligence and research in early 1985. He argued that there would be no improvement in the Philippines

---

23. Kline interview with CIA Philippines analyst.

until Marcos left the scene. Some officers in State's Bureau of East Asian Affairs agreed.

President Reagan, however, did not want to abandon Marcos. The NSC and the Defense Department shared his view. Even those arguing that Marcos should step down also realized that for the United States to withdraw support from Marcos with no identifiable alternative would be hazardous. U.S. stakes in the Philippines were high; the removal of Marcos risked bringing to power someone less favorably disposed to the presence of U.S. military bases. Assistant Secretary of Defense Armitage later explained that the new policy took a middle road "to put pressure on Marcos," because "he could either make the reforms or he would fall. We felt it was not a good thing to immediately put him in a corner." One reason the NSC and DOD were loath to push Marcos too far too fast, according to Armitage, is that the opposition had not coalesced. Moreover, the position of the Philippine military was far from clear, although "we were aware from intelligence of the grumblings in the army, and the splits and the divisions."

The NSC's Childress has acknowledged that the State Department "wanted to move faster...[but] we knew the influence that Ronald Reagan had with Ferdinand Marcos, and that was going to be the last step in the drama. We had to preserve that influence until the right moment." Childress said:

> The president also wanted to give Marcos every chance in the world to reform, rather than take the final step [of leaving]. It became a matter of timing, a matter of making sure there was a Philippine solution, that it was developed and the Filipinos could feel they carried out the revolution, not the Americans.[24]

In line with the new policy, Wolfowitz, Armitage, and Childress visited the Philippines in January 1985, urging reform. They were followed by Under Secretary of State Armacost, Pacific Forces Commander Admiral William Crowe, and CIA Director William Casey.

Marcos: "Part of the Solution?"

In the meantime, CIA intelligence analysts were continuing to evaluate whether the Marcos government was serving U.S. interests. The senior DI

---

24. Kline interview with Richard Childress. All further Childress quotations not otherwise attributed are from this interview.

manager recalls that these assessments switched in 1985 from a confrontational to a more nuanced tone. Using language that unmistakably echoed the policy dispute taking place downtown, a July 1985 assessment noted that DI analysts "are divided over whether or not Marcos can be part of the solution."

Some analysts, it said, argued that Marcos was in the strongest position to begin the process of "redirection" himself. But "the alternative view—and the one that has been gaining strength as conditions in the Philippines deteriorate—is that a continuation of Marcos's rule ensures the worst of all possible outcomes." The assessment avoided coming down firmly on one side or the other, saying that Marcos's performance over the coming year would settle the question. It did note, somewhat delicately, that "the burden of proof must rest on those who argue that he can be part of the solution."

In reality, there was virtually no dissent among the analysts: the vast majority believed that Marcos should go. According to a senior DI analyst:

> The real split, of course, was between the analysts and the Administration. We were struggling to get the Reagan people to see us as objective. If we came down strongly on the side of Marcos being an obstacle—as we did in most of our assessments— they wouldn't read [our reports]. So we judiciously posed and fully examined both views of the problem, hoping to get the White House to read the analysts' views and see that they were coherent and respectable.

Adding to the problem was the perception that Director of Central Intelligence (DCI) Casey, a member of the Reagan inner circle, was a Marcos supporter. "I think he began to come around," says the senior DI officer, "when he first saw the evidence of military complicity in Aquino's killing. But he probably continued to believe for some time that U.S. interests were best served with Marcos in power."

A couple of months later, CIA analysts produced another memorandum, this one devoted to the likelihood that the Marcos government could suddenly collapse. Subtitled "Thinking the Unthinkable," this paper, too, waffled enough to avoid offending Marcos's friends. "We didn't think sudden collapse was unthinkable," recalls the CIA Philippines analyst, by then the Philippine branch chief, "but we knew many people downtown did."

The CIA paper argued that it would be a mistake to discount the possibility of "an abrupt catastrophic turn of events in Manila," and it went on to list some potential "shocks" that might, singly or in combination, precipitate such an outcome. One of these potential shocks was "heavy-handed manipulation of the pre-election process...or flagrant fraud during elections." Any "collapse," the analysis concluded, would confront the United States with a confused and rapidly changing environment requiring quick decisions about which individuals or groups to support.

In the meantime, Marcos was not responding to U.S. encouragement to effect reform, in part because he was confident of Reagan's backing. Instead, in the spring of 1985 he charged publicly that the American media and certain elements in the U.S. government were out to get him. His resentment was spurred by revelations in the *San Jose Mercury News* that the Marcoses and several of their associates had made secret investments in the United States. Manila newspapers picked up the story.

At the same time, the opposition was gaining ground. Speculation on the succession was voiced ever more openly in media such as *Veritas*, a Catholic newspaper, and a radio station of the same name. UNIDO sought to impeach Marcos for his secret overseas investments, but lost the battle in the Assembly, controlled by the ruling party. Filipinos also reacted angrily when it became clear that General Ver and others on trial for Aquino's murder would be acquitted; the three-judge panel threw out the Agrava Board's testimony on the grounds that it violated the rights of the accused. The public assumed that Marcos was behind the court decision.

To get a better reading of the situation, Senate Foreign Relations Committee staffer Frederick Brown visited the Philippines again in August 1985. After a lengthy conversation with Marcos, he reported:

> Marcos believes that he enjoys the support of the highest levels of the Executive Branch of the U.S. government. Congress may huff and puff, assistant secretaries may harass him, and some of his military aid monies may be transferred to economic aid, but in the end, he believes, the U.S. will not pull its support. Many Filipinos seem to share this view.[25]

Given the circumstances, Reagan adopted a suggestion from Wolfowitz and Ambassador Stephen Bosworth that he send Senator Paul Laxalt (R-Nev.), a friend and confidant, to see Marcos. Laxalt was to communicate that Reagan personally was concerned "about the general political instability in the Philippines," and to assess whether Marcos still enjoyed the support of the people.[26] Reagan was also worried about the decline of the Philippine economy and the Communist insurgency.

---

25. *New York Times*, October 27–28, 1985.

26. Paul Laxalt, "My Conversations with Ferdinand Marcos," *Policy Review*, Summer 1986. Unless otherwise noted, all Laxalt attributions come from this source.

Bosworth and other administration officials had already communicated these concerns to Marcos, but the Philippine president seemed to suspect these messages were not coming from Reagan, but rather had been invented by the State Department.

Laxalt visited Manila in October 1985. His message was that congressional pressure to abandon Marcos was building. Marcos listened but, according to Bosworth, who attended, gave no sign that he intended to pursue reform. Laxalt came away from the meeting feeling that Marcos was isolated and that this distorted his perception of his country's problems and of his own popularity. Laxalt says he encouraged a proposal Marcos had floated in August of holding an early election instead of waiting for the scheduled one in 1987 (a subject that DCI Casey had also discussed with Marcos). But now Marcos told Laxalt he saw no need for an early election.

Later in October, Laxalt telephoned Marcos from the United States and again advanced the idea of moving up the election. Laxalt suggested that an announcement be made on David Brinkley's television news show for maximum effect in the United States. On November 3, Marcos implemented Laxalt's suggestion in all its details, but this meant that the announcement on U.S. television came in the middle of the night in the Philippines, one more indication that Marcos was out of touch with his own people. In yet another sign of how isolated Marcos had become, he kept his decision to call for an early election secret even from his close political advisers.[27]

On December 1, Marcos set the election date for February 7, 1986.[28] He knew the opposition was badly divided and no doubt hoped it would be unable to agree on a candidate in time. He may also have had an inkling of the coup plot developing in his defense ministry.

A group of Philippine Army officers, led by two colonels in Defense Minister Juan Ponce Enrile's security unit, had begun in mid-1985 to plot a coup.[29] The group, called "Reform the Armed Forces Now Movement" (RAM), planned at first to make their move after the originally scheduled presidential election in May 1987, on the assumption that Marcos would rig the election and that they could capitalize on the public reaction. But

27. Paul Wolfowitz, "A U.S. Strategy for Philippine Snap Elections," November 5, 1985, DNSA "Philippines," document no. 3047.

28. On "This Week with David Brinkley" of November 3, 1985, Marcos had announced that the election would be held January 17, but he then changed the date in response to opposition protests that the first proposed date allowed scant time to organize.

29. Lewis M. Simons, *Worth Dying For* (New York: William Morrow, 1987), p. 257–277.

after the early election announcement, the coup plotters also changed their schedule, to February 23, 1986.

They planned to storm the presidential palace, remove Marcos, and install a civilian-military leadership to include Enrile, Lieutenant General Ramos, and Corazon Aquino. The plotters reportedly hoped to invite Cardinal Jaime Sin, a cleric highly esteemed by Philippine Catholics, to join the new government, along with other respected military and political figures.

The United States was well aware of the coup plot. According to Armitage,

> The defense attaché's office had very good contacts in the RAM group. The U.S. policy was to discourage the RAM from premature coups. They were talking about moving here, moving there. We were not so much disinclined to moving as we were about the timing. We did not believe the armed forces of the Philippines [as a whole] had come to the decision that they should not support Marcos.

The intelligence community judgment on the prospects for a coup was divided. Many felt that, although members of RAM were unhappy with Marcos, most senior Philippine military officers would side with Marcos if RAM attempted a coup. At least one Philippines analyst, however, believed RAM could stage a coup and win the support of many senior military officers disenchanted with Marcos.

Congress decided, once again, to send its own representatives to the Philippines to test the waters. The Senate Select Committee on Intelligence (SSCI) wanted first-hand reports. Committee staffers visited the Philippines in August 1985 and reported to Chair David Durenberger (R-Minn.). They acknowledged some threat from the Communist-led NPA, but identified as well "a significant noncommunist, moderate opposition," although it was not united. As for Marcos, the staffers concluded that "the Marcos government is unlikely to pursue the changes necessary to stop the economic hemorrhaging, to slow or halt the insurgency, or to heal the major lesions that are infecting the political process."[30]

From October 1985 to January 1986, the Senate Foreign Relations Committee held three hearings to review administration policy on the Philippines. The committee's purpose was to focus public attention on the developing crisis, to strengthen the possibility of democratic change there, and to bring direct pressure to bear on Marcos. On October 30, Assistant

---

30. *New York Times*, November 2, 1985 (derived from an interview with Durenberger).

Secretary of State for East Asian and Pacific Affairs Paul Wolfowitz told the Foreign Relations Committee:

> The Philippines, one of our closest and most important allies, is in deep trouble. U.S. interests of immense importance are at risk. But it is not just our interests that are at stake. A Communist takeover in the Philippines would threaten the stability of the East Asian region and the many countries in it who have so successfully focused their efforts in recent years on economic development.

Wolfowitz also said that Washington had "made unmistakably clear to the Philippine leadership, to President Marcos personally, the need for early dramatic progress toward fundamental reforms if we are to be of effective assistance."[31] Two weeks later, Wolfowitz told Solarz's House Subcommittee on Asian and Pacific Affairs that Marcos's decision to call a snap election opened up the possibility of reviving the democratic process in the Philippines. But he noted that the election also raised the stakes for Marcos. If Filipinos did not see the elections as fair, Wolfowitz warned, there would be "increased polarization of Philippine society, a deepening of the present crisis and further growth of the Communist insurgency."[32]

In another administration comment on the elections, Under Secretary of State Armacost told the World Affairs Council on December 5 that "we can confidently expect to work with any government produced by an election which Filipinos consider to have been fair and honest." Armacost then noted that Congress had passed a resolution affirming the U.S. interest in fair and free elections.[33] In December, the Solarz subcommittee began an investigation into the Marcos property holdings in the United States. Testimony revealing the vast extent of those holdings received wide press coverage in the United States and in the Philippines.

The reports by the Senate Select Committee on Intelligence and two reports by the Foreign Relations Committee staff received wide circulation in Congress and in the Executive Branch. The staff reports contained broad assessments of the situation in the Philippines: they commented on the strength of the NPA, the economy, and the capability of the democratic opposition, and included assessments of Marcos as a leader and of his staying power. However, the reports and their relevance were quickly overtaken by events.

---

31. *New York Times*, October 31, 1985.

32. *New York Times*, November 13, 1985.

33. *New York Times*, December 6, 1985.

On December 2, 1985, Corazon Aquino announced her candidacy as head of the Laban Party. On December 11, Aquino and Salvador Laurel, head of UNIDO, agreed to run for president and vice president respectively on a joint ticket.

Despite the emergence of Aquino as a viable candidate, Marcos remained confident of victory. He campaigned hard on the Communist threat to the Philippines, arguing that Aquino would be incapable of dealing with the NPA insurgency. Marcos frequently recalled his World War II experiences, claiming to have been a guerrilla fighter against the Japanese and to have been wounded five times. Just two weeks before the election, however, Marcos's war record was called into question by an American historian who had discovered in official files that the U.S. military had never accepted Marcos's claims. This revelation received wide coverage in the Philippine media, as well as the *New York Times* and *Washington Post*. Marcos's health also became a campaign issue.

Aquino's campaign appearances drew huge crowds, generally much larger than Marcos's. Aquino pulled no punches. At an appearance in Manila on January 23, 1986, she answered Marcos's frequent charge that she had no experience: "I concede that I cannot match Mr. Marcos when it comes to experience," she said. "I admit that I have no experience in cheating, stealing, lying or assassinating political opponents."[34]

But despite the evidence of her growing support in the Philippines, Aquino's standing with President Reagan was uncertain. Secretary of State George Shultz recalled that both Reagan and Chief of Staff Don Regan were strongly influenced by a personal account of Aquino from *New York Times* columnist A.M. Rosenthal. After a trip to Manila, Rosenthal reported that he found Aquino to be an "empty-headed housewife" and a "dazed, vacant woman." Rosenthal's words, said Shultz, left a "deep and lasting impression" on Reagan and Regan.[35]

A month before the election, the U.S. intelligence community produced an estimate evaluating the likelihood of various outcomes. Noting Marcos's determination to stay in power, it predicted "substantial padding of the votes...to ensure his victory" or the use of some legal or quasi-legal stratagem to annul any unwelcome results. It also judged that the combination of a "sweeping" Aquino victory and strong U.S. pressure could induce Marcos to acquiesce in his defeat, after bargaining for conditions

---

34. Foreign Broadcast Information Service (FBIS) report of Agence France Presse, Hong Kong, January 23, 1986.

35. George Shultz, *Triumph and Turmoil: My Years as Secretary of State* (New York: Charles Scribner's Sons, 1993), p. 617.

and guarantees. The estimate's bottom line, however, was that Marcos would probably remain in power and things would get worse.

Most public polls predicted a Marcos victory. By January, the election was too close to call. On the eve of the vote, the intelligence community predicted that Aquino would actually win, but that Marcos would rig the results in his favor. This view was shared by the State Department.[36]

On January 30, 1986, President Reagan announced that a bipartisan U.S. observer delegation would visit the Philippines during the election. Foreign Relations Committee chair Senator Richard Lugar (R-Ind.) and Congressman John Murtha (D-Pa.) were to co-chair the delegation. This decision reflected Secretary of State Shultz's growing ability to overcome Reagan's reluctance to take any action that might be interpreted as anti-Marcos. State had argued that "just as the opposition cannot afford to boycott, we cannot afford to stand by and watch, and then wring our hands."[37]

In a statement announcing the delegation, drafted in the State Department and endorsed by DOD and the NSC, Reagan asserted that "Filipinos believe in elections—as long as they are fair—to resolve their political differences." He continued: "A free and fair election, if also followed by a genuine reform effort in the economic and security areas, will assist the Philippines along a path of growth, prosperity and stability that will benefit the whole region." Under such circumstances, Reagan declared, "we should consider, in consultation with the Congress, a significantly larger program of economic and military assistance for the Philippines for the next five years."

The U.S. observer delegation went to the Philippines and fanned out to witness voting at various polling stations. Many observers reported fraud by the ruling party. Many people were kept from voting and, although the vote count may have been accurately recorded at polling places, the totals made public in Manila suggested that the figures were being changed to insure a Marcos victory.[38] Moreover, the official vote count was suspiciously slow. Under U.S. pressure, Marcos had agreed to allow NAMFREL to tabulate the election results along with COMELECL, the official Committee on Elections. While NAMFREL reported results showing Aquino ahead, COMELECL began to delay the returns; it finally reported Marcos the winner with 53 percent of the vote.

---

36. Armacost to Shultz, November 7, 1985, DNSA "Philippines," document no. 3053.

37. Wolfowitz, "A U.S. Strategy for Philippine Snap Elections."

38. Kline interview with Larry Niksch. Niksch was a member of the observer delegation, and all further statements about the delegation not otherwise attributed are from this interview.

The day after the election, members of the U.S. observer group met in Manila to discuss their findings. That evening some thirty COMELECL workers left their posts and sought refuge in a nearby church, then declared that the government was rigging the results to insure a victory for Marcos. Members of the U.S. observer team visited the COMELECL defectors and found convincing evidence of fraud. Apparently, however, that was not enough to persuade President Reagan.

"The Time Has Come"

On February 10, 1986, Reagan told a group of regional editors that he was reserving judgment on the charges of fraud in the Philippine election. "In spite of all these charges," said Reagan, "there is at the same time the evidence of a strong two-party system now in the islands." Reagan hoped Marcos and Aquino "could come together to make sure the government works."[39] The following day, after Lugar had returned to Washington and reported to Reagan, the White House released a statement: "Since no definite judgment has yet been rendered by either the official or the unofficial Filipino electoral bodies, it is not appropriate for the United States to make such a judgment at this time. Nonetheless," the statement continued, "it is a disturbing fact that the election has been flawed by reports of fraud, which we take seriously, and by violence. This concerns us because we cherish commitment to free and fair elections and because we believe the government of the Philippines needs an authentic popular mandate in order effectively to counter a growing Communist insurgency and restore health to its troubled economy."[40]

Despite the strong evidence that fraud had occurred, the White House feared that condemning Marcos outright might cause him to declare the election null and void. After hearing Lugar's report, Reagan decided on February 11 to send Ambassador Philip Habib to assess the situation. Habib, a veteran of the Foreign Service upon whom Reagan had previously relied for sensitive fact-finding missions, set off to meet with Marcos, Aquino, and other Philippine leaders.

Meanwhile, at a news conference on the evening of February 11, Reagan replied to a question by saying: "we're concerned about the violence that was evident there and the possibility of fraud, although it could have been that all of that was occurring on both sides. But at the same time, we're encouraged by the fact that it's evident that there is a two-party

39. *New York Times*, February 11, 1986.
40. *New York Times*, February 13, 1986.

system in the Philippines and a pluralism that I think would benefit their people."

This statement pleased Marcos—who had the videotape played over and over on Manila television—and infuriated Aquino. "I would wonder at the motives of a friend of democracy who chose to conspire with Mr. Marcos to cheat the Filipino people of their liberation," Aquino said. Ambassador Bosworth assured Aquino that the U.S. position was evolving and urged her to be patient, hinting that she would be pleased with the eventual U.S. position. Bosworth also had to calm down his own staff, several of whom were upset by the president's statement.

On February 14, the Catholic bishops of the Philippines issued a statement condemning fraud in the election and urging nonviolent resistance. Two days later, the pope supported the bishops' statement. Meanwhile congressional pressure was mounting. On February 13, Senator Sam Nunn, ranking Democrat on the Armed Services Committee, and Senator Robert Dole, Republican majority leader, both declared that the United States should cut off aid to the Philippines if Marcos was elected by means of fraud.

The intelligence community was also providing considerable evidence to the NSC staff and the president that the ruling party had engaged in fraud on a massive scale. "We found hundreds of abuses by the Marcos people and only a couple by Aquino. But it was a real struggle to get the Reagan people to accept the scale of the Marcos abuses," recalls a senior DI manager.

To try to get its message accepted by the administration, intelligence officers bent over backwards to identify and examine any allegations of fraud by the Aquino forces. By this point, they had learned they had no choice but to follow such a strategy. Even the normally sympathetic Secretary of State Shultz had cautioned the intelligence community against "getting involved in policy views, especially in hotly contested issues."[41] The resulting assessments, in the view of the senior DI manager, went to extremes in seeking to appear balanced: "We wanted to be as credible and thorough as possible so we couldn't be accused of prejudice. Luckily we had very good information to work with, and we made our point that Aquino might have won a fair ballot."

On February 15, the White House signaled a major U.S. policy shift with a statement which said: "It has already become evident, sadly, that the elections were marred by widespread fraud and violence perpetrated largely by the ruling party." The evidence of fraud was so strong, the statement said, "that the election's credibility has been called into question."

---

41. Shultz, *Triumph and Turmoil*, p. 619.

The "fraud-on-both-sides" line had been dropped. Moreover, unnamed White House officials told the press that Marcos should start planning for the succession.

Two days later, Senator Lugar publicly called on Marcos to resign. A moderate-conservative Republican, Lugar was generally regarded as unprejudiced on the Philippines, and his statement clearly had an impact on thinking at the White House. Testifying before the Senate Budget Committee on February 18, Secretary of State Shultz acknowledged that Marcos supporters had carried out "fraud and violence on a systematic and widespread scale." On February 19, the Senate passed a resolution 85 to 9 condemning the election as fraudulent.

The following day, the House Foreign Affairs Committee voted unanimously to stop all military aid to the Philippines. Wolfowitz and Armitage had privately urged Solarz to avoid this step, arguing that it might cause the collapse of Philippine military morale. Solarz responded that Marcos was the best thing the Communists had going in the Philippines.

Despite public acknowledgement by the White House that Marcos had cheated to win the election, a major problem remained. COMELECL, the official body, said Marcos had won the election; NAMFREL maintained that Aquino was the victor. Aquino had announced a policy of non-violent resistance to bring Marcos down, and she seemed to enjoy widespread voter support. Marcos had several options: he could claim the presidency and wait Aquino out; he could declare the election null and void; or he could legally declare martial law and rule by decree. At this juncture, the military coup plot was revealed.

The coup was still scheduled for February 23. On or about February 20, Marcos learned of the plot.[42] He arrested some of the lower-ranking officers involved, who upon interrogation implicated Defense Minister Enrile. On February 22, Enrile learned that Marcos was aware of the coup. Fearing arrest, he convinced Lieutenant General Ramos to join him at Camp Aguinaldo in Metro Manila to announce that they had broken with Marcos. "I remember coming in on a weekend to do a 'spot commentary'," recalled the Philippine analyst, now the DI's Philippine branch chief. "I wrote that Marcos was finished."

Enrile and Ramos called a press conference at Camp Aguinaldo, where Enrile declared that "Marcos did not really win this election." He described how he had stolen votes for Marcos in Cagayan Province. Enrile and Ramos did not mention the coup plot. Marcos later did, and actually had one of the junior officers testify on television. But by that time no one

---

42. Simon, *Worth Dying For*, p. 270.

any longer believed the Philippine president. Most Filipinos believed the coup report was just another Marcos trick.

Corazon Aquino meanwhile was in Cebu City, some 400 miles south of Manila. At Enrile's request, Aquino phoned supporters and asked them to go to Camp Aguinaldo. While Aquino was in Cebu City, the United States offered her sanctuary on a U.S. Navy ship. She declined the offer.

After Enrile and Ramos announced their break with Marcos, the press arrived, and reports from Camp Aguinaldo were soon televised around the world. Aquino supporters flocked there, especially after Cardinal Sin urged them to show their support for the Marcos defectors. At one point, an estimated one million Filipinos surrounded the base. Ramos moved his military headquarters to Camp Crame, adjacent to Camp Aguinaldo.

As popular support for the rebels mounted, it became clear that any military suppression would involve many civilian casualties. Marcos had the force available. In fact, General Ver, who had been acquitted of Benigno Aquino's murder the previous December and reinstated as chief of staff, reportedly ordered a marine general to attack Camp Crame, and at one point a column of marine tanks, armored personnel carriers, and trucks of armed marines drove toward Crame. The column stopped just short of the people surrounding the camp, however. In the front rows of the Aquino supporters stood clergy and young women bearing flowers. When the marines stopped, the crowd cheered and the young women pressed flowers on the marines.

Within hours of the press conference by Enrile and Ramos, the White House reacted, saying, "these statements strongly reinforce our concerns that the recent presidential elections were marred by fraud, perpetrated overwhelmingly by the ruling party, so extreme as to undermine the credibility and legitimacy of the election."[43] On February 23, Habib returned to Washington, where he reported that Aquino had won the election "and deserved our support. Marcos was finished, and we ought to offer him asylum in the United States."[44]

Secretary of State Shultz called a meeting at his house late that morning, a Sunday, attended by Secretary of Defense Weinberger, Chairman of the Joint Chiefs of Staff Admiral Crowe, National Security Assistant John Poindexter, and the CIA's deputy director for intelligence, Robert Gates. All present unanimously shared the view that Marcos must go. Shultz decided to present that judgment to President Reagan at an NSC meeting that had already been scheduled for that afternoon.

---

43. *New York Times*, February 23, 1986.

44. Karnow, *In Our Image*, p. 415.

At the NSC meeting, Shultz observed that it was clear Marcos could no longer govern the Philippines. Secretary of Defense Weinberger supported Shultz. The only person present who argued for continued support for Marcos was Chief of Staff Donald Regan, who had not been at Shultz's house that morning. Regan may have been raising objections that he believed the president shared, but in the end Reagan, not without sadness, agreed with Shultz: Marcos would have to go.[45]

After the NSC meeting, Reagan approved a White House statement saying, "The President appealed earlier to President Marcos to avoid an attack against other elements of the Philippine armed forces." Noting that the United States was providing military assistance to the Philippines, the White House statement went on: "We cannot continue our existing military assistance if the government uses that aid against other elements of the Philippine military which enjoy substantial popular backing. The president urges in the strongest possible terms that violence be avoided as Filipinos of good will work to resolve the ongoing crisis."[46]

Ambassador Bosworth read this statement to Marcos before it was made public.[47] Marcos was incredulous. "What do you mean I can't use force?" Marcos asked Bosworth. "I'm the duly elected president of the Philippines. This is a military coup attempt. It's a revolution."

Bosworth then recommended to Wolfowitz that the White House state unmistakably that the time had come for a transition to a new government. Bosworth felt strongly that the word "transition" must be in the statement. That would make it crystal clear to Marcos that he must go. The State Department drafted a statement and sent it to the NSC staff. On Monday February 24, the White House issued a statement that concluded: "Attempts to prolong the life of the present regime by violence are futile. A solution to this crisis can only be achieved through a peaceful transition to a new government." Bosworth conveyed this statement to Marcos and it was then made public.

Still clinging to the hope that Reagan would save him, Marcos telephoned Senator Laxalt and asked him to discuss with Reagan the idea of Marcos sharing power with Aquino. Laxalt checked with Reagan and then telephoned Marcos back to say Reagan felt it would be "impractical and undignified" for Marcos to share power, then said that Marcos would be welcome to live in the United States. Marcos asked whether, in Laxalt's view, he should step down. Laxalt replied, "I think you should cut and cut

---

45. Kline interviews with Robert Gates, Armacost, and Armitage.

46. *New York Times*, February 24, 1986.

47. Kline interview with Stephen Bosworth.

cleanly. I think the time has come." Marcos replied: "I am so very, very dis-appointed."[48]

At 9:05 p.m. on February 25, 1986, two U.S. military helicopters took Marcos, Ver, and their families from Malacanang Palace to Clark Air Base, from which the U.S. Air Force flew them to Guam and then to exile in Hawaii.

---

48. Laxalt, "My Conversations with Ferdinand Marcos."

Chapter 6

Iraq, 1988–1990: Unexpectedly Heading toward War

Zachary Karabell and Philip D. Zelikow,
with assistance from Ernest R. May,
Kirsten Lundberg, and Robert D. Johnson

In mid-1989, President George H.W. Bush attended a meeting of the National Security Council to discuss the final draft of National Security Directive 26 (NSD-26), which defined U.S. policy toward the Persian Gulf. Acknowledging that Saddam Hussein, the dictator of Iraq, had actually used poison gas and that he aspired to have biological and nuclear weapons, the document said that continued Iraqi development of such weapons might necessitate U.S. military action. Its emphasis, however, fell on "economic and political incentives for Iraq to moderate its behavior and to increase [American] influence."[1]

At the table was Richard Kerr, deputy director of the Central Intelligence Agency (CIA). To the meeting, Kerr brought a report that described Hussein as a brutal dictator who had murdered thousands of his own people, including large numbers of Kurds in the north. Given that NSD-26 hinged on the possibility that limited incentives might lead Hussein to moderate his behavior, Bush had a simple question: Could Hussein really change? Kerr had a simple answer: No.

Nonetheless, no one at the meeting dissented from the policy proposed in NSD-26. As one senior Defense Department official present at the meeting described it, "The consensus was—what did we have to lose?" Robert Gates, the deputy national security advisor, echoed this sentiment: "The general attitude was that this was an approach you had to try, to try to get him to mend his ways. But no one was particularly optimistic that it would succeed or that Hussein would change his spots."[2]

---

1. National Security Directive 26 (NSD-26), "U.S. Policy Toward the Persian Gulf," October 2, 1989, in Christopher Simpson, ed., *National Security Directives of the Reagan and Bush Administrations* (Boulder, Colo.: Westview Press, 1995), p. 896.

2. Zelikow interviews with a senior Defense Department official, who prefers not to be identified, and with Gates. All further quotations from "senior Defense Department official" or Gates, unless otherwise attributed, are from these interviews.

NSD-26 codified a policy of "constructive engagement" toward Iraq, a policy that had developed after the end of the Iran-Iraq War in 1988. U.S. policymakers hoped that Hussein, if offered agricultural credits and generous loan terms, might see reason to moderate human rights abuses and stop developing nuclear, chemical, and biological weapons. The policy of "constructive engagement" would be severely tested throughout the spring and summer of 1990 as the U.S. government struggled to form an appreciation of the self-isolated and unpredictable dictator in Baghdad.

Background

When George H.W. Bush became president in January 1989, he had already served as Ronald Reagan's vice-president for eight years. He inherited an approach to Iraq that had been carefully crafted over the previous decade; U.S. policy toward Iraq was a by-product of U.S. policy toward Iraq's neighbor, Iran, which had been an ally under the shah and then an enemy under the revolutionary leaders who came to power in 1979. The Reagan administration, which took office in 1981, deemed Iran a threat to regional stability and resolved on a policy of containment, aimed at preventing any increase in Iran's power or influence, using any and all allies, including possibly Iraq.

Iraq and Iran had a history of confrontation and Iraq's leader, Saddam Hussein, viewed the Iranian revolution as a golden opportunity. Hoping to take advantage of Iran's instability, Hussein invaded Iran on September 22, 1980. Later CIA assessments concluded that Hussein had made the decision to invade on an impulse the night before and with very little planning. The United States reacted passively to the invasion. Conservative Arab monarchies—including Saudi Arabia—actively endorsed Saddam Hussein's move. Hussein's aims were limited: he wished to gain full control of the Shatt al-Arab waterway, formed by the confluence of the Tigris and Euphrates rivers, which was Iraq's only outlet to the sea. The gamble failed, as Iranian resistance proved stiffer than expected. Iran eventually forced the Iraqis to retreat from southwestern Iran. By mid-1982, the Iranians had recovered their territory and had themselves invaded southern Iraq.

As the threat to Iraq grew, the United States began to establish closer ties to Baghdad. Soon Americans and Iraqis were sharing limited intelligence on Iran. Reagan's secretary of state, George Shultz, hoped that Saddam would perceive that his interests dictated alignment with the United States.[3] U.S. support for Hussein varied, however, depending on

3. See George Shultz, *Turmoil and Triumph: My Years as Secretary of State* (New York: Charles Scribner's Sons, 1993), pp. 236–241.

the ebb and flow of the war. When it looked as if Iraq might be losing, as in late 1982 and again in 1986–1987, the administration tilted toward Hussein; when Iraq seemed to be winning, American assistance to Iraq lessened. Few in Washington would have regretted an end to the Iran-Iraq War that would leave both countries seriously weakened. No one considered Iraq a reliable ally.

American policy was further complicated by the secret U.S. sale of arms to Iran in a bid to win the release of Americans held captive by terrorist groups in Lebanon. These secret dealings, managed by Reagan's National Security Council (NSC) staff, became public in 1986 as part of the scandal that became known as "Iran-Contra" (because proceeds from the arms sales to Iran were used illegally to aid anti-Communist Contra guerrillas in Nicaragua). Reagan's Gulf policy, although confused, could be neatly summed up, as Robert Gates put it, as "a plague on both their houses."

A centerpiece of the Reagan-Shultz strategy during the Iran-Iraq War was Operation Staunch. In place since early 1983, Staunch was an attempt to contain the flow of advanced arms to the Gulf. Despite U.S. support of Iraq's war effort, Operation Staunch included restrictions on arms sales to Iraq. Although curtailed following the Iran-Contra revelations, the operation remained in effect until the end of Reagan's presidency. The Reagan administration turned a blind eye, however, to loopholes in the arms interdiction program. U.S. policymakers knew that Iraq obtained arms easily from the Soviets, the French, and many other suppliers, yet they made little effort to dissuade these nations from selling conventional arms to Iraq.[4] The administration was also aware that the Saudis, the Gulf states, and the Kuwaitis—as well as U.S. and European banks—lent the Iraqi dictator the capital to buy weapons.

Congress opposed U.S. arms sales to Iraq because of Hussein's atrocious record of support for terrorism, grave violations of human rights, and hostility toward Israel. U.S. export and agricultural credit programs were, however, less objectionable. They were popular with business and with some members of Congress.

Saddam Hussein was practically unknown to the Western public until the 1980s. As the United States became more deeply involved in Gulf politics during that decade, more Americans learned about one of the world's most brutal dictatorships. Saddam Hussein began his political career in 1957 at the age of 20 when he participated in several violent

---

4. The exceptions included unsuccessful American efforts to persuade France not to sell Exocet anti-ship missiles and Super-Etendard fighter bombers to Iraq. The U.S. government wanted Hussein to be able to defend himself, but it did not want him so well-armed that Iraq could threaten U.S. forces or interests in the Gulf.

demonstrations in Baghdad; two years later, as a member of the Ba'ath (Renaissance) Party, he was part of a team that tried to assassinate the Iraqi dictator, General Abdul Karim Qasim. During subsequent years of roving exile, Hussein rose high in the ranks of the Ba'ath Party; when the Party came to power in 1968, he was made chief of internal security.

Over the next decade, Hussein eliminated his rivals. At a meeting of party officials on July 22, 1979, six days after Saddam's friend-turned-rival Hasan al-Bakr had resigned as president of Iraq, Hussein was "elected" president. Then, the names of various individuals were read out; they were told to stand and leave the room. They would all be executed in the following weeks. Through further use of violence and intimidation, partially offset by welfare programs, public works, and public education, Iraq became a "republic of fear."[5]

In the spring of 1988, in the latest of a series of campaigns to suppress Kurdish separatists in northern Iraq, the regime used poison gas to massacre the inhabitants of several Kurdish villages. It was already common knowledge that both Iran and Iraq had used chemical weapons during their war, but photographs of the corpses of gassed Kurdish villagers at Halabja brought home to readers of U.S. newspapers and magazines the brutality of Hussein's regime. Senator Claiborne Pell (D-R.I.) introduced a bill calling for economic sanctions to penalize Iraq for human rights abuses. The Rhode Island senator, long known for his support of human rights, denounced Saddam's policies as "a campaign that can only be described as genocide."[6]

Though Secretary of State Shultz publicly termed Hussein's actions "unjustifiable and abhorrent," the Reagan administration opposed the sanctions proposed by Pell. Terming unilateral sanctions "premature," State Department spokesman Charles Redman argued that the United States should act only after assembling an international coalition. The administration considered a variety of options, including recall of the U.S. ambassador, but finally decided that any punitive measures would hurt more than they would help. Assistant Secretary of State for Near Eastern Affairs Richard Murphy summed up administration thinking by saying that the Halabja massacre had "shaken the fragile U.S.-Iraqi relationship and been heavily criticized in the Arab world," but that the United States

---

5. See Judith Miller and Laurie Mylroie, *Saddam Hussein and the Crisis in the Gulf* (New York: Times Books, 1990); Samir al-Khalil [pseudonym for Kanan Makiya], *Republic of Fear* (Berkeley: University of California Press, 1989); Phebe Marr, *The Modern History of Iraq* (Boulder, Colo.: Westview Press, 1985); and Saïd K. Aburish, *Saddam Hussein, The Politics of Revenge* (London: Bloomsbury, 2000).

6. *Congressional Record*, 101st Cong., 2nd sess., pp. 29634–29638 (September 9, 1988).

needed "to move quickly" to be "seen as anti-CW [chemical warfare], not anti-Iraq or pro-Iran." In any event, said Murphy, "we believe that economic sanctions will be useless or counterproductive in terms of our ability to influence the Iraqis."[7]

The Iran-Iraq War ended abruptly in August 1988. Though Iranian troops outnumbered Iraqi troops and continued to hold positions inside Iraq, signs of exhaustion and ebbing morale had become plentiful. Almost without warning, Iran agreed to a UN-sponsored cease-fire.

Iraq emerged from the war intact and well-armed but badly damaged and heavily in debt to both the West and to Arab nations. In the Near East bureau of the State Department (NEA), hope flared that the United States could take advantage of Iraq's distress.

Previously a leader among Arab "rejectionists" who opposed all compromises with Israel, Hussein had denounced Yasser Arafat, the chairman of the Palestine Liberation Organization (PLO), because of his yielding to U.S. pressure to negotiate. During the Iran war, however, Hussein had moderated his stand, ceasing to oppose Arafat and drawing closer to the "moderate" Arab states: Jordan, Saudi Arabia, Kuwait, and the Gulf emirates. NEA also noted that the war had weakened Hussein's ties to the Soviet Union, while Iraqi purchases of European weapons and U.S. grain had drawn Hussein closer to the West. Officials in the bureau were, to be sure, aware of Iraqi programs to develop nuclear, biological, and chemical weapons, but they reasoned that Iraq's need for economic reconstruction would lead Hussein both to desist from these programs and to continue his evolution toward support of U.S. objectives in the region.

NEA and others in the Reagan administration were also influenced by other Arab governments, many of which believed that Hussein was moving "into the mainstream."[8] The Reagan team hoped that Hussein could become like Syria's Hafez Assad, a ruthless dictator within his borders who could nevertheless act prudently or at least cautiously in foreign affairs. It was this approach that George Bush inherited.

During the transition from Reagan to Bush, a dissenting voice could be faintly heard. Zalmay Khalilzad, a former professor at Columbia

---

7. State Department memo, Murphy to Armacost, "U.S. Policy Toward Iraq and CW Use," September 19, 1988, National Security Archive, "Iraqgate: Saddam Hussein, U.S. Policy, and the Prelude to the Persian Gulf War," microfiche file (hereafter cited as DNSA "Iraqgate"), document no. 650. In the end, the sanctions effort failed not because of administration efforts but because the bill to which Pell's initiative was attached, the omnibus foreign aid package, failed to clear Congress after a last-minute filibuster by Senator Jesse Helms (R-N.C.).

8. State Department memo, Abramowitz (Bureau of Intelligence and Research [INR]) to Armacost, "Iraq's Foreign Policy: Deeper into the Mainstream," March 3, 1988, DNSA "Iraqgate," document no. 519.

University, served on the staff of Under Secretary of State Michael Armacost. Khalilzad argued that, with the end of the war, Iraq had emerged as the regional hegemon. Under the logic of balance-of-power politics, it was only a matter of time before Hussein confronted the other regional power, the United States. Hussein had enhanced his military capabilities with the equipment the Iraqi army had seized from the collapsing Iranian forces. The only conceivable target of that new strength, according to Khalilzad, was the United States or its regional clients: Saudi Arabia or the Gulf emirates, including Kuwait. As Khalilzad later recalled:

> Iraq needed to be contained. The United States could have built up its military capabilities in the Gulf and contained Iraq by continuing Operation Staunch. In addition, we could have adjusted our policy toward Iran by eliminating the restrictions imposed on it during the war, while maintaining those restrictions having to do with terrorism. This would have allowed economic dealings with Iran; like Syria, Iran would have remained on the terrorism list. It would have been an undesirable ally, but it would have been manageable.[9]

Khalilzad, however, found no takers for this view in Washington. Especially after the embarrassing Iran-Contra scandal, no senior officials could see any basis for improving relations with the rabidly anti-American Iranian regime. If anything, the reaction was the opposite. A task force assembled by George Bush's transition team argued that the United States needed to "recognize Iraq's present and potential power in the region and accord it relatively high priority." The task force predicted that Iraq would in the future function as "a more responsible, status-quo state working within the system."[10]

One day before Bush was sworn into office, U.S. Ambassador to Iraq April Glaspie was instructed to stress America's concern over Iraq's development of biological weapons, which was being carried out in contravention of a treaty banning such work signed by most countries in the world (although not Iraq).[11] Ambassador Glaspie was one of the leading experts on the Arab world at the State Department. Fluent in Arabic, she had served in Egypt, Syria, and Kuwait, and had been commended on

---

9.   Zachary Karabell interview with Khalilzad. All further quotations from Khalilzad, unless otherwise attributed, are from this interview.

10.   Bush administration transition papers, "Guidelines for U.S.-Iraq Policy," quoted in Alan Friedman, *Spider's Web* (New York: Bantam, 1993), p. 133.

11.   State Department 17113, "Iraqi Biological Weapons," January 19, 1989, DNSA "Iraqgate," document no. 758.

numerous occasions for the quality of her reporting. Sent to Baghdad in March 1988, Glaspie was prepared for her job as few before her had been. Her only liability was a reputation in Washington for showing too much empathy toward the views of Arab radicals.[12]

"Constructive Engagement"

Soon after his decisive victory in November 1988, Bush had begun to assemble a seasoned foreign policy team. In the White House, his national security advisor would be Brent Scowcroft, a retired Air Force general who had held the same post under President Gerald Ford. Scowcroft's deputy would be Robert Gates, a career Soviet analyst in the CIA who had been Kerr's predecessor as the agency's deputy director. Bush's secretary of state would be James Baker, who had been White House chief of staff and secretary of the treasury under Reagan and had also managed Bush's presidential campaign. After the Senate rejected his first choice, former Texas Senator John Tower, Bush chose as secretary of defense Richard Cheney, who had been chief of staff for Ford.

For Bush and his foreign policy advisers, the problems of highest priority rose from revolutionary change in Eastern Europe, upheaval in the Soviet Union, moves toward the unification of Germany, and democratic unrest in China. Iraq was hardly even in the second tier among their concerns.

When Iraq did become a subject of discussion within the new administration, each department within the Executive branch had its own angle of vision. In the State Department, Iraq figured chiefly as one piece of a larger regional puzzle that centered, for Secretary of State Baker, on resolving the Arab-Israeli dispute. Given that Hussein had started to support negotiations between the PLO and Israel, Baker "saw Iraq as a potentially helpful Arab ally in moving the moribund Middle East peace process forward."[13] Baker had also stepped up efforts to resolve the intractable civil war in Lebanon. In October 1989, Lebanese politicians reached a tentative accord known as the Taif agreements; it remained unclear, however, whether the politicians could speak on behalf of those in Beirut who were

---

12.   Robert Kaplan, "Tales From The Bazaar," *Atlantic Monthly*, August 1992. Also see Elaine Sciolino, *The Outlaw State: Saddam Hussein's Quest for Power and the Gulf Crisis* (New York: Wiley, 1991), pp. 177–179.

13.   James A. Baker III, *The Politics of Diplomacy: Revolution, War, and Peace, 1989–1992* (New York: G.P. Putnam's Sons, 1995), p. 263; also various *New York Times* articles of October 3, October 9, October 12, and October 19, 1989.

holding the weapons.[14] Enforcing the Taif agreements would be easier with Iraq's cooperation.

Baker first met with a senior Iraqi official, Deputy Foreign Minister Nizar Hamdoun, in March 1989. The main subject was U.S. compensation claims for damage done to the USS *Stark*, a U.S. frigate on duty in the Persian Gulf which had been mistakenly hit and nearly sunk by an air-launched Iraqi missile on April 4, 1988. Iraq was willing to meet American demands, an attitude seen by U.S. government officials as an encouraging signal. Although Baker repeated U.S. concern about Iraq's use of chemical weapons during the Iran-Iraq War, he also expressed his interest in improved relations. Considerable discussion was devoted to continued Iraqi access to both Export-Import Bank short-term credit insurance and the Department of Agriculture's Commodity Credit Corporation (CCC).

In the Department of Defense (DOD), some attention went to Iraq as the new regional military power which could either pose a threat to U.S. interests or instead might help guarantee secure oil supplies from the Persian Gulf. Iraq's pursuit of high-tech and unconventional weaponry made some officials in the Pentagon uneasy, as was true also for analysts at the CIA. But no one high in DOD or the CIA had a reason for interest in Iraq comparable to that of Baker, with his focus on the Middle East peace process and Lebanon.

In the Department of Agriculture (USDA), Iraq was seen as a valued customer for American agricultural commodities. In the Department of Commerce, similarly, Iraq was seen as a customer for American manufactured goods. Some goods had the potential for so-called dual-use application, meaning they could serve both a military and a non-military purpose. Dual-use goods could be sold only under special licenses granted by the U.S. government.[15] As for the Justice Department, its interest in Iraq was piqued in the fall of 1989 by Iraqi links with the Atlanta branch of the Italian Banca Nazionale del Lavoro (BNL), suspected of violations of federal banking laws.

The Bush administration did attend briefly to Iraq in 1989. As is typical for a new president, Bush conducted a general review of policies relating to particular regions and problems. One review dealt with the Persian

---

14. Saudi Arabia, with the tacit acceptance of the Syrians, invited 62 of the 99 members of the last elected (in 1972) Lebanese parliament to the Saudi resort city of Taif, where they negotiated an accord increasing the Muslim role in the Lebanese government. See Deirdre Collings, *Peace for Lebanon? From War to Reconstruction* (Boulder, Colo.: Lynne Rienner, 1994).

15. Under American export laws, dual-use items such as certain computer components could not be exported except with the approval of the Commerce Department.

Gulf, including Iraq. It was conducted by the NSC staff member in charge of the Middle East, Richard Haass.[16] Since 1979, Haass had been a vocal opponent of closer relations with Iran. Therefore, he wanted to explore the possibility of warmer contact with Iraq. In February 1989, Haass asked various interested agencies—State, Treasury, Commerce, Agriculture, and the CIA—to contribute to the Persian Gulf policy review. After the agencies sent in their preliminary reports, Haass convened several Policy Coordinating Committee (PCC) meetings, attended by assistant secretaries from the concerned departments, to discuss options.

As a result of the PCC discussions, a draft presidential policy directive on the Persian Gulf was drawn up by one of the two staffers in Haass's office, Sandra Charles.[17] Her draft directive was discussed in April by the NSC Deputies Committee, chaired by Deputy National Security Advisor Gates. The other regular members were Under Secretary of State for Political Affairs Robert Kimmitt, Under Secretary of Defense for Policy Paul Wolfowitz, and Kerr for the CIA. Officials from other departments or agencies attended when asked.

Even at the time of the meeting on the draft directive, Iraq was a distant concern of the deputies. The Ayatollah Khomeini, the leader of Iran's revolution, had just died, leaving the future of Iran uncertain. Thousands of miles away, Chinese students had assembled in Tiananmen Square in Beijing to call for democratization. The Chinese government had broken up the demonstration with brutal force. It was no more clear what the future held for China than what it held for the disintegrating Communist regimes of Europe. The fact that President Bush did not sign NSD-26 until October was not because the document was controversial; rather it was indicative of the low priority the administration as a whole accorded Persian Gulf affairs in the summer of 1989.

NSD-26 represented a compromise between those who wanted to encourage Hussein to support the United States on Middle East issues, and those concerned over the pace and scope of Hussein's weapons programs. Pro-conciliation officials could point to evidence that the current

---

16.   Richard Haass, a former Rhodes Scholar, started his government career as a staff member in the Carter administration's Defense Department and then held positions at the State Department and at Harvard's Kennedy School of Government. In the administration of George W. Bush, he would be head of policy planning in the State Department, and he would subsequently become president of the Council on Foreign Relations. He was interviewed for this case study by both May and Zelikow. All further quotations from Haass, unless otherwise attributed, are from these interviews.

17.   Sandra Charles had joined the NSC staff at the end of the Reagan administration from her prior post as a civilian staff member in the Pentagon. Her portfolio at NSC included U.S. policy in the Persian Gulf.

U.S. policy of constructive engagement was bearing fruit. In addition to his support for a PLO-Israeli dialogue, Hussein had worked with Egypt's President Hosni Mubarak at the end of 1988 to urge the PLO to recognize Israel. In February 1989, Hussein drew still closer to the moderate Arab states when he joined with Egypt and Jordan to create the Arab Cooperation Council, which was modeled on the European Community and intended to integrate Arab states that were not major oil producers.[18] Saddam Hussein also sought good relations with his Gulf neighbors; in March he cemented a non-aggression pact with King Fahd of Saudi Arabia. Of course, many aspects of Hussein's regime still disturbed American officials. His unconventional weapons program had only expanded with the end of the war, and it was common knowledge that Iraq wished to develop nuclear weapons. Also, Iraq's human rights record showed no signs of improvement.

NSD-26 therefore combined its economic incentives with a continuing threat of sanctions if Iraq did not curtail its unconventional weapons program and clean up its human rights performance. It embodied the consensus of officials concerned with the region as of the summer of 1989. In the words of one State Department official, the administration hoped to "embrace Saddam in a cocoon of moderation."[19] Although NSD-26 was not signed until early fall, by June it had become de facto U.S. policy toward the Gulf. The declassified portion of NSD-26 relevant to Iraq is carefully phrased:

> Access to Persian Gulf oil and the security of key friendly states in the area are vital to US national security. The United States remains committed to defend its vital interests in the region, if necessary and appropriate through the use of US military force, against the Soviet Union or any other regional power with interests inimical to our own. The United States also remains committed to support the individual and collective self-defense of friendly countries in the area to enable them to play a more active role in their own defense and thereby reduce the necessity for unilateral US military intervention. Normal relations between the United States and Iraq would serve our longer-term interests and promote stability in both the Gulf and the Middle East. The United States should propose economic and political incentives for Iraq to moderate its behavior and to increase our influence with Iraq. At the same time, the Iraqi leadership must understand that any illegal use of chemical and/or

---

18. The Arab Cooperation Council (ACC) comprised Egypt, Jordan, the Yemen Arab Republic, and Iraq. Its founding meeting was in Baghdad.

19. Quoted in Friedman, *Spider's Web*, p. 134.

biological weapons will lead to economic and political sanctions....Any breach by Iraq of [international] safeguards in its nuclear program will result in a similar response. Human rights considerations should continue to be an important element in our policy toward Iraq. In addition, Iraq should be urged to cease its meddling in external affairs, such as in Lebanon, and be encouraged to play a constructive role in negotiating a settlement with Iran and cooperating with the Middle East peace process. We should pursue, and seek to facilitate, opportunities for US firms to participate in the reconstruction of the Iraqi economy....Also, as a means of developing access to and influence with the Iraqi defense establishment, the United States should consider sales of non-lethal forms of military assistance.[20]

There were few, if any, arguments about the portion of the document that dealt with Iraq. As one senior administration official recalled — without being willing to be quoted by name:

> The basic outline of policy was: Stand by your friends in the Gulf and use limited economic tools to encourage Hussein to be more moderate. The concern over Iranian fundamentalism was a given, but there was no need to shift gears or do anything radically different. Everybody knew Hussein's reputation, and no one thought he was a potential member of the Kiwanis Club. But could he become a better member of the region? It was worth exploring the possibility, and we didn't have a lot to lose, especially because we couldn't get either the Arabs or the Europeans to sign on to anything more confrontational.[21]

NSD-26 was based on the assumption that both Iran and Iraq would be occupied with rebuilding their economies after the devastation of the war. While the prevailing sentiment may still have been "a plague on both their houses," almost everyone believed that Hussein was easier to deal with than Iran. While Iran was expected to continue its harsh anti-Americanism and reject all ties with the West, Iraq was expected to seek expanded contact with the West, particularly in the form of trade and aid. NSD-26 offered economic aid and encouraged American businesses to deal with Iraq.

---

20. NSD-26, in Simpson, *National Security Directives of the Reagan and Bush Administrations*, p. 896.

21. Zelikow interview with a senior administration official. All further quotations from "senior administration official," unless otherwise attributed, are from this interview.

The BNL Scandal and CCC Credits

Since the mid-1980s, the Department of Agriculture had been a strong proponent of good relations with Iraq. USDA's Commodity Credit Corporation (CCC) extended credit guarantees to Iraq for purchases of more than $1 billion a year worth of American agricultural commodities.[22] It had lobbied consistently against congressional action that might jeopardize the access of American agribusiness to the valuable Iraqi market. By 1989, Iraq had become the ninth largest purchaser of American agricultural products, and it was the largest importer of U.S.-grown rice.[23] The United States, in turn, was Iraq's largest supplier of non-military goods.

Iraq also received short-term credit insurance from the Export-Import Bank of approximately $200 million per year. This program generated controversy. Representative Howard Berman (D-Calif.) introduced a bill to deny Export-Import loans to any nation classified by the State Department as a terrorist state, which would include Iraq. Berman's bill sailed through the House of Representatives, but encountered strong resistance in the Senate. Before October 1989, when it became law, a conference committee that included Senators Daniel Inouye (D-Hawaii) and Robert Kasten (R-Wisc.) inserted a provision allowing the president to waive the restrictions in the name of national security.

Meanwhile, the Export-Import Bank was growing concerned about Iraq, due to conditions in the Iraqi economy and Iraqi payment practices regarding development loans, as well as the potential for the overthrow of Hussein, fluctuation of U.S.-Iraqi relations, and renewed war in the region.[24] In fact, although Iraq had temporarily defaulted on some credits extended during the Iran-Iraq War, Baghdad had scrupulously made all its payments to American banks whose letters of credit were secured by CCC guarantees. These guarantees were important to Iraq.

---

22. State Department briefing memo, Paul Hare to Baker, "Meeting with Iraqi Under Secretary Nizar Hamdoun—March 24, 1989," March 23, 1989. DNSA "Iraqgate," document no. 828.

23. State Department memo for Baker, "CCC Credits for Iraq," October 11, 1989, reprinted in the *Congressional Record*, March 2, 1992; State memo from Kelly and Sofaer (Legal Advisor) through Kimmitt and McCormack to Baker, "The Iraqi CCC Program," October 26, 1989, DNSA "Iraqgate," document no. 1089.

24. *Export-Import Bank Country Risk Analysis of Iraq*, April 18, 1989, predicted that Iraq would continue to default on loans except to "favored creditors." While Hussein was seen as eager for medium-term credit from Ex-Im, it was the opinion of the report that the Iraqi economy and Iraqi payment practices regarding development loans did not warrant the risk.

Outside events, however, disrupted this relationship. On August 4, 1989, federal agents raided the Atlanta branch of the Italian-owned Banca Nazionale del Lavoro (BNL) and seized thousands of documents. Coming in the midst of a scandal over U.S. savings and loan institutions, the seizure made instant news. It was soon revealed that BNL-Atlanta had loaned over $2 billion to Iraq during 1988 and 1989, with few visible guarantees of repayment. From 1985 to 1988, BNL-Atlanta had also been a leading participant in the CCC program, lending money to pay American agricultural exporters under letters of credit to Iraq, with Iraqi repayment to BNL secured by CCC guarantees. Media attention to BNL-Atlanta quickly led to press discussion of the CCC program and a widespread though inaccurate perception that the CCC program gave or lent cash to Iraq.[25]

At issue was what had been done with the money BNL-Atlanta had lent to Iraq. As Justice Department investigators probed in the summer and fall of 1989, they began to suspect that BNL somehow had "diverted" CCC-guaranteed credits to fund Iraqi purchases of arms or dual-use technology. In fact, CCC-guaranteed credits provided money only to American businesses. Wheat and rice, not cash, went to Iraq. Iraq then had to pay cash to American banks, including BNL, in fulfillment of the letters of credit under which the banks had advanced money to the American exporters. By 1989 and 1990, the cash Iraq was paying to American banks actually greatly exceeded the value of new agricultural purchases. But this situation was apparently not fully understood at first by Justice, nor by State. Initially, they thought American CCC credit guarantees were connected to BNL-Atlanta's separate, inadequately secured loans of cash to Iraq, which Iraq had used to buy military equipment.

As public outcry over BNL grew in the fall of 1989, State, Treasury, and Agriculture learned from the Justice Department that the BNL affair might have political repercussions. Alarmed at the negative press about BNL, State Department officials privately conceded that some of the $2 billion lent in 1988–1989 by BNL-Atlanta was probably used to fund Iraq's weapons programs.[26] The Atlanta U.S. Attorney's office, conducting its

---

25. CIA—Directorate of Intelligence, "Iraq-Italy: Repercussions of the BNL-Atlanta Scandal," November 6, 1989, DNSA "Iraqgate," document no. 1114. The CIA report reflected the press's misunderstanding, since the CIA analysts who wrote the memo were simply recycling what they had read in the press. In fact, the CCC guaranteed to U.S. farmers that, if Iraq did not pay them, the CCC would. Thus, Iraq would buy rice, for example, from U.S. farmers, and would pay for the rice by offering a letter of credit issued on its behalf by BNL. The U.S. farmer would take the letter of credit to BNL and get cash. BNL would turn around and recover the cash from Iraq, or from the CCC if Iraq were to default.

26. State Department memo, Kelly to Reginald Bartholomew, "The Banca del Lavoro Scandal," September 22, 1989, DNSA "Iraqgate," document no. 1015.

investigation of BNL, initially developed a theory that BNL loans under-
written by the CCC had been used for the Iraqi nuclear program. In early
October 1989, the assistant U.S. attorney in Atlanta briefed Department of
Agriculture Counsel Kevin Brosch. Brosch in turn informed State officials
of the possible ramifications of the BNL investigation, apparently including the mistaken CCC money-for-weapons hypothesis. That, at least, was
the impression of Frank Lemay, special assistant to Under Secretary of
State for Economic Affairs Richard McCormack, who warned in an
October 13 memo "that the investigation could blow the roof off the
CCC."[27] The Department of Agriculture was also investigating allegations
of mismanagement of the CCC program on the Iraqi side. Indeed, by the
fall of 1989, the Federal Bureau of Investigation, the Pentagon, the
Agriculture Department, the Internal Revenue Service, and Congress were
all investigating aspects of the U.S.-Iraq relationship.[28]

Against a backdrop of increasing tensions within the administration
over the best approach to Iraq, Secretary of State Baker and Iraqi Foreign
Minister Tariq Aziz met for the first time on October 6, 1989. In line with
Bush administration policy during its first year in office, Baker's primary
goal was not to contain Iraq or limit its chemical weapons program, but to
seek Aziz's "help in moving along the peace process in the Middle East."[29]
Nonetheless, the two men discussed broader aspects of the U.S.-Iraqi relationship. Baker assured Aziz that the United States desired better relations
with Iraq, but warned that the BNL investigation could adversely affect
the relationship. Baker expressed concern over unconventional weapons
proliferation, but reassured his counterpart that Iraq was not being singled
out for criticism: these were "worldwide concerns." He also noted that
"the administration never supported sanctions on Iraq and that he had
personally so testified." Such congressional actions were "limited to Iraqi
use of CW [chemical weapons] during the war," and now "we need to look
forward, not backward."

Aziz initially responded in kind, noting that Iraq was eager for good
relations "on the basis of mutual respect and understanding." Indeed,
Baker at first had the impression of Aziz as an "urbane, cosmopolitan
man." However, the Iraqi quickly shifted tone, charging that the Bush
administration was interfering in Iraqi internal affairs, seeking to retard

27. Memorandum of conversation, "USDA Comments on Investigation of Iraq and the
Banca Nazionale del Lavoro, Atlanta Branch, Scandal," October 13, 1989, DNSA
"Iraqgate," document no. 1066.

28. Friedman, *Spider's Web*, p. 140.

29. State Department 327801, "Secretary's October 6 Meeting with Iraqi Foreign
Minister Tariq Aziz," October 13, 1989, DNSA "Iraqgate," document no. 1068.

Baghdad's efforts to expand its "technological base" (the code-word for the nation's military buildup), and authorizing "some American agencies" to destabilize Saddam Hussein's government. Recalling this outburst in his memoirs, Baker described it as a display worthy of a "latter-day von Ribbentrop."[30]

Less than a week after this meeting, a State Department memo to Baker counseled caution in deciding whether to continue the CCC program with Iraq. However, the memo also emphasized the importance of constructive relations with Iraq. It said:

> Given the apparent problems with the Iraq CCC program, it would seem wise to proceed with caution and prudence. We should not jump to conclusions before all the facts are known; nor should we continue with business as usual. USDA, acting against the advice of the Fed and Treasury, but with the support of other NAC [National Advisory Council] members (including State), recently approved a "first tranche" of $400 million in FY 1990 CCC credits for Iraq....[31] They have told the Iraqis that approval of additional credits will depend on the outcome of the ongoing investigations into the [BNL] scandal and charges of corruption in the operation of the CCC program....In the meantime, the situation should be kept under close policy review because the stakes are big. We need export markets, and Iraq is a potential market and as the war-induced imports are replaced by commercial purchases, this market will undoubtedly increase in the next decade.[32]

At the same time, the Iraqis let the United States know that CCC was integral to Iraq's economic survival. Deputy Foreign Minister Hamdoun, speaking to Ambassador Glaspie on October 8, stressed that CCC credits were important not just to buy food but as a sign to the international monetary community that Iraqi credit was still good.[33]

---

30. Baker, *Politics of Diplomacy*, pp. 264–265.

31. The National Advisory Council (NAC) is an interagency policy group that oversees foreign loan programs such as Export-Import and CCC. It is chaired by the Treasury Department and consists of representatives, usually at the assistant secretary level, from other concerned agencies. In October and November, it met on several occasions to discuss the future of Ex-Im loans and CCC credits for Iraq.

32. State Department memo for Baker, "CCC Credits for Iraq," October 11, 1989, DNSA "Iraqgate," document no. 1060.

33. Baghdad 5379, "CCC Negotiations," October 9, 1989, DNSA "Iraqgate," document no. 1051. Haass later recalled his belief that Iraq would have been able to find other sellers of rice or wheat willing to offer generous credit terms.

While CCC and BNL were of major concern at the Department of Agriculture and Justice, and of lesser but still substantial interest to State in the fall of 1989, for other segments of the bureaucracy they were not a issue. Top officials at the White House did not discuss U.S.-Iraqi relations. There were no Deputies Committee meetings on Iraq between June 1989 and April 1990. "With the fall of the Berlin Wall and revolutions in Europe," Gates commented later, "no one really cared about Iraq" in the fall of 1989. Indeed, Iraq was not even among the top five regional priorities for Middle East specialists in the Bush administration. The Arab-Israeli peace process, the U.S. hostages in Lebanon, the volatile situation in Afghanistan after the Soviet pull-out, and the simmering crisis between India and Pakistan all ranked well above Iraq in importance.

For analysts at the CIA and planners at the Defense Department, the only reason to pay attention to Iraq was the mounting evidence of Hussein's continued military buildup. The CIA reported that Hussein had not begun demobilizing his armed forces after the end of the war with Iran. In the early fall of 1989, the CIA obtained photographic evidence of fixed missile sites in Iraq's western desert. These missiles could have only one purpose: to strike Israel. The CIA also monitored the traffic of high-tech components into Iraq from Europe and elsewhere, and informed the White House of Iraq's progress in building its own missile launchers and crude rockets. There was also evidence that Iraq was engaged in nuclear research and development of unconventional weapons. It was no secret that Iraq sought to evade non-proliferation controls and was trying to find non-U.S. suppliers of the desired technology.[34] Iraq was also suspected of attempting to evade Commerce Department dual-use export controls to obtain such items as specialized furnaces, which could be used for ballistic missiles, and machine tools, which could be used for weapons factories. A number of front companies made these purchases for Iraq in the United States.[35] The CIA followed such proliferation dangers but was not closely following BNL-Atlanta; the case was viewed as a law enforcement matter and therefore a domestic issue, outside of the CIA's lawful purview.

Only the Pentagon took concrete measures in response to what it perceived as a significant change in Iraq's status, caused by the imminent collapse of the Soviet Union and the devastation suffered by Iran in the 1980s.

---

34. See, for example, State Department, Bureau of Oceans and International Environmental and Scientific Affairs," SNEC Cases of Interest," November 21, 1989, DNSA "Iraqgate," document no. 1149; State Department 46278, "Possible Iraqi Missile and Nuclear-related Procurement," February 1990, DNSA "Iraqgate," document no. 1201; Kenneth Timmerman, *The Death Lobby* (Boston: Houghton Mifflin, 1991).

35. CIA—Directorate of Intelligence report, November 6, 1989, DNSA "Iraqgate," document no. 1114. The most prominent of these companies was Matrix-Churchill.

At the end of 1989, according to a senior Defense Department official, military planners reassessed U.S. military strategy in the Persian Gulf and designated Iraq as the primary threat to America's friends in the region: Saudi Arabia, Kuwait and the other Gulf states. Planners prepared for the contingency of an Iraqi attack south, against Saudi Arabia or Kuwait.

In November 1989, the debate over CCC credits came to a head. The State Department argued forcefully for their continuation. Baker himself advocated continuing the CCC program. Concerned with the region as a whole, not with administrative irregularities in the CCC or a banking scandal in Atlanta, Baker stuck to the policy articulated in NSD-26. Assistant Secretary of State for Near East Affairs John Kelly was a staunch Baker ally in supporting the CCC program for Iraq.[36] On October 26, the Near East and South Asian Affairs Bureau (NEA) headed by Kelly recommended that Baker telephone Secretary of Agriculture Clayton Yeutter to urge agreement to the proposal to extend a further $1 billion in CCC credit guarantees to Iraq. Kelly argued that "in view of the evidence available, State believes that, to wall off an FY90 CCC program from the BNL investigation, it is sufficient to exact Iraq's promise to cooperate in the investigation of past practices." Offering a $1 billion CCC program "would strengthen relations with Iraq, in line with NSD-26, and help U.S. exporters."[37] Baker promptly contacted Yeutter; by the end of the call, Yeutter had agreed with his colleague.

Although Treasury and the Federal Reserve Board worried about Iraq's general credit record and debt burden, in the end neither agency felt strongly enough about the CCC issue to kick the matter up to the White House for a higher-level decision. Treasury concluded that "given Agriculture's expertise and State's backing...we seem to have no choice but to indicate our concerns, encourage USDA to improve program controls, and allow the program to go forward."[38] Baker later termed this policy development "squarely within the parameters of NSD-26."[39]

Considering these arguments and following its own inclination, the Agriculture Department concluded that the costs of jettisoning the CCC program far outweighed any benefits. The department concluded that

---

36. John Kelly had joined the Foreign Service in 1964 but, apart from a stint as ambassador to Lebanon in the mid-1980s, he was not known for his Middle East expertise.

37. Kelly and Sofaer through Kimmitt and McCormack to Baker, "The Iraqi CCC Program: Whether to push for a full CCC program for Iraq," October 26, 1989, DNSA "Iraqgate," document no. 1089.

38. Treasury Department memo, "Overview" pursuant to NAC meeting, October 1989, DNSA "Iraqgate," document no. 1122.

39. Baker, *Politics of Diplomacy*, p. 266.

suspending the CCC assistance would have three negative consequences. First, it would be seen as an insult by the Iraqi government, undermining a process by which the U.S.-Iraqi political relationship "has been carefully nurtured during the years of the Iran-Iraq War, and more particularly during the 10 months since the ceasefire." Second, a cutoff could harm the U.S. image in the region as a whole, providing evidence to suspicious Arab nations "of their second class treatment in U.S. foreign policy." Finally, the Agriculture Department was concerned—as it had been throughout 1989—with the domestic ramifications of sanctions. U.S. agricultural producers, "nearing the end of their patience," would undoubtedly protest strongly against any cutoff of aid, resulting "in considerable one-sided, negative publicity." Therefore, the Department of Agriculture endorsed the October proposal of the State Department and the National Advisory Council (NAC) for $1 billion worth of continued CCC credit guarantees for Iraq in FY90.[40]

On November 8, the NAC decided to continue the CCC program for Iraq. State clearly had the deciding voice. The State Department representative at the meeting, wrote the notetaker from Treasury, "stated that, despite possible future revelations, overwhelming foreign policy considerations led him to urge support of the proposal."[41] The program's $1 billion in credits would be released in two tranches, with the first $500 million in credit guarantees available immediately; the second $500 million would be forwarded in early 1990, provided that neither the BNL investigation nor the Agriculture Department's review of the CCC administration uncovered wrongdoing within the Iraqi government.[42]

---

40. USDA Draft Report for NAC, November 5, 1989, DNSA "Iraqgate," document no. 1127. The USDA was not the only agency with such concerns: on October 26, 1989, Kelly had penned a memo pointing out that "trade has become the central factor in this relationship," ibid., document no. 1089.

41. Treasury Department notes, NAC Deputies Meeting, November 8, 1989, DNSA "Iraqgate," document no. 1127.

42. The Justice Department finally handed down indictments of BNL-Atlanta officials in March of 1991, charging them with more than 300 counts of conspiracy to defraud. Whom BNL defrauded remains a troublesome question. By 1986, the Atlanta branch manager, Christopher Drogoul, had begun concealing loans to Iraq from both his home office in Rome and from U.S. bank examiners. The actual role of BNL-Atlanta's Italian managers in approving loans to Iraq remains cloudy. The U.S. intelligence community had fragmentary knowledge about BNL's activities but never connected this information either to a domestic law enforcement issue or to potential foreign policy concerns. See Staff Report, Senate Select Committee on Intelligence, "The Intelligence Community's Involvement in the Banca Nazionale del Lavoro Affair," 103rd Cong., 1st sess., February 1993.

To critics, the administration could answer that there was no proof that Iraq was using food bought with CCC credit guarantees to purchase weapons.[43] U.S. officials were certainly aware that if Hussein could buy food on credit, he could use the hard currency thus saved to buy weapons on the world market. However, Iraq's hard-currency repayments to U.S. banks exceeded the value of the new credits available with CCC guarantees. Another reason for administration complacency was a National Intelligence Estimate (NIE) on Iraq, drafted in the summer and circulated in the fall of 1989, which reflected the general view among U.S. government experts on Iraq.

The October 1989 NIE was neutrally entitled "Iraq: Foreign Policy of a Major Regional Power." It argued that Hussein would focus on internal reconstruction rather than external expansionism for the next several years. Robert Gates recalled its conclusions:

> People's concerns about Iraq as a geopolitical problem were probably mitigated by the NIE…which said that we think this guy is going to focus on rebuilding for the next few years. The NIE said that Hussein may well flex his muscle or do some sabre rattling, but his policy would not be particularly expansionist or interventionist. The NIE contributed to the complacency, but didn't create it. The conclusions of the NIE were consistent with what the policy-makers were hearing from their Arab counterparts: that Hussein was in desperate economic straits, and that he might put the squeeze on his Arab buddies to get the price of oil raised.

The NIE discussed Iraqi attempts to violate the Nuclear Non-Proliferation Treaty, and it detailed what was known about Iraq's nuclear weapons research and development. It also noted the existence of fixed missile sites and a number of other weapons systems whose target was assumed to be Israel. It pointed out Iraq's war-weariness and chronic shortage of cash. The estimate acknowledged that the United States Central Command was reorienting strategy with Iraq as a potential adversary, and even discussed Iraqi claims on Kuwaiti territory: the Kuwaiti islands of Bubiyan and Warba were mentioned as potential targets of Iraqi expansion. The NIE concluded, however, that Iraq would in all likelihood seek a way short of force to occupy the islands. Furthermore, although Iraqi aggression against Kuwait was mentioned as a possible danger, that possibility was not highlighted in the "key judgments" section of the document, the only section most policymakers would read.

---

43. Even subsequent investigations never uncovered such proof. See Kenneth I. Juster, "The Myth of Iraqgate," *Foreign Policy*, No. 94 (Spring 1994), pp. 105–119.

Overall, the NIE assumed that Iraq under Saddam Hussein would behave rationally and predictably. It did not analyze the choices that might face Hussein as a result of his economic problems. Although analysts were aware that Iraq had substantial debts and ever-mounting military expenditures, the estimate did not explore just how Hussein would get the money to pay for them.

CIA veterans said later that the principal author of the NIE was comparatively new to Persian Gulf affairs, and Kerr told the authors of a book on the Gulf War that the members of the National Foreign Intelligence Board had not thought the estimate sufficiently important or controversial as to require their meeting to discuss it. They cleared it in a round of telephone calls. "It was kind of a sloppy NIE," said Kerr, "The estimate did not do a good job of looking to the future."[44]

Answering questions about the future would have been even harder than asking them. American intelligence on Iraq was weak. Even during the Iran-Iraq War, American officials had concluded that intelligence resources on Iraq were not adequate to offset Hussein's ability to disguise his plans and to hide his intentions from both friend and foe. As of 1989, the CIA had few reliable sources of human intelligence on Iraq. While technical intelligence from such sources as satellites gave the United States a good sense of Iraq's military capabilities, these were of little use in assessing Saddam Hussein's intentions. The United States therefore relied heavily on diplomatic reporting and on the perceptions of America's friends in the region, especially the Gulf emirates and the Saudis. In 1989, these sources consistently asserted that Hussein was becoming more moderate.

The one constant note of worry in intelligence reports on Iraq was Baghdad's effort to acquire new weapons of mass destruction, such as nuclear weapons. Yet this unease did not cause American policymakers to reconsider the strategy of constructive engagement. As one senior State Department official reflected later (without wishing to be quoted by name), violations of the Nuclear Non-Proliferation Treaty had not led to breaks with Pakistan, South Africa, or Israel, either:

> Had the full extent of Hussein's violations been known, there might have been an attempt to slow down or delay the program,

---

44. Michael R. Gordon and Bernard E. Trainor, *The Generals' War: The Inside Story of the Conflict in the Gulf* (Boston: Little, Brown and Company, 1995), pp. 10–11. John A. Gentry, *Lost Promise: How CIA Analysis Misserves the Nation: An Intelligence Assessment* (Lanham, Md.: University Press of America, 1993), p. 149. The period in which this estimate was prepared was also a period in which numerous analysts in the Office of Near East and South Asian Analysis in CIA's Directorate of Intelligence were experiencing morale problems and in many cases finding employment elsewhere.

but not necessarily confrontation. Much depends on the reading of intent. If we had suspected regional ambitions on the part of Iraq, we might have acted differently. But with the NIE saying that Iraq would seek power and prestige through means other than intervention, why get overly worried? Saddam was perceived more as a new Assad than as a new Khomeini.[45]

A Villain Still

It was only with a change in Iraq's policies toward its neighbors that serious concern emerged among top officials in the spring of 1990. The catalyst was money. In debt to the tune of $80 billion as a result of the war with Iran, Hussein carefully kept current in his payments to U.S. banks. But the bulk of his debt was to creditors in the region, notably the oil-rich, cash-rich Gulf states. Hussein owed $10 billion to Kuwait alone. Just paying the interest would have forced Hussein to curtail or terminate many of his weapons programs, as well as subsidies for domestic social programs. Hussein began to exert more and more pressure on Arab creditors to forgive his debts. The result was increasingly to make Hussein's appearance of being a moderate seem a façade.

The first open break between Iraq and its neighbors appeared at the February 1990 meeting of the Arab Cooperation Council (ACC) in Amman, Jordan. Arguing that the Iran-Iraq War had been a struggle not between Iran and Iraq but between Iran and the whole Arab world, Hussein now asked that other Arab states compensate their champion. He claimed that Iraq had provided the manpower; it was only fair that the Gulf states provide the money. Iraq should no more repay its "loans" than the other Arab countries should supply Iraq with men to replace those who were lost in the war. Anticipating some resistance to his demands, Hussein declared: "Let the Gulf regimes know that if they do not give this money to me, I will know how to get it." At the same meeting, Hussein made another noteworthy declaration: that the U.S. military presence in the Gulf was no longer necessary. Now that the war was over, he argued, its only purpose could be to help Israel. It was time, Hussein said, for American warships to leave the Gulf. Hussein's remarks provoked Egyptian President Mubarak to leave Amman early.[46]

---

45. Zelikow interview with a then–high State Department official who preferred not to be named.

46. Lawrence Freedman and Efraim Karsh, *The Gulf Conflict, 1990–1991: Diplomacy and War in the New World Order* (Princeton, N.J.: Princeton University Press, 1993), p. 45.

Since the fall of 1989, with the NIE on Iraq and President Bush's endorsement of NSD-26, relations with Iraq had received little high-level attention in Washington. The first tranche of $500 million in CCC credit guarantees was advanced on schedule, with the second tranche due for release in the spring of 1990. Other U.S. assistance that might strengthen the strategy of constructive engagement was under consideration. In January, the Joint Chiefs of Staff (JCS) discussed the possibility of extending "low-level, non-lethal military assistance." While acknowledging that Iraq's past use of chemical weapons made the climate unfavorable for improved military-to-military relations, the JCS recommended proceeding with those assistance programs that did not require notification to Congress, such as training missions or officer exchange programs.[47] On January 17, 1990, meanwhile, President Bush signed a national security waiver, as the Senate negotiators on the Berman bill had provided in the conference committee. This enabled the Export-Import Bank to continue its short-term credit insurance program with Iraq even though Iraq remained on the State Department list of countries that supported terrorism.

Two weeks before the Amman ACC summit, Assistant Secretary of State for Near East Affairs Kelly had made a highly publicized visit to Baghdad to meet with Hussein and Iraqi Foreign Minister Aziz. Hussein discussed the decline of the Soviet Union and the resulting increase in U.S. leverage in the Middle East. He expressed the hope that America would use its preeminence for more than simply supporting Israel. Kelly raised the issue of Iraq's dismal human rights record, but also assured Hussein that the United States viewed Iraq as an important potential contributor to regional stability. When Kelly returned to Washington, he was called to testify before the House Foreign Affairs Subcommittee on European and Near Eastern Affairs. Though speaking several days after the Amman summit, Kelly said:

> Iraq seeks improved relations with the United States. Trade will be a key factor in our future relationship. Though the country faces a difficult period of reconstruction, I saw firsthand that the effort is well under way. There are important opportunities for American business in Iraq.... This is not an easy relationship, but it is an important one in which we have made significant progress in recent years.

---

47. Joint Staff Washington to U.S. Central Command (Schwarzkopf), "Proposed U.S.-Iraq Military Initiatives," January 3, 1990, DNSA "Iraqgate," document no. 1184. These proposals were never implemented. See Gordon and Trainor, *The Generals' War*, pp. 11–12.

In view of Hussein's provocative comments at the Amman summit, some American officials did begin to question whether constructive engagement was really having any effect. Haass, who had been a defender of the Iraq policy, convened several interagency meetings to review it. At the Defense Department, Assistant Secretary for International Security Affairs Henry Rowen decided that Hussein was the real source of instability in the Middle East and should be treated as such. In coming to this position, Rowen was influenced by a recent RAND study organized by Zalmay Khalilzad, the "dissenting voice" who had warned about Saddam Hussein in 1988.[48]

While these reviews were underway, the Department of Agriculture was deciding whether to issue the second tranche of CCC credit guarantees. In early February, Iraq had announced that it intended to request the additional $500 million for 1990. Under normal conditions, the Department of Agriculture would have based its decision solely on its internal investigation of the CCC program. Conditions, however, were not normal: the CCC program reflected the recommendations of NSD-26, and any decision on the CCC was likely to have wider implications for U.S.-Iraq policy. Moreover, from the Amman summit on, Hussein seemed bent on testing the U.S.-Iraqi relationship.

On March 10, 1990, British journalist Farzad Bazoft was condemned to death by an Iraqi court on charges of spying. Despite international appeals for clemency, Bazoft was executed on March 15. Less than two weeks later, British customs officials at Heathrow airport in London seized a shipment of clandestinely purchased U.S.-made nuclear-bomb triggers bound for Iraq. On April 10, British customs officials, aided by U.S. law enforcement agents, again intercepted an illegal shipment bound for Iraq, this time a cargo of components apparently intended to form part of a long-range "super gun." Major U.S. newspapers and television networks reported extensively on these episodes, and the tone of the reports was overwhelmingly negative. An entire segment of the television news magazine "Nightline" was devoted to Iraq's police state.

This shift in the tone of U.S. public opinion convinced Saddam Hussein that the U.S. government was turning against him. His suspicion of America was never far from the surface. Tolerating no free press in Iraq, he apparently attributed American media criticism to the Bush administration. He had already interpreted a February 15 *Voice of America* broadcast condemning secret police in numerous countries, including Iraq, as official U.S. censure. The State Department, not wishing to alienate

---

48. Karabell interview with Henry Rowen.

Hussein, instructed April Glaspie to make clear that the management of *Voice of America* did not take direction from other elements of the U.S. government, and that hence the broadcast did not represent U.S. policy.

On April 2, 1990, Hussein delivered a lengthy speech defending Iraq and the decision to execute Bazoft. He claimed that the West, and the United States in particular, had been trying to sell him enriched uranium for years and now—after the trigger seizure—they were trying to frame him for the crime of developing a nuclear weapon, which he denied Iraq was trying to obtain. He called the United States hypocritical for condemning him for Bazoft's death, but not inquiring too closely into the murder of Dr. Gerald Bull, a renegade Canadian scientist helping Iraq build unconventional weapons who was assassinated in Brussels at the end of March 1990 by gunmen whose identities are still unknown. Hussein, of course, suspected that they were Israelis, and he threatened that if Israel tried to thwart Iraq's military progress by attacking, as it had in 1981 by bombing Iraq's Osirak nuclear reactor, then "by God, we will make fire eat up half of Israel."

These events set off alarm bells in Washington. State Department spokesperson Margaret Tutwiler termed Hussein's remarks "inflammatory, irresponsible, and outrageous." Those in the administration and Congress who had never placed much faith in Hussein's supposed moderation concluded that the Iraqi leader was finally revealing his true intentions. Under Secretary of State Robert Kimmitt, for instance, said to Baker, "these are tough guys. We have to deal with them toughly. Incentives haven't worked; it's time to go to disincentives."[49]

For the time being, however, the administration went no further than strong rhetoric. On Capitol Hill, the situation stimulated renewed calls for sanctions and other concrete action. In contrast to 1989, Congress seemed prepared to act in a unified way. Berman reintroduced his bill terminating aid programs to Iraq, and added a provision banning the export of dual-use goods to Iraq. In the Senate, Inouye and Kasten dropped their opposition to Berman's proposal and indicated their support for a general trade ban against Baghdad.[50]

The U.S. intelligence community did not prepare a new National Intelligence Estimate to update its 1989 judgment that Iraq would become more moderate because of the need to rebuild after the war with Iran. Instead, the community issued specific reports about Iraq's arms proliferation efforts and its worrying military buildup. The CIA warned that Hussein's April 2 speech might be a harbinger of Iraqi aggression against

---

49. Baker, *Politics of Diplomacy*, p. 269.
50. *Congressional Quarterly Weekly Report*, April 28, 1990, pp. 1281–1282.

Israel. Analysts concluded that, even if Iraqi-Israeli relations deteriorated further, it would be difficult for the United States to line up a coalition against Iraq: even America's Arab allies were unlikely to side with Israel. To make things worse, the U.S.-PLO dialogue, quietly in progress for several years, had collapsed following a terrorist attack against Israel, which appeared to have been ordered by the PLO and which PLO chairman Arafat refused to disavow or condemn. America's stock was particularly low in the region.

Officials were torn about what to do. One White House official recalled a late-March PCC meeting which produced "no clear consensus." One complicating factor, the official recalled, was continued insistence by U.S. allies in the Arab world that "we got this guy under control, we can work with him." No one in the U.S. government wanted to make a martyr of Hussein by attacking him unilaterally. The official noted:

> The question by April was whether you keep the relationship open or shut it down. There was pressure from the Hill with the Berman bill, and some publicity which forced us to think about Iraq. We all agreed that we didn't like the way Saddam was acting. The question was tactical. Were you more likely to maintain leverage and influence through continued, limited contact, or through severing it?

While the CIA noted Hussein's increasingly radical rhetoric, the head of the State Department's Intelligence and Research Bureau urged a better understanding of the Iraqi leader. He wrote:

> Despite the bluster, Iraqi President Saddam Hussein's April 2 speech illustrates a real and abiding fear that Israel (with US and UK backing) is planning another strike against Iraq. While the media has focused primarily on his claims of "dual chemical" capabilities, Saddam did not directly threaten Israel with a first strike chemical attack.... Recent incidents, coupled with a lack of understanding of the West (especially the press), have exacerbated Saddam Hussein's traditional paranoia.[51]

On April 11, several Republican senators and one Democrat, Howard Metzenbaum of Ohio, made a well-publicized visit to Iraq to meet with Saddam Hussein in Mosul. They listened sympathetically to Hussein's complaints about the negative tone of American media reports on Iraq.

---

51. Mulholland to Kimmitt, "Iraq's Threat Against Israel," April 12, 1990, DNSA "Iraqgate," document no. 1316.

Alan Simpson (R-Wy.) told Hussein that he, too, had been attacked by America's "haughty and pampered press." Senator Robert Dole (R-Kansas)—whose home state had benefited substantially from CCC credit guarantees—said that he opposed any curtailment of U.S. aid to Iraq and that he spoke for the president in expressing the hope for a better relationship between the two nations. "Please allow me to say," Dole added, "that only twelve hours earlier President Bush had assured me that he wanted better relations, and that the U.S. government wants better relations, with Iraq."[52]

Clearly, the administration was of two minds: it did not want to jettison the relationship with Hussein, but it could not defend the relationship publicly. The lack of consensus at the March Policy Coordinating Committee meeting was indicative of the administration's difficulty. Although there was a general inclination to move away from constructive engagement, Iraq was still seen as too important to alienate completely. Moreover, those Arab states friendly to the United States were unwilling to push Hussein into a corner.

In the midst of this inconclusive reassessment, the Department of Agriculture came to a decision on the second tranche of the CCC credit guarantees. Based on an internal USDA investigation and report, the department concluded that although the suspected culprits were mostly U.S. exporters rather than Iraqis, there were too many irregularities. Agriculture Department officials worried that further investigation might reveal kickbacks and other crimes. Against the background of public complaint against the government's costly bailout of badly-managed U.S. savings and loan institutions, these officials feared being accused of mismanaging public funds. What with the outrage against Hussein of pro-Israel members of Congress, they feared also being exposed to lengthy inquisitions on Capitol Hill.[53]

At the beginning of April, therefore, Under Secretary of Agriculture Richard Crowder circulated a draft press release announcing that the department was suspending the second $500 million tranche of CCC credit guarantees to Iraq. The USDA review, said the release, "has raised a number of questions regarding contract pricing, purchasing practices, shipments, requests for additional services and imposition of special taxes

---

52. Sciolino, *The Outlaw State*, pp. 175–176; Freedman and Karsh, *The Gulf Conflict*, pp. 36–37.

53. Agriculture Department memo from Crowder to Scowcroft, "USDA's Position on Options in NSC Deputies Committee Review of PCC Paper on Iraq," May 21, 1990, DNSA "Iraqgate," document no. 1386.

and fees." At the same time, Crowder apparently notified several congressional staffers of the Department's decision.[54]

The NSC staff and the State Department's NEA protested Crowder's draft announcement. At the beginning of March, the Iraqi ambassador had complained to National Security Advisor Scowcroft about delay in releasing the second tranche, and Haass and Charles had contacted the Agriculture Department to press for action.[55] But they had not anticipated a USDA move to cancel the program without coordinating such a significant policy decision with the rest of the government.

Over the next six weeks, the NSC staff and NEA jointly fought a holding action to protect the CCC program to Iraq. The NSC staffers called for a searching examination of existing and future policy options. As one senior White House official remembered: "USDA was prevented from suspending CCC in April because it was no longer a solely technical agricultural issue. You couldn't have GS-11s [mid-level bureaucrats] in Agriculture making decisions of this nature. And until we heard otherwise, Scowcroft, Bush, and the rest of us felt that it was best to continue the CCC program."

At an April 12 PCC meeting that was convened to set the agenda for an NSC Deputies Committee meeting scheduled for April 16, NEA Chief Kelly declared that NSD-26 should be the basis for future action.[56] As he interpreted that document, this meant Iraq should receive the remainder of the $1 billion in FY90 CCC credits as well as $200 million in pending short-term Export-Import Bank credits. In addition, Kelly recommended increased contacts with Saddam Hussein and other Iraqi officials to stress in person the importance of moderation. Richard Haass reminded the group of the other themes of NSD-26: concern about Iraqi human rights abuses and the need to involve Iraq in the overall Middle East peace process. He feared that a strategy of economic sanctions or containment would forfeit any chance to influence Hussein, and that it would be ineffective, earning no support from Europe and only harsh criticism from moderate Arabs who wished to work with Hussein. Haass also stressed

---

54. USDA Draft Press Release, April 1, 1990, DNSA "Iraqgate," document no. 1295; see also Representative Henry Gonzalez's floor statement in the *Congressional Record*, July 9, 1992.

55. Recounted in NEA to Kimmitt, March 5, 1990, DNSA "Iraqgate," document no. 1247.

56. Kelly was coming under increasing criticism from Congress. At an April hearing, Representative Mel Levine (D-Calif.) blasted Kelly's approach, noting that he was "very, very worried that the benign Administration, looking the other way and holding out the olive branch toward Iraq, may yield the same kind of exasperating results" as after the Tiananmen Square incident in China. *National Journal*, April 13, 1991, p. 891.

the need for a coordinated policy, not agency-specific nor piecemeal, toward Iraq. The Department of Defense did not participate in the debate.

Meanwhile, the diplomats were worried. Ambassador Glaspie reported from Baghdad that she had met with Deputy Foreign Minister Hamdoun on April 1, the day of Hussein's disturbing speech, and "stressed the serious problem which now exists between our two governments." She tried, however, to make him understand that "this does not mean that there is an effort to 'get' Iraq."[57] Briefing Under Secretary of State Kimmitt before the upcoming Deputies Committee meeting, Kelly conceded that Iraq's recent actions had "virtually eliminated political support for efforts to build useful relations with Iraq." But he was more worried that the State Department was losing influence within the Executive branch to rivals such as the Commerce Department and the Agriculture Department. "In order to regain control of policy toward Iraq," he reasoned, "we need to establish a political framework that provides a strong response to irresponsible Iraqi actions in the near term, and lays down some longer-term markers for gradually rebuilding the relationship."[58]

Finding such a framework, however, had eluded the Bush team for over a year, and it continued to do so. As Kelly observed, "the dilemma we face is that the relationship is already paper-thin." Baghdad was, in fact, gaining increasing leverage in the relationship: U.S. oil imports from Iraq, which had totaled 80,000 barrels per day in 1987, skyrocketed more than eight-fold to 675,000 per day in early 1990 and reached fully 1.1 million barrels per day in July.[59] Terminating Export-Import loans or CCC guarantees would, in the end, hurt U.S. exporters even more than Iraq. The dilemma, Kelly admitted, was that "we [needed] to send a signal to both Iraq and the Congress that we [were] prepared to take action against Iraq as a sign of our displeasure," while simultaneously preserving "our ability to deal with the Iraqis in the longer term." Apart from urging preservation of the CCC program, however, Kelly offered no ideas for how the United States could accomplish those goals.

The Deputies Committee meeting on April 16 was inconclusive. Kimmitt, unconvinced by Kelly's argument, advocated terminating both Export-Import loans and CCC guarantees for Iraq.[60] Gates agreed, as he

---

57. Baghdad 1888, "Smuggled Electrical Components: Iraq Asserts Innocence," April 1, 1990, DNSA "Iraqgate," document no. 1294.

58. Kelly to Kimmitt, "NSC Deputies Committee Meeting on Iraq—April 16, 1990," DNSA "Iraqgate," document no. 1326.

59. Friedman, *Spider's Web*, p. 160.

60. Kimmitt note to Secretary Baker, April 17, 1990, DNSA "Iraqgate," document no. 1333.

recalls, that "the policy needed to be changed to one that was more confrontational." Under Secretary of Defense Paul Wolfowitz also agreed that Hussein could not be curbed, yet he saw little significance to the CCC issue one way or another, and worried about the reaction of domestic farm business lobbies. Gates, in the chair, ordered several follow-up studies for another Deputies Committee meeting sometime in May.

In Baghdad, Glaspie was absolutely opposed to any cutoff of CCC credit guarantees. She assured the Iraqis that the Bush administration still hoped for good relations.[61] In public, NEA chief Kelly remained supportive of the CCC program. When he testified before the House in late April, Kelly claimed that President Bush himself opposed food-related sanctions. Moreover, he said, "experience has shown that economic sanctions are most effective when they are imposed on a multilateral basis. There is no prospect of this in the case of Iraq."[62] While Kelly admitted that the relationship between the United States and Iraq had taken a turn for the worse, he stated that so long as Iraq acted responsibly, relations would improve: "The potential for improvement in conduct is certainly there."

Responding to pleas from his staff, National Security Advisor Scowcroft tried to delay as long as possible the official suspension of CCC credit guarantees. He called Secretary of Agriculture Yeutter on May 18, asking the Agriculture Department once more to hold off on a press release announcing termination of the program.[63] Haass personally traveled to Baghdad to impress on Hussein the seriousness of the current impasse. Haass told Foreign Minister Aziz that the future of the U.S.-Iraqi relationship lay in Iraq's hands. With Congress pushing for sanctions, the Iraqis, Haass warned, were giving the administration little help in resisting Iraq's opponents within the United States. Aziz complained that the recent bad press on Iraq in the United States and the continued American military presence in the Gulf showed the Iraqis that Bush had adopted an anti-Iraq policy. "No," Haass remembers replying: "we are simply pursuing a pro-U.S. policy."

As Gates had requested, an options paper was prepared for another meeting of the Deputies Committee on the subject of Iraq. The State-drafted paper noted that "suspension of CCC at this point would be a strong political statement." The memo raised the possibility of normalizing relations with Iran, but dismissed the idea as one that "would send paranoia-meters

---

61. Baghdad 2907, May 18, 1990, DNSA "Iraqgate," document no. 1381.

62. Kelly testimony before the House Subcommittee on Europe and the Middle East, April 26, 1990, DNSA "Iraqgate," document no. 1355.

63. According to Treasury Department notes, reprinted in *Congressional Record*, July 9, 1992.

in Baghdad off the end of the scale. It would raise basic questions about our policy in the Gulf and the region as whole that would have to be addressed here."[64] Any proposal to rally moderate Arabs into an anti-Iraq coalition seemed quixotic. In the spring of 1990, the primary Middle East policy concern was the Arab-Israeli dispute. Neither U.S. officials nor Arab leaders dwelt on the possibility of an Iraqi military move against a brother Arab state.

Fearing that the tide was turning against continuation of CCC credits, Glaspie cabled Baker on May 18 to protest the move.[65] But her objections were overridden. On May 29, the Deputies Committee met, again with Gates in the chair. The Agriculture Department reported on the results of its administrative review of the program and described some irregularities which, while not egregious, were still loose ends.[66] Gates went around the table to ask what each department recommended. Deputy Secretary of Agriculture Ann Veneman responded first: "I don't even know why we are discussing this. USDA has already decided to suspend the program. There's nothing left to decide." For State, Kimmitt still held to his April view, opposing further assistance to Iraq as punishment for Iraq's misconduct. The Justice Department joined the chorus. Attorney General William Barr explained that, quite apart from the CCC program irregularities, his prosecutors in Atlanta were preparing to indict Iraqi officials for their complicity in BNL-Atlanta's unauthorized and unsecured loans of cash to Iraq in 1988 and 1989.

Gates later recalled that the sentiment for CCC suspension was unanimous "with the sole exception of the Defense Department because of their argument that we shouldn't use food as a weapon; it was not related to Iraq at all." The meeting also featured a long discussion about how to strengthen and tighten export controls, and all agreed that licensing requirements for dual-use exports to Iraq should be tightened. Haass and Charles from the NSC tried to soften the blow to U.S.-Iraqi relations. The Iraqis were told that the second tranche was being withheld only temporarily, pending the outcome of the CCC and Atlanta investigations.[67]

---

64. State Department memo for Brent Scowcroft, "Options Paper on Iraq," May 16, 1990, DNSA "Iraqgate," document no. 1379.

65. Baghdad 2907, May 18, 1990, DNSA "Iraqgate," document no. 1381.

66. See USDA memo, Brosch, Dickerson, and McElvain to Crowder and Raul, "USDA Administrative Review of Iraq GSM-102 [CCC] Program," May 21, 1990, DNSA "Iraqgate," document no. 1386.

67. Commerce memo, Galvin to Kloske, "Interagency Meeting on Iraq," June 11, 1990, DNSA "Iraqgate," document no. 1422; Staff Report, Senate Select Committee on Intelligence, "The Intelligence Community's Involvement in the Banca Nazionale del Lavoro Affair," 103rd Cong., 1st sess., February 1993, p. 69.

The Iraqis took the suspension of CCC guarantees as yet more evidence of an anti-Iraq conspiracy in Washington. Diplomats at State, as well as the NSC staff, were pessimistic about future relations with Baghdad; they began to pay more attention to Hussein's militancy. At the end of June, the State Department even considered putting Iraq back on the list of states formally designated as supporting terrorism, which would preclude any significant economic interaction between the two countries.[68] Although NSD-26 was still on the books, it had clearly been overtaken. The Bush administration decided for the time being against any further public advocacy of better relations with Iraq. At the end of June, Wolfowitz gave an interview to the United States Information Agency (USIA), in which he commented that, while the Soviet Union had collapsed, there remained someone in the Middle East who had threatened to use missiles on his neighbors.[69]

Although there was some ambivalence within the administration over the wisdom of halting CCC credits, there was more consensus on the need to tighten export controls. Officials developed new guidelines for export licensing in the weeks after the May 29 Deputies Committee meeting. Even before the new guidelines were in place, Haass made sure that tungsten furnaces manufactured by the Consarc Company were not shipped to Iraq: the Iraqis claimed that the furnaces were for the production of artificial limbs, but the CIA judged that they were more likely to assist in the manufacture of nuclear weapons. Because the legislative revision was still incomplete, Haass was able to stop the shipment only by invoking an obscure provision of the 1978 Nuclear Non-Proliferation Act. The furnaces were seized on the docks just before they were due to be loaded onto ships bound for Iraq in late June.

Hussein in Trouble

In July, Hussein's position worsened appreciably. The United States was growing antagonistic. The Soviet Union was gone. Iraq's debts were mounting. While the French, Germans, Chinese, and many others remained willing to sell Iraq high-tech arms, they were no longer willing to lend Iraq money or let its government buy goods on credit. The CIA learned that Hussein personally received confirmation of this bad news from bankers in Europe before a July 1990 meeting of the Paris Club (the

---

68. State Department 208957, "Iraq and Terrorism," June 27, 1990, DNSA "Iraqgate," document no. 1441.

69. *State Department Bulletin*, July 10, 1990, p. 8.

198 I DEALING WITH DICTATORS

informal coordinating committee for big lenders). Hussein had nowhere to turn but back to the very Arab states to which he was indebted. Foremost among these was the small but wealthy emirate on Iraq's southern border: Kuwait.

Hussein's plight was exacerbated by the falling price of oil, which had been steadily dropping over the previous six months. Almost all of Iraq's earnings came from oil, and by July the price had dropped below OPEC's agreed price floor. For every dollar reduction in the price of a barrel of oil, Hussein lost tens of millions of dollars of cash he needed to pay the interest on his loans. By 1990, he was regularly defaulting on payments to his Arab creditors, particularly Kuwait, which held some $10 billion of Iraq's debt. If the price of oil continued to drop, Hussein would begin defaulting on his payments to Western creditors, and that could spell economic collapse for Iraq. The drop in oil prices was no accident of nature: Kuwait and the United Arab Emirates were producing almost two million barrels more per annum than the 22-million-barrel quota established by OPEC.[70] This overproduction drove the price of oil down and, with it, Iraq's hopes of sustaining both a military build-up and an economic recovery.

Hussein focused his anger on Kuwait. At a meeting of the Arab League in Baghdad on May 30, he accused the Kuwaitis not just of overproducing, but also of siphoning oil from the Rumaila oilfield which lay underneath the Iraq-Kuwait border. Over the next weeks, he repeated a demand that Kuwait impose a moratorium on Iraqi war debts, and he insisted that Kuwait repay Iraq for the oil that Kuwait had "stolen" from the Rumaila oilfield. Although neither of Hussein's accusations was without foundation, the Kuwaitis rejected all of Hussein's demands, especially that for the $2.4 billion alleged by Iraqi Foreign Minister Aziz to represent the value of the Rumaila oil. His verbal threats having failed, Hussein on July 15 moved several divisions of Iraqi Republican Guards to the Iraq-Kuwait border.

The Bush administration was slow to react to the developing crisis between Iraq and Kuwait. Other foreign policy concerns drew attention away from the Gulf. A crisis between Pakistan and India seemed more intense and far more dangerous, for each nation was believed to possess nuclear weapons. In the middle of May, Gates, Haass, and Kelly were all in South Asia trying to talk the Indians and Pakistanis into backing off from war.

Neither in Washington nor in Baghdad did State Department representatives take a position on the merits of the Iraqi-Kuwaiti dispute. They did, however, insist that it be settled peacefully. On July 19, Baker sent to

---

70.   Freedman and Karsh, *The Gulf Conflict*, pp. 41ff.

all American ambassadors in the Middle East a circular intended to clarify official U.S. policy on the Iraq-Kuwait clash:

> A central principle in international relations is that disputes
> should be settled by peaceful means, not through intimidation
> and threats of the use of force. The United States takes no position
> on the substance of the bilateral issues concerning Iraq and
> Kuwait....US policy is unchanged: We remain committed to
> ensure the free flow of oil from the Gulf and support the sover-
> eignty and the integrity of the Gulf states....We also remain com-
> mitted to supporting the individual and collective self-defense of
> our friends in the Gulf, with whom we have deep and longstand-
> ing ties.[71]

From July 15 on, the CIA monitored the situation on a daily basis.
Hussein dispatched more and more troops to the border with Kuwait. On
July 25, CIA Director William Webster briefed President Bush and top officials that the intelligence community was issuing a formal "warning of
war." The warning was based on troop movements, not on special knowledge of Hussein's intentions: the CIA reported that the degree of military
mobilization indicated that Iraq would be capable of advancing through
Kuwait and deep into Saudi territory. The intelligence community did not
predict where Hussein would strike, where he would stop, or what he
intended to do, but it did warn that an attack was coming.

This intelligence analysis was, however, contradicted by Iraq's neighbors. Jordan, Egypt, Saudi Arabia, and even Kuwait and the UAE urged
the United States not to become involved in the dispute and cautioned that
Hussein was unlikely to carry out his threats. Bush telephoned the
Egyptian president, the king of Saudi Arabia, and the king of Jordan: all
assured him that, knowing Saddam Hussein as they did, they believed
that no attack was imminent. The war warning from CIA stated flatly that
the Kuwaitis were wrong in supposing that Hussein was bluffing, however. Bush and his advisers had to wonder, Gates remembered, "Who knows
Saddam Hussein better? King Fahd, the Amir of Kuwait, or a GS-15 analyst out in Langley, Virginia?"

The conventional wisdom in Washington was that any attack would
be limited to the border areas. Gates recalled that most people believed
Hussein would take the Rumaila oilfield and possibly the islands of
Bubiyan and Warba. A Defense Department summary of intelligence
analysis concluded: "If Iraq did attack Kuwait, its goal would likely be

---

71. State Department 235637, "Iraqi Letter to Arab League Threatening Kuwait," July
19, 1990, DNSA "Iraqgate," document no. 1465.

focused on obtaining a port in the Persian Gulf, rather than completely conquering Kuwait."[72] The administration was not pleased by the prospect of an Iraqi attack, even a limited one, but no one believed that much could be done about it. At a July 25 press conference, State Department spokesperson Margaret Tutwiler emphasized that the United States was not committed to defending the territorial integrity of the Gulf states. "We do not have any defense treaties with Kuwait," she said. "There are no special defense or security commitments to Kuwait." She added, however, that "coercion and intimidation" had no place "in a civilized world."[73]

Even these veiled American warnings were too much for Kuwait, Saudi Arabia, and other moderate Arab states. They feared that such sentiments expressed publicly would provoke or embarrass Hussein and that he would respond violently in order to save face. The only Arab country willing to send a cautionary signal to Iraq was the United Arab Emirates. On July 24, the United States conducted aerial refueling exercises with the UAE as a show of support for Kuwait. But when Tutwiler publicly mentioned these exercises at her press conference, the UAE reacted angrily to what it perceived as America's heavy-handedness. At this juncture, and without any warning, Saddam Hussein invited April Glaspie for a private audience.

Glaspie had no time to get special instructions for her meeting. So, like Tutwiler the day before, Glaspie stated to Hussein that the United States had no defense treaty with Kuwait and no opinion on the substance of the border dispute. She told him that Bush had "instructed her to broaden and deepen our relations with Iraq and...had very recently reaffirmed his desire for a better relationship and has proven that, for example, by opposing sanctions bills."[74] She again emphasized that the United States could not endorse anything but a peaceful settlement. According to her report, Hussein agreed, stating that he wished to see the issue resolved without violence at an OPEC meeting scheduled for July 28 in Jeddah, Saudi Arabia.

Glaspie later claimed that she informed Hussein in no uncertain terms that the United States would respond forcefully to any Iraqi incursion.[75] These claims are not substantiated by what she reported to Washington.

---

72. DoD Intelligence Information Report, July 28, 1990, DNSA "Iraqgate," document no. 1481.

73. *New York Times*, July 26, 1990.

74. Baghdad 4235, "Iraq/Kuwait: Ambassador's Meeting with Saddam," July 25, 1990, DNSA "Iraqgate," document no. 1482; Baghdad 4237, "Saddam's Message of Friendship to President Bush," July 25, 1990, ibid., document no. 1484.

75. See House International Relations Committee, Subcommittee on Europe and the Middle East, *Hearings*, March 21, 1991.

Nor is there evidence that Washington had decided on such a momentous warning, which would have required backing at least from Kuwait and Saudi Arabia. Nor, in any case, does it seem likely that a firm statement from Glaspie would have carried much weight with Hussein. Any assertion to the contrary, Gates said later, "is post facto lint picking.... The fact is that Saddam Hussein was convinced that the United States would not act, and there was nothing we could have done beforehand to persuade him otherwise."

At the White House, the arrival of Glaspie's cable reporting on her meeting with Hussein was greeted with relief. The White House took Hussein's assurances that he looked to a diplomatic solution at the upcoming OPEC meeting as a sign that the Arabs were finally going to settle the dispute amongst themselves. Haass even pulled back from a stern memo he had sent to President Bush, hours before hearing the news of Glaspie's meeting. In it, Haass had urged that Hussein be warned in no uncertain terms against a violent settlement of his grievances with Kuwait. After reading Glaspie's cable, Haass and Charles drafted a letter for Bush to send to Hussein, trying to build on this seemingly positive turn of events. Once again, it seemed, Arab diplomacy was at work. The crisis appeared to be subsiding.

At the July 28 OPEC meeting, the Iraqis agreed to a further meeting with the Kuwaitis in Jeddah, with the Saudis as arbiters. That same day, the State Department prepared a cable to Baghdad with the message from Bush that Haass and Charles had drafted. To some officials at the Defense Department, the proposed language seemed too balanced, nuanced, and non-threatening. Henry Rowen and Under Secretary Wolfowitz tried to convince State to send instead a sharp warning against any Iraqi military action, but both the State Department and the White House believed that too strong a message would torpedo Arab diplomatic efforts.[76] The message ultimately went out without Pentagon concurrence. In the message President Bush said:

> I was pleased to learn of the agreement between Iraq and Kuwait to begin negotiations in Jeddah to find a peaceful solution to the current tensions between you. The United States and Iraq both have a strong interest in preserving the peace and stability of the Middle East. For this reason, we believe that differences are best resolved by peaceful means and not by threats involving military force or conflict. I also welcome your statement that Iraq desires friendship rather than confrontation with the United States. Let

---

76. *New York Times*, October 25, 1992.

me reassure you, as my ambassador, Senator Dole and others have done, that my administration continues to desire better relations with Iraq. We will also continue to support our friends in the region with whom we have had long-standing ties. We see no necessary inconsistency between these two objectives. As you know, we still have certain fundamental concerns about certain Iraqi policies and activities, and we will continue to raise these concerns with you, in a spirit of friendship and candor....Both our governments must maintain open channels of communication to avoid misunderstandings and in order to build a more durable foundation for improving our relations.[77]

But the July 31 meeting in Jeddah came to naught. On August 1, the intelligence community upgraded its formal "warning of war" to a "warning of attack," reflecting a judgment that the outbreak of fighting was imminent. The Deputies Committee hastily convened a meeting. Gates was out of town. Kimmitt asked Kerr, the deputy head of the CIA, to estimate the chance of an Iraqi attack on Kuwait. Kerr said the probability was "99.9" percent. That was not what Iraq's Arab neighbors are saying, Kelly pointed out.

Kimmitt and Haass considered sending a second message from Bush, more strongly worded than the first, but Hussein took steps that preempted any further action: in the early morning of August 2, before the sun rose, hundreds of Iraqi tanks and thousands of troops began a rapid conquest of Kuwait.

---

77. State Department 247900, "President Bush's response to Saddam Hussein's message," July 28, 1990, reprinted in the *New York Times*, October 25, 1992.

Chapter 7

Learning from the Cases

Ernest R. May and Philip D. Zelikow

As the Preface explains, these cases were designed for and used in executive program classes for senior managers in the U.S. intelligence community. In this final chapter, we review some of the ways in which participants in that executive program approached these cases in order to learn from them.

The pointers here say little about intelligence analysis per se. We did not think it the purpose of the executive program to try to teach grandmothers how to suck eggs. The pointers are designed to stimulate thought about what happens to information and analysis — reality judgments — when they come to be blended with value judgments and action judgments to form appreciations, as Vickers used the term (see Introduction).

China, 1945–1948

One of the best ways of experiencing the case of U.S. policy toward China and Chiang Kai-shek in the period between 1945 and 1948 is to imagine oneself a staff aide to Secretary of State Marshall in 1947 when he was reviewing the recommendations of General Wedemeyer. Like Marshall, this hypothetical staff aide would know that if Marshall rejects Wedemeyer's recommendations, no amount of effort will prevent the fact from leaking and resulting in an outcry from supporters of Chiang both on Capitol Hill and elsewhere, including Henry Luce's widely-read magazines, *Time* and *Life*. The aide also knows that, if Marshall accepts Wedemeyer's recommendations, the decision will be questioned by the State Department's China experts, critics of Chiang elsewhere, and large numbers of influential members of the Eastern establishment who oppose any diversion of attention or resources away from Europe. The secretary has to expect to be pressed about the reasons for his choice, whatever it is, and later to be grilled by committees of Congress. He has to be ready to answer in-depth questions about the relative importance of China to the

United States, feasible alternative courses of action, and the possible consequences of each such course.

Providing staffwork for a high official is hard even if the official is a gentle taskmaster; Marshall was anything but that. General Omar Bradley recalled serving on Marshall's staff as a young officer. Marshall had thrown out an idea and asked his staff to analyze it. Bradley reported that he could find nothing to criticize, whereupon Marshall blew up, saying that it was the job of a staff officer to find every possible fault in his boss's thinking. Preparing Marshall for press conference questions or executive session hearings on Capitol Hill would have required the staff aide to follow to its limit every argument involving almost every distinguishable contingency, after which Marshall would ask: are there factors I did not consider?

The most challenging line of speculation concerns the possible domestic political consequences of alternative U.S. strategies. In fact, Marshall's decision did produce horrendous domestic fall-out. When in 1949 his successor, Dean Acheson, issued a fat "White Paper" on U.S. relations with China, making the argument that Chiang had been beyond rescue by the United States, Republicans and conservative Democrats would attack it ferociously. So would Luce and many others. In the meantime, Alger Hiss, once a high-ranking State Department officer, would be exposed as a probable Soviet spy, and many of the critics of Marshall and Acheson would charge that Hiss and other undercover Communists in the State Department had engineered decisions aimed deliberately at undermining Chiang and allowing the Chinese Communists to win the civil war.

In the spring of 1950, Senator Joseph R. McCarthy of Wisconsin would take up this charge. A barroom brawler, McCarthy had little concern for either accuracy or consistency. More responsible Senators promptly opened hearings on McCarthy's allegations with the intention of disgracing him. The summer and autumn of 1950, however, brought the Korean War, and American defenders of South Korea were initially driven into a narrow corner of the peninsula. Then, after recovering and marching into North Korea, they were thrown again into retreat as a result of large-scale intervention by Communist China. During that autumn, McCarthy toured the United States attacking those of his critics who were up for reelection, and nearly all went down to defeat.

For the next several years, McCarthy would be a power on Capitol Hill. "McCarthyism"—irresponsibly indiscriminate allegations of treason, espionage, and subversive activity—rampaged across the whole nation. McCarthy even attacked Marshall himself as having been party to "a conspiracy so black that its principals shall be forever deserving the maledictions of all honest men." So influential was McCarthy for a time that even Dwight Eisenhower, as the 1952 Republican presidential candidate, smilingly shared a platform with him, in spite of the calumnies McCarthy had spread about George Marshall, Eisenhower's friend, mentor, and former chief.

McCarthyism as it flourished in the early 1950s could not be clearly foreseen in 1947 and 1948. But one of the challenges posed by this case study is to imagine how the possibility of something like the furor over "who lost China" could have figured in the staffwork done for Marshall in that earlier period.

Marshall was resolutely and austerely non-political. He did not vote, holding that it was improper for military leaders to entertain preferences regarding those who might become their commanders-in-chief. He disapproved of the very idea that electoral considerations might influence decisions on foreign policy or national security policy. In 1948, President Truman had surprised Marshall, and the rest of the world, by suddenly recognizing Israel as an independent state. Suspecting that, as many observers thought, Truman had done so partly in hope of stronger support from American Jews in the approaching presidential election, Marshall considered resigning in protest. When he found Truman's political aide Clark Clifford at a White House meeting on the Middle East, Marshall bristled and, in effect, demanded that he leave. Clifford went away complaining of Marshall's "righteous God-damned Baptist tone."

The challenge presented by this case is to think about how to integrate all the considerations that bear on a difficult and uncertain choice. It would hardly be realistic to imagine an aide to Marshall arguing for a totally different policy line on account of possible domestic reverberations, but it is not equally unrealistic to imagine a staffer prodding the secretary to think ahead about such reverberations and perhaps to prepare for them.

The point of trying to participate vicariously in the choices of 1947–1948 is not to decide whether Marshall made the right choice or not; it is to reflect on the process of making choices. Although we suggest that readers think hardest about questions to which Marshall might have given more thought, we believe that simply identifying the questions that Marshall did ask can be immensely rewarding. One objective of immersing oneself in a case study is to reflect on rules of thumb worth remembering at future moments of choice. And for this purpose there may be no better model than Marshall in this case. Indeed, we hope that as readers or students enter imaginatively into other episodes chronicled here—and as they make their own real-time choices—they will ask themselves: how would Marshall have thought about this issue?

The Congo, 1960–1963

The case of U.S. policy toward the African nation of the Congo may strain the reader's imagination more than any other in our collection. The context for U.S. decision-making in the late 1950s and early 1960s was the high Cold War. "McCarthyism" had subsided after the mid-1950s: the Senate had voted to censure McCarthy himself for his excesses. Fear of domestic subversion had subsided, but this fear was displaced by one more firmly based in reality. The Soviet Union had developed nuclear and thermonuclear weapons, had displayed long-range bombers capable of dropping atomic bombs on the United States, and had sent up its Sputnik satellites, showing that it was also capable of building and deploying ballistic missiles with intercontinental range. The Soviet Union thus seemed to be ahead of the United States in long-range rocketry, and the American public had good reason to fear an annihilating Soviet attack. Reminders of this peril were soon on every hand. "Fallout Shelter" signs became common in U.S. cities, and schoolchildren regularly rehearsed crouching under their desks for protection against nuclear attack.

Meanwhile, the arena of the Cold War expanded. American officials had boasted in the early 1950s of thwarting Communist efforts to take over Iran, Guatemala, and the Philippine Islands. But the late 1950s saw Communists successfully push the French out of northern Indo-China and gain strength elsewhere. Stalin's successor, Nikita Khrushchev, promised support for "wars of national liberation." Many anti-colonial nationalists aligned themselves with the Soviet Union, or at least declared that they would not side with the United States. In 1959, Americans had the shock of seeing Cuba, ninety miles from their own shores, declare itself committed to Communism and a member of the Soviet camp. Dread of nuclear war thus had as its accompaniment a growing sense that Communism might sweep over the non-European world and even most of the planet.

To enter vicariously into decision-making on the Congo, one must somehow internalize the anxieties of this period. It can help to look at some films popular at the time such as, for example, "On the Beach," in which all civilization disintegrates under radioactive clouds, or "The Manchurian Candidate," in which an American war veteran is brainwashed into becoming a puppet of all-knowing Communist masters. If one does make the investment needed to get vicariously into this case, the payoff can be quite high, not least for seeing in sharp perspective the problem of how to mount an analytical attack on strong, widely-shared presumptions that actually have foundations as flimsy as cobwebs.

In this case, the Joint Chiefs of Staff—the senior officers of the U.S. armed services, and individually men of discernment and wide experience—unite in declaring that the United States should be prepared for unilateral military action on the premise that "we will not tolerate a Soviet military takeover of the Congo." Here, Dwight Eisenhower, a protégé of Marshall and a man of the highest intelligence, completing his second term as president, asserts at a National Security Council meeting that the situation resulting from UN withdrawal from the Congo would be "too ghastly to contemplate." Here, senior officials with shining academic credentials and broad experience believe that the president has ordered the assassination of Lumumba, and they sponsor one attempt after another to carry out that order.

How could a staffer for the president or for one of his key advisers suggest effectively that the underlying reasoning be probed? How could they see that the kinds of questions get asked that Marshall asked about China? For example, what exactly did the Soviet Union stand to gain in the Congo and the West stand to lose? If the Soviet Union did effect a military takeover, what would be the chances that the Congo would turn into a liability, where the cost of preserving order outran any returns, whether in propaganda or in copper and precious stones? What might be the costs to the United States and its allies of assuming the commitment recommended by the Joint Chiefs? How could one cause a serious exploration of the question that even Marshall did not pursue as far as he might have done with regard to China: what could be the domestic consequences of making such a commitment?

To list these questions is not to suppose that merely asking them could have caused the chiefs, the president, and others to strike their foreheads and declare that they had been foolish. There were plausible scenarios in which Soviet success in the Congo would indeed have had domino effects elsewhere. In a world in which survival might turn on Soviet leaders' belief that, to prevent their taking over West Berlin, the United States would initiate a mutually suicidal nuclear exchange, it was not foolish for U.S. officials to worry about any action that might lead Moscow to question U.S. resolve. In purely humanitarian terms, indeed, there were "ghastly consequences" following the UN withdrawal from the Congo, especially as the U.S. protégé Joseph Mobutu transformed himself into the tyrant Mobutu Sese Seko.

The opportunity here is for an experience complementary to that of participating vicariously in the decision-making regarding China in 1947–1948 described in the first case in this book. There, General Marshall chose the most cautious of possible action options. The challenge was to come up with ways to get Marshall to think a little more about preparing for the possible adverse consequences of caution. Here, the challenge is to invent ways of getting members of the Eisenhower administration to think more about the possible adverse consequences of bold action, and the possible rewards of caution.

This case also offers the opportunity to worry through questions of implementation as well as policy. Even if the premise stands that developments in Congo are important to the United States, does it follow that the U.S. government should attempt to assassinate Lumumba? Surely, ethical considerations ought not to be simply brushed aside. What would make assassination of a foreign leader an act that could be publicly justified, if it came to light as, eventually, it surely would? Are circumstances such as to make the killing of Lumumba comparable to killing Hitler before or during World War II? How sure was the basis for belief that Lumumba's removal would make conditions better for the Congolese, or for the United States?

Although this case comes from the comparatively distant past, it may have more utility for the present than any other case in our volume, because analytical questions concerning the Congo of Lumumba's time are strikingly similar to those inherent in a global war against terrorism. How does one gauge the seriousness of a supposed threat? How does one weigh a hoped-for reduction in threat against possible costs? How should one take account of an adversary's reading of a U.S. decision not to take action that is within its capabilities? How should one evaluate courses of action that might be open to objection on ethical grounds such as, most obviously, targeted assassinations? Precisely because this case is from a remote era, an effort to enter into it imaginatively can sharpen one's ability to identify and pose questions worth asking today.

Nicaragua, 1977–1979, and Iran, 1978–1979

The Somoza case and the case of the Shah of Iran both come from the presidency of Jimmy Carter. Both involve essentially the same policy issue: how to manage a relationship with a weakening dictator who is an ally of the United States, who is threatened by domestic opponents potentially hostile to the United States, but who might conceivably be replaced by an alternative regime that would not only remain a U.S. ally but be marginally more democratic.

In the near or immediate background were events that made the context for decision-making drastically different from that of the late 1940s or the early 1960s. The combination of moral certainty and comparative ruthlessness evident in decision-making about the Congo figured also in decision-making about Vietnam: Americans of both parties attached high importance to keeping South Vietnam out of Communist hands. Many officials with firsthand experience in Vietnam came to view South Vietnam's dictator, Ngo Dinh Diem, as someone whose stubbornness, personal pride, and misplaced family loyalties jeopardized the campaign to contain a Communist-led insurgency. Most American reporters who covered Vietnam adopted this view and broadcast it to audiences at home. A coterie of advisers to President John F. Kennedy, working with Henry Cabot Lodge, the U.S. Ambassador in Saigon, had therefore encouraged a coup by South Vietnamese military officers, one result of which was Diem's murder.

By coincidence, Kennedy's own murder followed soon afterward.[1] His successor, Lyndon B. Johnson, inherited not only concern about possible expansion of the Communist sphere but also a sense of additional responsibility accruing from awareness that the United States had helped bring to power the generals now ruling in Saigon. Johnson was very conscious of this responsibility. One of his first acts as president was to fire Roger Hilsman, the assistant secretary of state for Far Eastern Affairs, whom Johnson thought had authored what he called "the kill Diem cable." Johnson also looked at Vietnam with the eyes of someone who had been in the Senate with Joe McCarthy and witnessed the adverse domestic effects of the Truman administration's cautious approach to China. In characteristically earthy language, Johnson said to a confidant that the uproar if the United States lost Vietnam would make the uproar over the loss of China "look like chickenshit."

But in the event, when South Vietnam was eventually taken over by Communist North Vietnam, the public reaction was not at all like that attending Communist success in China at the end of the 1940s. Commitment of a half-million American combat troops, accompanied by a massive strategic bombing campaign, had failed to rescue South Vietnam. Debate at home about the wisdom of and even the moral justification for the war had ruptured the near consensus that had developed during the high Cold War after the ebbing of "McCarthyism." Partly in reaction to radical antiwar protests, Johnson's successor, Richard M. Nixon, employed at home some of the "dirty tricks" associated with covert action abroad. Members of the president's immediate staff arranged the burglary of the opposition party's offices in the Watergate building. Investigations by a special prosecutor and by congressional committees traced subsequent efforts to cover up this crime back to Nixon himself. Facing certain impeachment and probable conviction, Nixon resigned, giving way to Vice President Gerald Ford, who then lost in 1976 to Jimmy Carter.

In the meantime, Congress had conducted other investigations, including far-reaching inquiries into Cold War covert operations. Reports from special committees, particularly the one headed by Senator Frank Church of Idaho, detailed and denounced the CIA's efforts to assassinate Lumumba and Cuba's Fidel Castro. Congress passed legislation forbidding any such efforts in the future. It also set up permanent select committees to oversee the intelligence community. Congressional leaders

---

1. Charles McCarry, a onetime CIA officer, has written several thrillers built around the premise that Kennedy's murder was revenge for Diem's, but only the imagination of a thriller writer could piece together a plausible causal connection between the two events.

negotiated with the White House a series of agreements limiting the extent to which presidents could authorize covert action without prior closed-door congressional consent.

The Carter administration thus operated in circumstances quite different from those of its predecessors. It could not expect Congress and the public to accept uncritically its judgments as to the best means for dealing with dictators such as Somoza or the Shan of Iran. It had to expect debates in which significant numbers of citizens would condemn whatever choice the administration made: some would say that no dictator should receive U.S. support, while others would insist that the United States should back almost any regime so long as it was anti-Communist, and the opinions of still others would range across numerous points in between.

Carter and his aides had to expect, moreover, that whatever policy the administration pursued, each stage of implementation would be subject to congressional and public scrutiny. This was not solely because of additional congressional oversight. Indeed, the two intelligence oversight committees proved to be models of discretion. It was rather because post-Vietnam, post-Watergate Washington was teeming with investigative reporters who could ferret out information about almost all of the foreign policy debates in the executive branch. Officials to whom journalists would reveal another official's disclosure would make disclosures of their own, in hope of getting fair reportage for their side of an issue. Most things came to light, sooner or later.

Many officials had a further incentive for disclosure because of the multiplication in layers of bureaucracy, begun early in the Cold War, that had been deliberately built up by Nixon and his National Security Advisor, Henry Kissinger, in an effort to dilute departmental autonomy and to concentrate policymaking in the White House. Not even cabinet officers could be sure that their written memoranda reached the president, but the president was bound to read any prominent story in the *New York Times*, the *Washington Post*, or one of the major weeklies; thus these seemed, to such officials, attractive alternative routes of communication.

These conditions have not changed. Someone who can successfully imagine taking part in one of these Carter-era cases gets an opportunity to reflect on how a combination of greater openness and more intricate organization can complicate decision-making. Consider an intelligence or policy analyst a layer or two below a departmental assistant secretary or the equivalent: how might that person try to ensure that important questions are seriously addressed, bearing in mind that any words on paper (or in e-mail) might appear in the next day's newspaper? How might he take into account the fact that this worry will be even more pronounced in the minds of men and women higher up in the decision chain, mixed with temptation to use the newspaper as a conduit for communicating with one another or with the president? How might she further take into account the fact that any piece of evidence or argument sent through ordinary channels must make its way through a maze of offices and committees?

Taking part vicariously in one of these Carter-era cases can help one think about how a mid-level analyst might try to be persuasive even in post-Vietnam, post-Watergate Washington. One thought-experiment which has proved useful for our students is to imagine making use of techniques suggested in *Thinking in Time*.[2] What follows deals only with the Iran case, but the questions are easily transferred to the case of Nicaragua, the chief difference being the level of public visibility. Events in Iran were likely to lead network prime-time news shows, while this was rarely true for events anywhere in the Americas.

Step one is to try to identify the presumptions in the minds of decision-makers. They know certain facts, but they base their decisions in large part on presumptions of fact. In September 1978, Carter and his aides knew that there had been large demonstrations in Iran which the Shah's troops had put down with heavy loss of life. They knew that the Shah had installed a new and allegedly reformist cabinet. They presumed that further demonstrations would occur, but that the Shah would retain control, and that some measures of reform would eventually quiet the opposition. One did not have to be in government to identify these presumptions: they were evident to anyone who read news stories citing high-level sources.

Step two, which is much harder, is to develop a strategy for probing key presumptions. *Thinking in Time* suggests two preliminary measures. The first is to assess the strength of a given presumption in the mind of a given decision-maker. If there had been a betting pool, what odds would President Carter have required to place a serious bet that the Shah would be in power in September 1978? What about National Security Advisor Zbigniew Brzezinski? Secretary of State Cyrus Vance? William Sullivan, the U.S. ambassador in Teheran? The second measure is to ask what new facts could either strengthen or weaken a key presumption; in this case, what could cause one of the major actors to change his estimate of what was likely? What facts could cause Vance, for example, to begin to think that the odds of the Shah's staying in power were nearer fifty-fifty than two out of three?

Step three is to start a search for facts that will either bolster or weaken an important presumption. As of September 1978, everyone in the administration presumed that the Shah had control of his army and would retain it. What specific evidence could have provided a test: perhaps

2. Richard E. Neustadt and Ernest R. May, *Thinking in Time: The Uses of History for Decision Makers* (New York: Free Press, 1986).

trends in desertion rates? numbers of demonstrators recognizable as out-of-uniform soldiers? numbers of disgruntled officers speaking to foreign reporters? The facts sought would have had to be facts that could work either way, not just support one thesis or another.

This approach was implicit in Marshall's analysis of the China problem. It could have been applied by an analyst involved in the Congo case. Here it is particularly worth imaginative deployment, for the case features two analysts—Gary Sick on the NSC staff and Henry Precht in the State Department—who could in fact have followed this methodology. Someone thinking about whether he or she could have done so, if in Sick's shoes or Precht's, has to recognize that the search for facts could itself appear to be evidence of a policy decision if reported in the press. A *Washington Post* story in September 1978 indicating that someone in the U.S. government was asking questions about the Iranian army's loyalty to the Shah could have had effects comparable, on a small scale, to those of President Carter's comment in December that the future of the Shah was "in the hands of the people of Iran," which seemed in Teheran to signal that the United States was giving up on the Shah.

Taking part vicariously in either of the Carter-era cases forces one to think not only about how to develop effective intelligence and policy analysis but also how to cope with the politics of contemporary decision-making in the United States.

The Philippines, 1983–1986

In 1980, Ronald Reagan defeated Jimmy Carter. A former two-term Governor of California, Reagan was perhaps better known to the nation-wide public as a movie star and radio and television commentator. He had been a New Deal Democrat but had changed parties and gone on to become a leading spokesman for right-wing Republicans. In 1976 he had been defeated for the Republican nomination by the more moderate incumbent, Gerald Ford. Since Reagan was already in his mid-sixties, most people took his concession speech to be a swan song, both for himself and for the militantly anti-Communist Republicans who had never entirely repudiated Joe McCarthy and who had forced the nomination of Barry Goldwater in 1964. These were the Republicans who had never reconciled themselves to the détente with the Soviet Union effected by Nixon and Kissinger.

Events during Carter's presidency helped to moot these expectations. After Carter allowed the fallen Shah to enter the United States for medical treatment, supporters of the Ayatollah Khomeini seized the U.S. embassy in Teheran and made several dozen American officials their hostages. An attempted rescue mission failed. Meanwhile, the domestic economy sagged. Business periodicals focused on Japan as a competitor likely to surpass the United States. Carter himself made a speech deploring America's "malaise." Détente with the Soviet Union gave way to renewed Cold War as the Soviets displayed large new nuclear-armed missiles and sent armed forces into Afghanistan to restore an overthrown Communist regime.

In 1980, Reagan's defeat of Ford for the Republican nomination and his subsequent defeat of Carter seemed evidence that the spirit of the Goldwater campaign survived and thrived. While Reagan's inauguration did not quite mark a return to the Cold War of the 1950s and early 1960s, it certainly marked the beginning of a new period in which moral and other questions about backing dictators gave way to moral concern about containing and, if possible, rolling back Communism. The person Reagan chose to be Ambassador to the United Nations, political scientist Jeane Kirkpatrick, had supplied the rationale in an article that distinguished between authoritarianism and totalitarianism. Authoritarian regimes, she wrote, were merely dictatorships lacking democratic institutions. They could be allies against Communist totalitarianism and could eventually be reformed, humanized, and democratized. By contrast, totalitarian regimes were committed in principle to suppressing individualism, human rights, and freedom of choice; they had to be overthrown.

This general view influenced U.S. dealings with dictators during Reagan's eight years as president. The administration bent itself to over-throw the Soviet-style Sandinista government that had replaced Somoza's in Nicaragua. Meanwhile, in the Democratically-controlled Congress, majorities passed legislation reflecting continuing misgivings about covert action of the type the United States had undertaken earlier in the Congo. Members of the White House staff, however, circumvented these legal constraints, secretly obtaining funding for the anti-Sandinista Contras from the likes of the Khomeini regime in Iran, which had only in 1981 released the U.S. hostages, and which continued to characterize the United States as "the great Satan." Disclosures of these deals led to the protracted "Iran-Contra" investigations, reviving the principle that U.S. dealings with dictators must be judged to be ethically and morally justifiable not only by presidents and their aides, but also by elected members of Congress.

What distinguishes the Marcos case not only from the Iran-Contra affair but from the other cases in this volume is the fact that the key difference in judgment was between the entire well-informed establishment on the one hand and the president of the United States on the other. Everyone knowledgeable about Philippine affairs, whether on Capitol Hill, in an executive department, or in the intelligence community, concluded fairly early on that Marcos had lost or was losing popular support. It eventually became an expert consensus that the United States should not continue to be identified with him. The chief practical ground for hesitancy was the possibility that the opposition might not cohere and that as a result the removal of Marcos would result in anarchy.

President Reagan, by contrast, believed that Marcos had been a loyal U.S. ally throughout his long reign. In the president's mind, practical considerations had to be very powerful to overcome obligations created by past cooperation. Where others in public life drew historical analogies, Reagan often drew parallels from movies in which he had performed. For example, the faith he expressed that technology could be developed to shield the United States from any missile attack, dubbed "Star Wars" by critics, owed something to a film role in which his character had saved the world by stealing the technology of a mad scientist.

The Marcos case study offers readers an opportunity to focus on processes of persuasion. The problem faced by Congressional Research Service analyst Marjorie Niehaus was how to get individuals higher in the action chain to adopt her conviction that "it was not in our interest to have [Marcos] as leader of the Philippines." The problem faced by those who came to share her view was how to get President Reagan to conclude that Marcos's was a lost cause.

Someone assuming Ms. Niehaus's role has to think of how to muster facts and arguments, much as does a lawyer when facing a jury. She had to think of how the credibility of her sources would be judged by those whom she hoped to influence. She had to take account of other evidence they might hear or see that would suggest a conclusion different from hers. But her arena was not a courtroom: she also had to decide which individuals to target, to think about their relations with one another and with their own agency networks, and to calculate how the Philippines might rank among their priorities. It can be instructive to try to think through a game plan for Ms. Niehaus or someone similarly situated, perhaps following the format suggested above where we discuss the Carter-era cases.

If Ms. Niehaus persuaded the people she could reach in the Executive branch and on Capitol Hill, there would remain for them the problem of how to approach President Reagan. This too would involve the mustering of evidence, and also thinking hard about the president's criteria for weighing sources. Aware that the president and his director of central intelligence, William Casey, believed the CIA to have a liberal bias, its analysts, as emphasized in our Introduction, chose to muffle their certainty about Marcos's doom, hoping that the president might read and not simply discard out of hand an "on the one hand...on the other hand" estimate. Was this wise? Would you, the reader, have been more forthright in urging a particular conclusion?

The group enlisted conservative Republicans whom the president respected. This involved risks. Senators Richard Lugar and Paul Laxalt might have delivered harsh reports on Marcos's snap election. But they might not have. They might instead have reinforced Reagan's instinctive view that, if Marcos cheated, the opposition had probably also cheated. How can such risks be calculated? How can they be minimized?

With this case, a reader or student can also engage in the mental experiment of trying to calculate emotional appeals that might offset those affecting the president's loyalty to Marcos. The book *Thinking in Time* argues for "placing" individuals whom one hopes to influence: that is, seeing them in their own histories and thinking about experiences from which they may have carried away lessons.

Here, it could be worthwhile to look back over Reagan's entire career and ask two questions. First, of what public events was he aware that might seem to him analogies for his situation vis-à-vis Marcos? Second, were there semi-private events, as in movies he had made, which might either enter his conscious thinking or be called to his attention and thus perhaps influence his judgment?

The public events most likely to have been on his mind were the fall of the Shah and the nearly coincident fall of Somoza. Among President Reagan's circle, it was a commonly held view that the Carter administration should have bolstered these two dictators, not undermined them by pressing for reform; they were to be counted among Ambassador Kirkpatrick's "authoritarian" regimes. Another such event was the fall of Fulgencio Batista in Cuba in 1959 and his replacement by Fidel Castro.

Thinking about how to persuade President Reagan could have involved thinking hard about these apparent precedents and especially about how their details differed from those of the case in hand. For one thing, the Philippines had no counterpart for Khomeini, the Sandinistas, or Castro. In fact, by contrast, the opponents of Marcos were admirers of the United States, who could be likened to the democratically inclined civilians who had taken over from military dictators in Latin America.

A quick search through the president's movie memories might have uncovered films in which obligations of comradeship ceased to be binding because the onetime friend or ally turned bad. A way might have been found to remind him that, in his own lone role as a villain, in the 1964 film "The Killers," his character had not deserved loyalty.

The case here does not show any of the president's advisers making deliberate use of such analogical reasoning. Vicariously experienced, however, it offers the opportunity for thinking not only about how to pose analytical questions such as those suggested in connection with other cases, but also about possible uses of "placement."

Iraq, 1988–1990

In our Introduction, we dealt with the Iraq case as an example of how rapidly the balance among value judgments can change. To draw out this lesson, one needs first to identify the full range of U.S. values and interests potentially affected by events in Iraq in the period when George H.W. Bush succeeded Reagan as president. Then, the challenge is to identify the particular mix of values dominant at each moment when Iraq became a focus of attention among high-level decision-makers. Why did the mix change? Was the change in any way foreseeable? Would it have been possible at one moment of decision to take into account the possibility that the mix might be different next time?

Each case in this book offers opportunities for thinking about the collection and analysis of intelligence as well as about the use of intelligence in policymaking. The intelligence available as a basis for policymakers' reality judgments was in every instance partial, though in varying degrees, and surrounded by uncertainties. How should intelligence analysts acknowledge such limitations without giving up their ability to be helpful in the formation of appreciations? After 9/11, with the U.S. intelligence community in flux, these questions may deserve especially close scrutiny.

In any event, we put before the public this collection of cases on intelligence analysis and policymaking believing, that they offer many opportunities for learning, most of which we ourselves have not yet discovered. As our Introduction makes clear, we set our own uses of these cases in a framework taken from Sir Geoffrey Vickers' book *The Art of Judgment*. Regarding the use of case studies for learning, we cite the authority of an even greater thinker, Immanuel Kant, who wrote in *Critique of Pure Reason* that: "Examples are the go-cart of judgment."[3]

---

3. Immanuel Kant, *Critique of Pure Reason*, 2nd ed. (1787), p. 174: "So sind Beyspiele der Gangelswagen der Urtheilskraft."

About the Editors

Ernest R. May is Charles Warren Professor of History at Harvard University. His writings include *Knowing One's Enemies: Intelligence Analysis before the Two World Wars* (1985); (with Richard E. Neustadt) *Thinking in Time: Uses of History for Decisionmakers* (1986); *American Cold War Strategy: Interpreting NSC 68* (1995); (with Philip D. Zelikow) *The Kennedy Tapes: Inside the White House during the Cuban Missile Crisis* (1997); and *Strange Victory: Hitler's Conquest of France* (2000). In 2003–2004 he was Senior Adviser to the 9/11 Commission. He is a member of the Intelligence Science Board and the Board of Visitors of the Joint Military Intelligence College. At Harvard he is a member of the Board of Directors of the Belfer Center for Science and International Affairs.

Philip D. Zelikow is former Director of the Miller Center of Public Affairs and White Burkett Miller Professor of History at the University of Virginia and is currently serving as counselor of the State Department. Zelikow recently served as the Executive Director of the National Commission on Terrorist Attacks Upon the United States, better known as the "9/11 Commission." Zelikow is co-author, with Ernest R. May, of *The Kennedy Tapes: Inside the White House During the Cuban Missile Crisis.*

Kirsten Lundberg is a senior writer of case studies on public policy issues at the Kennedy School of Government at Harvard University. She has written on such topics as public policy and intelligence; domestic preparedness; education management; corruption; privatization; and non-profit governance. Her published cases include: *Piloting a Bipartisan Ship: Strategies and Tactics of the 9/11 Commission; Convener or Player? The World Economic Forum and Davos; The Anatomy of an Investigation: the Difficult Case(s) of Wen Ho Lee;* and *Politics of a Covert Action: The US, the Mujahideen and the Stinger Missile.* Before Harvard, Ms. Lundberg was a correspondent for United Press International in Brussels, London, Stockholm, and

Moscow. Her journalism has been published in the *New York Times, Newsweek, Boston Globe* and others.

Robert D. Johnson is Professor of History at Brooklyn College and the CUNY Graduate Center. His writings include *Congress and the Cold War* (2005); *Washington, 20 January 1961* (1999); *Ernest Gruening and the American Dissenting Tradition* (1998); *The Peace Progressives and American Foreign Relations* (1995); and *On Cultural Ground: Essays in International History* (as editor, 1994). He is director of CUNY's Free Institutions Initiative and has served as a research associate for the Miller Center's Presidential Recordings Project.

Index

BCSIA Studies in International Security
Published by The MIT Press

Sean M. Lynn-Jones and Steven E. Miller, series editors
Karen Motley, executive editor
Belfer Center for Science and International Affairs (BCSIA)
John F. Kennedy School of Government, Harvard University

Agha, Hussein, Shai Feldman, Ahmad Khalidi, and Zeev Schiff, *Track-II Diplomacy: Lessons from the Middle East* (2003)

Allison, Graham T., Owen R. Coté, Jr, Richard A. Falkenrath, and Steven E. Miller, *Avoiding Nuclear Anarchy: Containing the Threat of Loose Russian Nuclear Weapons and Fissile Material* (1996)

Allison, Graham T., and Kalypso Nicolaïdis, eds., *The Greek Paradox: Promise vs. Performance* (1996)

Arbatov, Alexei, Abram Chayes, Antonia Handler Chayes, and Lara Olson, eds., *Managing Conflict in the Former Soviet Union: Russian and American Perspectives* (1997)

Bennett, Andrew, *Condemned to Repetition? The Rise, Fall, and Reprise of Soviet-Russian Military Interventionism, 1973–1996* (1999)

Blackwill, Robert D., and Michael Stürmer, eds., *Allies Divided: Transatlantic Policies for the Greater Middle East* (1997)

Blackwill, Robert D., and Paul Dibb, eds., *America's Asian Alliances* (2000)

Brom, Shlomo, and Yiftah Shapir, eds., *The Middle East Military Balance, 1999–2000* (1999)

Brom, Shlomo, and Yiftah Shapir, eds., *The Middle East Military Balance, 2001–2002* (2002)

Brown, Michael E., ed., *The International Dimensions of Internal Conflict* (1996)

Brown, Michael E., and Šumit Ganguly, eds., *Government Policies and Ethnic Relations in Asia and the Pacific* (1997)

Brown, Michael E., and Šumit Ganguly, eds., *Fighting Words: Language Policy and Ethnic Relations in Asia* (2003)

Carter, Ashton B., and John P. White, eds., *Keeping the Edge: Managing Defense for the Future* (2001)

de Nevers, Renée, *Comrades No More: The Seeds of Political Change in Eastern Europe* (2003)

Elman, Colin, and Miriam Fendius Elman, eds., *Bridges and Boundaries: Historians, Political Scientists, and the Study of International Relations* (2001)

Elman, Colin, and Miriam Fendius Elman, eds., *Progress in International Relations Theory: Appraising the Field* (2003)

Elman, Miriam Fendius, ed., *Paths to Peace: Is Democracy the Answer?* (1997)

Falkenrath, Richard A., *Shaping Europe's Military Order: The Origins and Consequences of the CFE Treaty* (1994)

Falkenrath, Richard A., Robert D. Newman, and Bradley A. Thayer, *America's Achilles' Heel: Nuclear, Biological, and Chemical Terrorism and Covert Attack* (1998)

Feaver, Peter D., and Richard H. Kohn, eds., *Soldiers and Civilians: The Civil-Military Gap and American National Security* (2001)

Feldman, Shai, *Nuclear Weapons and Arms Control in the Middle East* (1996)

Feldman, Shai, and Yiftah Shapir, eds., *The Middle East Military Balance 2000–2001* (2001)

Forsberg, Randall, ed., *The Arms Production Dilemma: Contraction and Restraint in the World Combat Aircraft Industry* (1994)

George, Alexander L., and Andrew Bennett, *Case Studies and Theory Development in the Social Sciences* (2005)

Hagerty, Devin T., *The Consequences of Nuclear Proliferation: Lessons from South Asia* (1998)

Heymann, Philip B., *Terrorism and America: A Commonsense Strategy for a Democratic Society* (1998)

Heymann, Philip B., *Terrorism, Freedom, and Security: Winning without War* (2003)

Heymann, Philip B., and Juliette N. Kayyem, *Protecting Liberty in an Age of Terror* (2005)

Howitt, Arnold M., and Robyn L. Pangi, eds., *Countering Terrorism: Dimensions of Preparedness* (2003)

Hudson, Valerie M., and Andrea M. den Boer, *Bare Branches: The Security Implications of Asia's Surplus Male Population* (2004)

Kayyem, Juliette N., and Robyn L. Pangi, eds., *First to Arrive: State and Local Responses to Terrorism* (2003)

Kokoshin, Andrei A., *Soviet Strategic Thought, 1917-91* (1998)

Lederberg, Joshua, ed., *Biological Weapons: Limiting the Threat* (1999)

Mansfield, Edward D., and Jack Snyder, *Electing to Fight: Why Emerging Democracies Go to War* (2005)

Martin, Lenore G., and Dimitris Keridis, eds., *The Future of Turkish Foreign Policy* (2004)

May, Ernest R., and Philip D. Zelikow, eds., with Kirsten Lundberg and Robert D. Johnson, *Dealing with Dictators: Dilemmas of U.S. Diplomacy and Intelligence Analysis, 1945–1990* (2006)

Shaffer, Brenda, *Borders and Brethren: Iran and the Challenge of Azerbaijani Identity* (2002)

Shaffer, Brenda, ed., *The Limits of Culture: Islam and Foreign Policy* (2006)

Shields, John M., and William C. Potter, eds., *Dismantling the Cold War: U.S. and NIS Perspectives on the Nunn-Lugar Cooperative Threat Reduction Program* (1997)

Tucker, Jonathan B., ed., *Toxic Terror: Assessing Terrorist Use of Chemical and Biological Weapons* (2000)

Utgoff, Victor A., ed., *The Coming Crisis: Nuclear Proliferation, U.S. Interests, and World Order* (2000)

Williams, Cindy, ed., *Holding the Line: U.S. Defense Alternatives for the Early 21st Century* (2001)

Williams, Cindy, ed., *Filling the Ranks: Transforming the U.S. Military Personnel System* (2004)

The Robert and Renée Belfer Center for Science and International Affairs

Graham Allison, Director
John F. Kennedy School of Government
Harvard University
79 JFK Street, Cambridge MA 02138
Tel: (617) 495–1400; Fax: (617) 495–8963
http://www.ksg.harvard.edu/bcsia   bcsia_ksg@harvard.edu

The Belfer Center for Science and International Affairs (BCSIA) is the hub of research, teaching and training in international security affairs, environmental and resource issues, science and technology policy, human rights, and conflict studies at Harvard's John F. Kennedy School of Government. The Center's mission is to provide leadership in advancing policy-relevant knowledge about the most important challenges of international security and other critical issues where science, technology and international affairs intersect.

BCSIA's leadership begins with the recognition of science and technology as driving forces transforming international affairs. The Center integrates insights of social scientists, natural scientists, technologists, and practitioners with experience in government, diplomacy, the military, and business to address these challenges. The Center pursues its mission in four complementary research programs:

- The **International Security Program** (ISP) addresses the most pressing threats to U.S. national interests and international security.

- The **Environment and Natural Resources Program** (ENRP) is the locus of Harvard's interdisciplinary research on resource and environmental problems and policy responses.

- The **Science, Technology, and Public Policy Program** (STPP) analyzes ways in which science and technology policy influence international security, resources, environment, and development, and such cross-cutting issues as technological innovation and information infrastructure.

- The **Program on Intrastate Conflict** analyzes the causes of ethnic, religious, and other conflicts, and seeks to identify practical ways to prevent and limit such conflicts.

The heart of the Center is its resident research community of more than 140 scholars: Harvard faculty, analysts, practitioners, and each year a new, interdisciplinary group of research fellows. BCSIA sponsors frequent seminars, workshops and conferences, maintains a substantial specialized library, and publishes books, monographs, and discussion papers.

The Center's International Security Program, directed by Steven E. Miller, publishes the BCSIA Studies in International Security, and sponsors and edits the quarterly journal *International Security*.

The Center is supported by an endowment established with funds from Robert and Renée Belfer, the Ford Foundation and Harvard University, by foundation grants, by individual gifts, and by occasional government contracts.